SWEET

SWEET

VALERIE GORDON

PHOTOGRAPHS BY PEDEN + MUNK

ARTISAN

NEW YORK

Published by Artisan
A division of Workman Publishing Company, Inc.
225 Varick Street
New York, NY 10014-4381
artisanbooks.com

Published simultaneously in Canada by Thomas
Allen & Son, Limited

Library of Congress Cataloging-in-Publication Data

Gordon, Valerie.
    Sweet / Valerie Gordon.
        pages   cm
 Includes index.
 ISBN 978-1-57965-468-9
 1. Desserts. 2. Confectionery. I. Title.
TX773.G65   2013
641.86—dc23   2013006288

Design by Michelle Ishay-Cohen

Printed in China
First printing, September 2013

10 9 8 7 6 5 4 3 2 1

FOR STANLEY

CONTENTS

INTRODUCTION

It's 2 a.m. on a night in the middle of July, and my partner, Stan, and I are talking about Christmas.

"I finalized the new holiday collection today," I say. "How are we going to work the new items into the holiday production schedule? What did we run out of last year? How many people do we need to hire this year? Have we ordered enough boxes?"

Every year it's the same thing, yet somehow each new pre-holiday season seems even more frenetic. A few short years ago, we were making fifteen different chocolates, all by hand, and it felt very complicated. Today we also make more than a hundred other products: preserves, petits fours, chocolate bars, cakes, pastries, cookies, and pies. It's no longer just complicated—it's controlled chaos.

When we started our company nine years ago, our motto was "For gifts and personal indulgence." Valerie Confections has evolved so much since then, but the same intention remains behind everything we make. Each chocolate is made by hand, dipped by hand, and packed by hand in boxes finished with hand-tied ribbons. I believe in making all of our products this way. For me, it is the same idea as preparing a home-cooked meal. There is true intimacy in a box of chocolates that are all slightly different because human hands, thankfully, cannot replicate the robotic movements of a machine. Handmade gifts and desserts create a special moment for the person on the receiving end. The next time you need to give a birthday present or a hostess gift, present a box of homemade cookies or a pie—the response will undoubtedly be surprise and gleeful anticipation.

EARLY MOMENTS

When I was six years old, I accompanied my mother, grandmother (Pau-Pau), and grand-father (Gung-Gung) on a house call to a business associate of Gung-Gung's. My relation-ship with Pau-Pau and Gung-Gung was tentative at best. They spoke Chinese exclusively, and communication was somewhat limited with their half-white, non-Chinese-speaking granddaughters. Gung-Gung was the patriarch of the family, and while I don't recall ever being told to obey him, I do remember feeling as if there wasn't an alternative. On this particular outing, Gung-Gung was carrying a large box of See's Nuts and Chews, which caught my eye. It wasn't Christmas or Chinese New Year, so I asked my mother, "Why is Gung-Gung bringing chocolate to his friend's house?" Gung-Gung responded in Chi-nese, and my mother translated. "Gung-Gung says, 'Never go empty-handed.'"

By third grade, I had developed a fairly serious baking habit and, whenever pos-sible, tried to sample more sophisticated desserts. We lived in San Francisco, and across town, in the tony Pacific Heights neighborhood, there was an amazing patis-serie, Fantasia. Decadent and fancy, it offered an impossible number of desserts: towers of cookies, chocolates, marzipan fruits, and tray after tray of perfect petits fours and tortes. The tables were occupied by beautifully coiffed ladies, and the entire picture was one of unspeakable joy to my eight-year-old eyes. It was almost too much to take, such beauty and splendor in one room. I never wanted to leave, but I could never choose what to eat. What would be the most delicious creation? I'd stare into the cases until my mother finally insisted that we go, and only then would I decide what to eat. The image of the petits fours is seared in my mind to this day. *My fairy-tale fantasies were filled with desserts, not Barbies or princesses.*

As the youngest of four children, I was frequently left alone to amuse myself or to navigate the world. And there was no "play" baking with an Easy-Bake oven. I used grown-up equipment and, with little guidance, somehow managed to teach myself how to bake and cook. I created things like monkey bread, dessert pizzas, and a wide array of cookies, including a masterpiece Victorian gingerbread house when I was in the fifth grade. That same year, I discovered a neighborhood dessert shop—

Tassajara—and visiting it became my favorite pastime. Its location couldn't have been more different from Fantasia's in Pacific Heights; the Haight-Ashbury neighborhood was decidedly bohemian. The patrons were dressed casually, and the desserts were rustic and organic, yet, in their own way, as beautiful as those at Fantasia. The cases held homey tarts, dense chocolate cakes, and nutty and buttery cookies. I often went out of my way to be able to enter the shop, missing my school bus so I was forced to take public transportation and then had no choice but to walk the three blocks to school, passing by Tassajara. My circuitous journeys to school also gave me the liberty of spending as long as I liked while making my choice in front of the bakery case. On my first visit there, after staring at the case for what felt like hours, I realized that there was no need to choose: I would enjoy *two* pastries, an almond croissant and a palmier. What fifth grader could ask for more at 7:30 a.m.?

The hours I spent gazing into bakery cases had an enormous impact on my life's path and on my own style of desserts. The casual organic approach of Tassajara and the classic elegance of Fantasia, the yin and yang of desserts, merged to create my hybrid perspective on sweets.

By the time I was eighteen, my relationship with desserts was well defined. My joyous moments have always been punctuated by dessert. The first time I fell in love, I could think of no better way of expressing my emotions than sending a package of homemade chocolate chip cookies to my boyfriend at college. And every Christmas, there were staples like Snowballs (page 254) and Brownies (page 266) for friends and family. Desserts can be a celebration, and desserts can also comfort us. The night my father died, the trauma seemed more than I could handle. I cocooned with my family at my childhood home for a few days. There were no activities to distract me, so I baked. Oatmeal cookies with dried apricots and almonds. The cookies were some of the best I had ever made— the centers chewy, the edges crispy, and the apricots' tartness perfectly balancing the nuts. I see those days in hazy snapshots, but I do recall with absolute clarity the taste of those cookies.

The early 1990s were an exciting time for restaurants in San Francisco. Because of the dot.com boom, there was an abundance of diners with hefty expense accounts. I was in college studying drama during the day, and I spent my evenings working at one of those bustling restaurants, Lulu's. It was an exhilarating place to be, as the farmto-table movement was starting to burgeon and celebrity chefs were emerging from under the surface of our consciousness. I ran the door at Lulu's, so it was my responsibility to know every name and face in the industry, to be familiar with the menu and wine list, and to orchestrate the seating of more than five hundred people a night. Every evening when we opened the doors, I was presented with a culinary who's who from Alice Waters to Marion Cunningham to Alfred Portale. The produce all came from the farmers' market, the beginning of what was to become the landmark market at Ferry Plaza. Dining out became my major source of recreation. Being surrounded by food gave me a rush and an enormous thrill, and I devoured it all. But I had no desire to work professionally in a kitchen. I treated my moments of creating food as an intimate activity and would never have predicted that that would change.

In 1997, I relocated to Los Angeles, having felt a pull in that direction for years. As cosmopolitan as it is, San Francisco is a very small town, and the idea of more anonymity and unfamiliar streets sounded like perfection. When I arrived, I immediately got a job managing Les Deux Cafés. Located on a run-down street in the middle of Hollywood, "the Café" was the vision of Michèle Lamy, a former fashion designer from Paris and the most forward-thinking individual I have ever worked with. The menu was market-driven French cuisine, but that wasn't the restaurant's main focus. If San Francisco was the food mecca, Los Angeles was the celebrity mecca, and each night the room was filled with a bevy of entertainment and other personalities: Madonna, Joni Mitchell, Al Pacino, Salman Rushdie, and David Bowie were frequent guests. Michèle taught me the art of detail, from the fabric-covered handwritten menus to the *mignardises* (tiny sweets) served in silver bowls from the flea market; her vision was compelling, honest, and consistent. The most valuable lesson I learned from my years there was simple: create something with what you have.

Unfortunately, it took an extended period of misfortune for me to realize what I had. Just after my thirtieth birthday, I suffered a broken back and found myself facing a painful and bleak future. I spent hours in solitude. I read *Swann's Way* (twice), and very unironically meditated on the importance of a cookie in one's life. And the concept for Valerie Confections was born. Like Scarlett O'Hara, I realized my life's true calling. It had always been there, ever obvious to others, but not at all to me. It took one of my greatest struggles to make me see what I had always wanted to do.

FOR GIFTS AND PERSONAL ENJOYMENT

Do you remember the last time you opened an exquisite box of chocolates? Untying the ribbon, lifting the lid, peeling back the wrapping, and gazing at them? Their different shapes and colors lie before you, and you want to take a tiny taste of all of them, to see which one you want to eat first. It makes you feel happy. It makes *me* feel happy. Every time.

Valerie Confections was started with that experience in mind, devoted to creating handmade chocolates that are both beautiful and delicious, each one a gift. Stan and I started the business in 2004 in our apartment with six flavors of toffee, a box that we called our Debut Assortment, and it's still one of our biggest sellers. The first Christmas was crazy. In the pre-online-shopping era, we took orders by fax and phone. Our small dining room was curtained off for packaging; the second bedroom was the office. I made family meals for us and our two part-time employees as we all tied ribbons around boxes late into the night.

In 2006, when I was pregnant with our son, August, we moved to our current location on an unglamorous street just south of Silverlake, an eclectic community nestled between Hollywood and downtown Los Angeles. Soon after the move, I tested petits fours over a period of eight months, intent on making my own version of the tiny cakes I'd seen at Fantasia. I wanted to create a collection that, like the toffee, we could ship across the country. Our petit four cakes are dense and buttery, layered with ganache, and dipped in chocolate. The décor isn't simply piped frosting—we candy individual rose petals, pansies, and citrus zest. The petits fours were the perfect bridge between the confections we were known for and the bakery we were becoming.

In 2008, our little factory on a weird street became our boutique. Michèle Lamy's "work with what you have" credo was a great model to follow. With the economy at rock bottom, we needed a new focus for our company to survive. I got in the kitchen and cooked, threw the rules out the door, and was no longer limited by the parameters of a chocolate or petits fours box. I found myself newly invigorated by the challenge of making our company work. Our basic philosophy stayed the same: create a moment—every bite should have a beginning, a middle, and an end; use the best ingredients; and make everything as delicious as possible. We established booths at the local farmers' markets and then purchased fruits from our neighboring vendors, creating a web of commerce with other small businesses. Every week we sent out a seasonal menu to our growing e-mail list. We offered the members of our community handmade sweet and savory pastries, and they responded.

Since the debut of our market booths, both our business and our family have grown. Despite the challenging economy, business has actually doubled. Following a more organic path of growth than the one we had originally set out on has allowed us to expand in ways we couldn't have predicted. And our second child, a girl named Lee, was born on Christmas Eve 2011, one week overdue (she was considerate enough to let me work through the Christmas rush before I gave birth).

Although the hours are long, I get tremendous gratification from my work. I'm in the enviable position of truly being inspired every time I walk into the kitchen. New ingredients continue to motivate me, I'm energized by the process of developing new recipes, and I am humbled by the response our products elicit.

Before we started the company, we had an abstract idea of who our customers would be, but now they are our friends. We have families who stop by our market booths every week, and we get to see their kids growing up. And we have people who order our chocolates as gifts every year, for whom we have become a part of their holiday tradition.

Over the years, just as often as people have asked for recipes, they've come to me for advice. They want to find out how they can do what I've done, where I went to school, and how I became a chef. Well, I'm a self-taught home baker, and I don't consider myself a chef. However, in a very real way, I was trained by all my favorite chefs, because I used their cookbooks to teach and inspire me. I started with a passion for learning, a willingness to experiment, and a stack of cookbooks. And I'm lucky enough to have turned my passion into a career.

I wrote this book to share some of what I've learned and, hopefully, to inspire you to feel confident in the kitchen. To make jam, or chocolates, for the first time. To attempt something that you haven't tried, or to revisit something you've done before with a new perspective. And to approach baking with a sense of adventure and possibility so that after spending some time with these recipes, you're able to expand not only your repertoire but also your understanding of the techniques and flavors involved, and start creating your own recipes—and telling your own stories through food.

I encourage you to experiment in your kitchen. Pair ingredients or components to suit your own palate, and feel free to alter recipes to your taste. It's this sense of exploration that drove me to create Valerie Confections. It's what I hope to inspire in anyone who tastes our desserts for the first time. And it's what I hope you discover in this book.

HOW TO USE THIS BOOK

I have tried to write the recipes in this book in the most approachable, nontechnical way possible in the hope that that simplicity will allow you to use them often. The array of desserts is large, so every season and occasion can be filled with delicious homemade treats. You'll find cakes for celebrations, refreshing sorbets, cookies, chocolates, and pies for any time of the year. There are jams and granolas to satisfy your desire for a homemade breakfast, and you can make petits fours and scones for afternoon tea. I've also given mix-and-match components for cakes (see page 110) and pies (see page 164) so you can create hybrid sweets to your liking. Make your own signature dessert and see what happens.

Although the individual recipes can stand on their own, they are also intended to complement one another. For example, embellish a creamy dessert from the Bowl chapter with a crunchy cookie from the Jar chapter. Or use recipes in tandem to create dessert parties (see page 121).

MISE EN PLACE

How many times have you started a recipe only to notice halfway through that you are missing a key ingredient? It's a frustrating experience, and the best way to avoid it is to prepare your *mise en place*—a French phrase that translates to "everything in place"—before you start baking. Begin every baking session by reading the recipe carefully, reviewing the ingredients and the equipment needed, the "prep," and the cooking process. Designate an area in your kitchen as your "station" and set everything up there: measure and prep all of your ingredients, and collect the tools and equipment called for.

INGREDIENTS

There is a group of key baking ingredients you will see repeatedly in these recipes. A well-stocked kitchen is a well-loved kitchen. Keep basic ingredients such as all-purpose flour, brown sugar, gelatin, confectioners' sugar, and fresh eggs on hand at all times so you can create your favorite desserts without delay. Specialty ingredients, like some of those included in this list, may be a bit pricier or more challenging to source, but they will maximize both flavor and richness in a variety of recipes.

Atomized 69% Bittersweet Chocolate

This ingredient sounds far more exotic than it is; atomized chocolate is very finely ground fully conched chocolate. The more common unsweetened cocoa powder can taste bitter or astringent when used as a coating on truffles or other desserts; atomized chocolate has a smooth mouthfeel and a strong chocolate flavor, with no acidity. See Resources, page 335.

Butter

I use Plugrá unsalted butter for all baking and confections. Plugrá contains more butterfat than most American butters, resulting in richer, more flavorful desserts. Unsalted butter allows you to control the level of salt in your recipe.

Citrus Zest

Adding grated citrus zest is an easy way to infuse maximum flavor into whatever you are making. For instance, in the Lemon Cake (page 78), the lemon juice imparts a subtle lemon flavor. Using more juice for a stronger lemon taste would make the batter too wet; zest adds concentrated lemon flavor. It is important to buy organic or "nonsprayed" fruits when you will be using zest, as the skin can absorb significant amounts of pesticides.

Crème Fraîche

Crème fraîche is rich soured cream that is thicker and less tangy than standard American sour cream. You can make your own by combining heavy cream with a small amount of buttermilk and leaving it in a warm environment to ferment. Crème fraîche contributes a buttery, slightly tangy flavor to cakes and other baked goods and ganaches. Crème fraîche also helps baked goods retain moisture.

Fleur de Sel

This French sea salt (literally "flower of salt") has larger crystals than table or kosher salt and brings out more flavor from the other ingredients, in both sweets and savory dishes.

Nut Flours

You will see nut flours in a variety of recipes in this book. Nut flour can be made easily by blitzing nuts in a food processor or coffee grinder for 2 to 3 minutes. Once the nuts are transformed into flour, stop pulsing. If you continue to grind them, they will turn into nut butter. Store nut flours in an airtight container in the refrigerator or freezer for 3 to 4 months. Blanched nut flour is made from blanched (skinned) nuts. For standard nut flours, or anything listed as raw nut flour, I tested the recipes using nuts with the skins intact. Toasted nut flour is made from nut flour that is toasted in the oven until it turns golden and smells toasty. Do not try to make toasted nut flour using roasted nuts; that will result in a mealy, oily nut mass. To make toasted nut flour, spread raw nut flour on a baking sheet and toast in a 350°F oven for 6 to 8 minutes, until the flour turns dark golden and smells roasted.

Nut flours are very popular today for use in gluten-free recipes. For the recipes in this book, nut flours are used specifically to create a forward, nutty flavor. See Resources, page 335, for information on where to purchase nut flours.

Nut Pastes

Almond paste, the nut paste I most commonly use, is sometimes confused with marzipan, which is substantially sweeter and softer. Nut pastes create rich, moist cakes with a fine crumb. The increased moisture also extends the shelf life of any baked good made with nut paste. See page 44 for a quick and easy recipe for almond paste.

Vanilla Bean Paste

Vanilla extract is a staple in most people's cupboards; it is alcohol that has been infused with vanilla flavor. Some of these recipes call for vanilla extract, but more often I prefer to use vanilla bean paste, which is vanilla beans blended into a sugar syrup. Vanilla bean paste is slightly more expensive than extract, but it imparts a more intense flavor and also leaves speckles of vanilla beans in a dessert. And vanilla bean paste is easier to blend into a batter than seeds scraped from a vanilla bean, which can clump and result in uneven flavor and color. See Resources, page 335.

MEASURING

You will find both volume and weight measurements (in ounces and pounds) for the ingredients used in the recipes in this book. Most home bakers are accustomed to volume measurements, but I urge you to experiment with weight measurements. It's the only way to ensure that your recipes will have consistent results, particularly when you're making chocolate confections (see the Box chapter, page 169). Using a digital scale is incredibly easy, and once you grow accustomed to it, you will see it's also faster, as well as more precise, to measure ingredients this way.

Measuring Dry Ingredients

When measuring dry ingredients like flour and sugar by volume, fill the measuring cup until the top is slightly rounded, then swipe a flat edge across the top. None of the dry ingredients used in these recipes, including brown sugar, were measured as "packed" cups.

EQUIPMENT

This list includes all the necessary pans and tools you would need to make every recipe in the book. For specialty equipment and paper products, see Resources, page 335.

Baking Pans
Four 9-inch round cake pans
One 9-inch round cake pan with a removable bottom
Three 9-by-2-inch round cake pans
Three 9-by-3-inch round cake pans
One 9-inch springform pan
One 10-inch springform pan
Two 9½-by-5½-inch loaf pans
One 10-inch tube pan
Two mini cake pans (twelve 3-inch molds per pan; optional)

Two 13-by-18-by-1-inch baking sheets
Three 9-by-13-by-2-inch baking pans
One 9-by-9-by-2-inch baking pan
Four 9-by-6-by-1-inch baking pans
Three 8-by-8-by-2-inch square baking pans

One 9-inch pie pan
One 9-inch fluted tart pan with a removable bottom
One 11-inch fluted tart pan with a removable bottom

Two large muffin tins
Two popover pans

Eight 3-inch ramekins (optional)

Baking Supplies
Parchment paper: 9-inch circles and full sheets (12 by 16 inches)
Silicone liners: 13-by-18-inch and (optional) 9-by-13-inch

Two 13-by-18-inch wire cooling racks
Cake turntable (optional)

Pots and Pans
Small, medium, and large saucepans
One 4- to 6-quart pot
One 8-quart pot
Copper or heavy stainless steel pot
Double boiler (optional)

Mixing Bowls
Small, medium, and large, including heat-proof bowls

Measuring Equipment
Measuring cups, both liquid and dry
Measuring spoons
Digital kitchen scale
Candy thermometer, preferably digital

Mixers and Food Processor
Stand mixer
Handheld mixer
14-cup food processor

Ice Cream Maker
I used the Cuisinart Frozen Yogurt, Ice Cream, and Sorbet Maker for all of the recipes in this book

Spatulas and Spoons
Small and large offset spatulas
Flexible rubber spatulas
Heatproof silicone spatulas
Wooden spoons

Knives

Long serrated knife
Cleaver or other heavy knife
Paring knife
9- or 10-inch chef's knife

Sieves and Sifters

Fine-mesh sieve
Fine-mesh sifter
Cheesecloth

Pastry Equipment

Bench/dough scraper
Bowl scraper
One 3-inch round cookie cutter
One 2-inch heart-shaped cookie cutter
One 4-inch ring mold
One 6-inch ring mold
Ice cream scoop (for portioning cookies)
Marble slab (optional)
Pastry bag and assorted tips
Pastry brush
Pastry cutter
Pastry wheel
Pie weights or dried beans
Pizza cutter
Rolling pin

Other Kitchen Tools

Cherry pitter
Citrus juicer
Coffee or spice grinder
Kitchen shears
Melon baller
Oven mitts
Ruler
Tea strainer or tea ball
Vegetable peeler
Wax paper
Wire whisks
Zester

Candy-Making Equipment

Dipping forks, preferably 2- and
    3-pronged
Candy cups
Chocolate depositor
Confectionery bars
Latex gloves

Canning Equipment

15- to 21-quart canning pot
Funnel
Jar lifter
Canning jars and lids

Paper Products

Cake boxes (optional)
Cellophane candy wrappers
Muffin papers
Paper containers for ice cream (optional)

PEDESTAL

CELEBRATION DESSERTS

IN March 2009, a good friend, food editor Lora Zarubin, approached me about contributing to a piece she was working on for the *Los Angeles Times Magazine*. The story revolved around wedding cakes, with the idea that a couple should be able to get their favorite cake transformed into a wedding cake for their special day. Lora chose a handful of bakers in Los Angeles and assigned each one a cake to execute in tiered form. "Have you ever heard of Blum's Coffee Crunch Cake?" Lora asked. I'm sure my heart skipped a beat. It was such an amazing question to be asked—I grew up with the Blum's cake. It was the most significant dessert of my life: literally every Christmas, Chinese New Year, birthday, and holiday of my childhood was defined by this cake.

Blum's Bakery had eight locations in California, the last of which closed in the late 1970s. In 1948, Blum's original baker, Ernest Weil, opened Fantasia in San Francisco, and the coffee crunch cake was served there, but, sadly, that too closed in the late 1980s. The impact that desserts have on our childhood psyches is remarkable. Desserts, and cakes in particular, represent defining moments of celebration in our lives. Very few people eat cake every day; cakes celebrate specific moments, and the memories of the excitement, anticipation, and taste are indelible. Blum's and Fantasia hold a special place in the hearts of thousands because of the coffee crunch cake.

I researched and tested every published version of the coffee crunch cake I could find until I finally arrived at a tiered version I thought best represented the cherished cake. When Lora's article was published, the response was astounding. We received more than a hundred phone calls that day from people with stories about the Blum's cake of their youth. We filled endless orders that week, and the demand has scarcely diminished. One grateful customer put her hand on mine and, with tears in her eyes, said, "I tasted my childhood in that cake."

After recovering from the whirlwind of crunch mania, I realized there must be many more "extinct" cakes that were due a revival. My research and recipe testing continued, and soon desserts from LA's historic Chasen's, Brown Derby, and Bullocks Wilshire Tea Room followed. I chose to re-create the most famous desserts from these establishments, because paying homage to the restaurants of Hollywood's Golden Era and their desserts in tandem is doubly satisfying.

This chapter also includes a number of my favorite cakes that define holidays—the cheesecake we make every Thanksgiving, the cake no birthday is complete without, the fruitcakes our customers eat at Christmastime, and more. I hope you will create new memories and traditions for yourself with these cakes—I would love for people to bake them for many years to come.

Blum's Coffee Crunch Cake

Blum's Bakery had eight locations in California until the last one closed in the late '70s; the bakeries were pink-and-gold palaces that served generations of dessert lovers. Being able to offer this historic cake to our customers has been one of the greatest privileges of my career. The cake component is a chiffon cake, an oil cake that was invented in 1927 and released to the broader public by Betty Crocker in a mix in 1948. Although similar to an angel food cake in texture, it has more heft and moisture and a slightly richer flavor. Layered with coffee whipped cream and coffee-flavored honeycomb crunch, the cake is a marriage of complementary textures. Be sure to apply the crunch just before serving the cake, or it will start to melt.

MAKES ONE 9-INCH CAKE; SERVES 8 TO 12

FOR THE CHIFFON CAKE

1¼ cups (6.25 ounces) all-purpose flour

1½ cups (10.5 ounces) sugar

½ teaspoon kosher salt

5 large eggs, separated, plus 2 large egg whites

2 tablespoons water

¼ cup (2 ounces) canola oil

1 teaspoon vanilla extract

1 teaspoon cream of tartar

1 teaspoon grated lemon zest

1 tablespoon lemon juice

FOR THE COFFEE CRUNCH

2¼ cups (15.75 ounces) sugar

⅓ cup (2.66 ounces) strong brewed coffee

⅓ cup (3.75 ounces) light corn syrup

1½ tablespoons baking soda

FOR THE COFFEE WHIPPED CREAM

2½ cups (20 ounces) well-chilled heavy cream

2½ tablespoons sugar

2½ teaspoons vanilla extract

2½ teaspoons instant coffee granules

TO MAKE THE CAKE

› Position a rack in the center of the oven and heat the oven to 350°F. Coat the bottom and sides of a 9-inch round cake pan with a removable bottom with nonstick baking spray.

› Sift together the flour, ¾ cup of the sugar, and the salt into a medium bowl.

› In the bowl of a stand mixer fitted with the whisk attachment (or in a large bowl, using a handheld mixer), whip the yolks and ¼ cup sugar on medium speed until thick and pale yellow, about 4 minutes. Gradually add the water, oil, and vanilla, mixing well. If using a stand mixer, transfer the mixture to a large bowl and wash and dry the mixer bowl and whisk (or wash the beaters).

› Add the egg whites to the large mixer bowl (or another bowl) and beat until frothy. Add the cream of tartar and continue beating until the egg whites form soft peaks. Add the remaining ½ cup sugar and beat until stiff, glossy peaks form. Add the lemon zest and juice and beat just until incorporated, about 15 seconds.

› Using a rubber spatula, fold the yolk mixture into the egg whites. Gradually fold in the dry ingredients, approximately 1 cup at a time, until fully incorporated.

› Pour the batter into the prepared cake pan and smooth the top with a spatula. Bake the cake for 55 minutes to 1 hour, until it is golden brown and a toothpick inserted in the center comes out clean.

› Let the cake cool completely on a cooling rack, about 45 minutes (removing the cake when it is still warm will cause it to deflate and likely tear).

› Run an offset spatula around the sides of the cake to loosen it from the pan. Holding the rim of the pan with one hand, press the bottom of the pan up and out. Run an offset spatula between the cake and the bottom to release it. Wrap the cake in plastic wrap and refrigerate until you are ready to assemble the cake.

TO MAKE THE COFFEE CRUNCH

> Attach a candy thermometer to the side of a 4- to 6-quart heavy pot. Add the sugar, coffee, and corn syrup to the pot and cook over medium-high heat, stirring occasionally with a heatproof silicone spatula until the mixture reaches 270°F, about 10 minutes.

> Meanwhile, heavily coat a 13-by-18-by-1-inch baking sheet with nonstick baking spray. Measure the baking soda into a ramekin or cup and place near the stovetop, along with a large whisk.

> When the crunch reaches 270°F, increase the heat to high and stir constantly until the crunch reaches 305°F. Remove from the heat and quickly whisk the baking soda into the crunch; the mixture will expand and aerate quickly, in a matter of seconds. Pour the crunch onto the baking sheet. Allow the crunch to cool, undisturbed, for at least 30 minutes.

> Using a cleaver or other heavy knife, chop the crunch into quarter-sized pieces. (The crunch can be made ahead and stored in an airtight container at room temperature for up to 2 weeks.)

TO MAKE THE COFFEE WHIPPED CREAM

> Combine the heavy cream, sugar, vanilla, and coffee in a large bowl and whip with a handheld mixer until medium peaks form.

TO ASSEMBLE THE CAKE

> Place the cake on a turntable or cake stand and, using a long serrated knife, slice the cake horizontally in half. Remove the top half and place cut side up on a plate. Cover both halves with whipped cream, using approximately ½ cup per side. Scatter 1 cup of the crunch evenly to cover the bottom half. Place the top half, cream side down, on the top of the crunch layer and press gently to even the layers. Frost the sides and top of the cake with the remaining whipped cream. Refrigerate until ready to serve.

> When you are ready to serve the cake, cover the sides and top with the remaining crunch (if you apply the crunch in advance, it will start to melt and lose its bite).

STORING

> This cake is best enjoyed the day it is assembled. Store it in a cake box or under a cake dome in the refrigerator.

SAVING THE EXTINCT DESSERT

AFTER RESURRECTING THE BLUM'S COFFEE CRUNCH CAKE, I was filled with excitement and an overwhelming desire to rescue other extinct desserts from our local culinary history. As I embarked on this journey, I quickly discovered a key problem—the Blum's cake was the only "famous" dessert that I had actually tasted. Chasen's and the Brown Derby were not part of my personal history, so I needed to piece together the stories of the desserts through recipes in print and online, and, most important, through the oral history of people who once frequented those establishments.

To date, the most challenging recipe in this ongoing project has been Scandia's apple cake (see page 57). Recipes from the 1950s and '60s were written in a style that is best described as bare-bones. For instance, a recipe I located for the apple cake listed "12 macaroons," with no specification as to what kind of macaroon: almond or coconut. So, I tested the cake with both kinds of macaroon, but neither one seemed to obviously overshadow the other. Clearly I needed to go deeper in my research. I searched for other dessert recipes from Scandia's and found one that listed almond macaroons as an ingredient, so that mystery was solved. But what about the type of apples, the sweetness of the whipped cream, and the mysterious toasted cake crumbs? I was forced to shelve the cake research for months, as I couldn't find anyone who had tasted the actual cake at Scandia's and had a clear memory of it.

Finally, a gentleman named Art Krauss came into the shop, asking if we had Scandia's apple cake. I was away from our store at the time but received a text message that read, "Art Krauss remembers Scandia cake; call him." I immediately picked up the phone and had an intimate conversation with Art about the cake. He gave me an in-depth description of the apples, the height of the cake, and the color of the currant jelly. Art has a very refined level of "taste memory," which was a true gift for someone in my position. I asked if he could feel the fork in his hand cutting the cake. He answered affirmatively. "Does the cake resist your fork a bit?" I asked. "*Yes, yes it does,*" he replied. "Did the taste remind you of a crustless apple pie?" I pressed. "Yes, it was like pie and the cream wasn't yicky." After my fifteen earlier tests of the cake, Art had provided me with all the answers to my lingering questions, and he is forever an official taster at Valerie Confections.

So much of our culinary history can be found on handwritten recipe cards and in obscure cookbooks picked up at yard sales. Some recipes are embedded in the memories of our parents and grandparents, and one short conversation may bring those desserts back to life. I urge you to unearth some of your most beloved desserts and catalog them for generations to come. Unlike pictures, books, or paintings, we can't just look at a recipe for a dessert to live on—we need to taste it.

Chasen's Banana Shortcake

Back in the day, every big star went to Chasen's. If you search for Chasen's on-line, you will find photos of Elizabeth Taylor and Richard Burton, Spencer Tracy, Marilyn Monroe, and Cary Grant laughing gaily in one of their storied booths. It was a glamorous destination for Hollywood royalty, renowned not only for its clientele but also for how it catered to the specific needs of its famous patrons. When Elizabeth Taylor was filming *Cleopatra* in Rome, Chasen's shipped orders of chili to her on set. Which brings me to a theory I have about this cake: it seems very likely that some food-fixated celebrity asked the owners of Chasen's to create a cake that tasted like a banana split. You'll see what I mean when you taste it—the chocolate sauce, sliced bananas, whipped cream, and melted ice cream are deliciously reminiscent of that ice cream shop favorite.

● MAKES ONE 9-INCH CAKE; SERVES 8 TO 10 ●

FOR THE CAKE

2 cups (10 ounces) all-purpose flour, sifted

1/4 teaspoon kosher salt

1 teaspoon baking powder

2 sticks (8 ounces) unsalted butter, softened

1 cup (7 ounces) sugar

4 large eggs

2 teaspoons vanilla bean paste (see Resources, page 335)

2 tablespoons heavy cream

FOR THE CHOCOLATE SAUCE

3/4 cup (3 ounces) unsweetened cocoa powder

1 cup (8 ounces) heavy cream

3/4 cup (5.25 ounces) sugar

1/2 cup (5.5 ounces) light corn syrup

FOR THE BANANA SAUCE

2 very ripe bananas

3/4 cup (6 ounces) heavy cream

1 tablespoon sugar

1 teaspoon vanilla bean paste (see Resources, page 335)

1 pint high-quality vanilla ice cream, softened

3 tablespoons light rum

FOR THE WHIPPED CREAM

2 cups (16 ounces) well-chilled heavy cream

1/4 cup (1.75 ounces) sugar

1 teaspoon vanilla extract

2 bananas, sliced into 1/2-inch disks

TO MAKE THE CAKE

▶ Position a rack in the center of the oven and heat the oven to 350°F. Coat the bottoms and sides of two 9-by-3-inch round cake pans with nonstick baking spray.

▶ Sift together the flour, salt, and baking powder into a medium bowl.

▶ In the bowl of a stand mixer fitted with the whisk attachment (or in a large bowl, using a handheld mixer), beat the butter and sugar on medium speed until pale and fluffy, about 3 minutes. Add the eggs one at a time, mixing well after each addition. Add the vanilla paste and mix well, about 30 seconds. Add the dry ingredients in two batches, mixing until fully incorporated. Pour in the cream and mix for 1 minute.

▶ Divide the batter between the prepared cake pans, spreading it evenly. Bake for 30 minutes, or until the tops appear dry and slightly golden and a toothpick inserted in the center comes out clean. Allow the cakes to cool for 15 minutes in the pans on a cooling rack, then remove the cakes and cool completely on the rack. Wrap the cakes in plastic wrap and refrigerate until you are ready to assemble the cake.

TO MAKE THE CHOCOLATE SAUCE

▶ Put the cocoa powder into a medium bowl. Combine the cream and sugar in a small saucepan and cook over medium-low heat, stirring, until the sugar dissolves. Pour in the corn syrup, increase the heat to medium, and continue stirring until the mixture boils.

▶ Pour the hot cream mixture over the cocoa powder and whisk until smooth. Pour the mixture back into the saucepan and cook over medium-low heat, stirring occasionally, until large bubbles form and the sauce appears glossy, about 5 minutes. Pour the sauce into a small pitcher or a bowl. (The sauce can be stored, covered, in the refrigerator for 1 week. Reheat over low heat before serving.)

TO MAKE THE BANANA SAUCE

› Slice the bananas into very thin rounds. Using a handheld mixer, whip the cream, sugar, and vanilla paste in a medium bowl until stiff peaks form. Using a rubber spatula, fold in the ice cream, sliced bananas, and rum, just until incorporated. Cover and refrigerate. (The banana sauce can be refrigerated for up to 3 hours. It actually holds well if refrigerated for longer, but the bananas will turn brown; if you need to make the sauce more than 3 hours ahead of time, add the bananas just before serving.)

TO MAKE THE WHIPPED CREAM

› Using a handheld mixer, whip the cream, sugar, and vanilla in a medium bowl until stiff peaks form.

TO ASSEMBLE THE CAKE

› Place one layer on a turntable or cake stand. Using an offset spatula, spread one-third of the whipped cream over the top of the cake. Cover with a layer of the sliced bananas. Spread another one-third of the whipped cream on top of the bananas. Top with the second cake layer. Frost the top of the cake with the remaining whipped cream, spreading it evenly. Arrange a circle of the remaining banana slices around the edge of the cake. (If assembling the cake ahead, do not add the circle of banana slices until just before serving.) To serve, drizzle a bit of chocolate sauce over the cake. Cut into slices, arrange on plates, and drizzle with the banana and remaining chocolate sauces.

STORING

› This cake is best enjoyed the day it is assembled. Store it in a cake box or under a cake dome in the refrigerator.

Bullocks Wilshire Coconut Cream Pie

If only Bullocks Wilshire Tea Room existed today. The building still stands—it is a gorgeous example of art deco architecture that was meticulously restored by Southwestern Law School. The tearoom itself is again in pristine condition and is now used as the student cafeteria, but, sadly, it lacks the carts filled with little sandwiches and coconut cream pies. Regulars of the tearoom know this pie was a favorite because of its heavenly soft coconut filling.

●— MAKES ONE 9-INCH PIE; SERVES 8 —●

FOR THE CRUST

1¼ cups (6.25 ounces) all-purpose flour

½ teaspoon kosher salt

½ teaspoon sugar

¼ cup (2 ounces) vegetable shortening, chilled

5⅓ tablespoons (⅓ cup/2.66 ounces) unsalted butter, cubed and chilled

1 tablespoon ice water

FOR THE FILLING

1 cup (8 ounces) evaporated milk

1 cup (8 ounces) heavy cream

½ cup (3.5 ounces) sugar

6 large egg yolks

1 tablespoon plus 1 teaspoon cornstarch

1 tablespoon unsalted butter, softened

¼ teaspoon vanilla extract

¼ teaspoon almond extract

3 tablespoons cream of coconut, such as Coco Lopez

FOR THE TOPPING

½ cup (1.87 ounces) sweetened shredded coconut

3 cups (24 ounces) heavy cream

¼ cup plus 2 tablespoons (2.75 ounces) sugar

TO MAKE THE CRUST

› Combine the flour, salt, and sugar in a food processor. Add the shortening and butter and pulse until they are in pea-sized bits, about 1 minute. Add the water and pulse until just combined; you should still see little pieces of shortening and butter in the dough. Remove the dough from the processor, shape it into a disk, and wrap it in plastic wrap or parchment paper. Chill for at least 30 minutes.

› Heat the oven to 325°F.

› Place the dough on a floured cool surface.

› Using a rolling pin, roll the dough into a 12-inch circle: Start from the center of the dough and roll outward, rotating the dough 2 to 3 inches after each roll—this will help create a true circle. After every four to five rolls, run a large offset spatula under the dough to release it from the work surface. Add a little flour to the surface, rolling pin, and/or dough if the dough sticks or becomes difficult to roll.

› Roll the dough up onto the rolling pin, then unroll into a 9-inch pie pan, centering the round. Gently press the dough into the bottom of the pan and against the sides, making sure there are no air pockets. Press the dough against the upper edges of the pan so it extends about ½ inch beyond the rim; trim any excess dough with kitchen shears. Chill the crust for 15 minutes, or until the dough is cool and firm.

› Prick the bottom of the dough with a fork about 10 times, evenly spacing out the score marks, then use the back of the fork to make symmetrical indentations all around the rim of the crust.

› Put the pie pan on a baking sheet and bake for 30 minutes, or until lightly golden. Let cool completely on a cooling rack. (Leave the oven on.)

TO MAKE THE FILLING

› Combine the evaporated milk, cream, and sugar in a medium saucepan and bring to a boil.

› Meanwhile, whisk together the yolks, cornstarch, butter, vanilla, almond extract, and cream of coconut in a medium bowl. Whisking constantly, gradually stream the cream mixture into the egg mixture. Return the mixture to the saucepan and cook over low heat, stirring constantly, for 10 to 15 minutes, until the custard thickens and coats the back of the spoon.

› Pour the custard into the baked pie shell. Bake for 35 minutes, or until the custard is set and lightly golden on top. Let cool completely on a cooling rack. (Leave the oven on to toast the topping.)

TO MAKE THE TOPPING

› Spread the coconut on a baking sheet and toast in the oven, stirring twice, for 6 minutes, or until golden. Let cool completely.

› In the bowl of a stand mixer fitted with the whisk attachment (or in a large bowl, using a handheld mixer), whip the cream with the sugar until very stiff peaks form.

TO FINISH THE PIE

› Scoop the whipped cream onto the center of the pie and, using an offset spatula, smooth it into a dome shape. Cover with the toasted coconut.

STORING

› This pie is best enjoyed the day it is made. Store it in a cake box or under a cake dome in the refrigerator.

TIP: PARBAKING, OR PARTIALLY BAKING, a piecrust is a technique used when the filling is exceptionally wet or requires only a shorter cooking time. Both criteria are true of this filling, so the parbaking time is longer than you may have seen in other recipes to ensure the crust is not underbaked.

The Brown Derby Grapefruit Cake

I drive past the original Brown Derby on my way to Valerie Confections every day. In a building distinctively shaped like a Derby hat, the most popular of the chain's four locations was across the street from the Ambassador Hotel and the Cocoanut Grove. The Brown Derby was famous for its wall of fame lined with caricatures of celebrities, its Cobb salad, and this cake.

● MAKES ONE 9-INCH CAKE; SERVES 8 TO 10 ●

FOR THE CAKE

1¼ cups (6.25 ounces) cake flour

¾ cup (5.25 ounces) sugar

1½ teaspoons baking powder

½ teaspoon kosher salt

2 tablespoons water

2½ tablespoons canola oil

3 large eggs, separated

2 teaspoons grated grapefruit zest

1 teaspoon grated lemon zest

1 tablespoon grapefruit juice

¼ teaspoon cream of tartar

FOR THE CREAM CHEESE ICING

10.66 ounces cream cheese, softened

6 tablespoons (¾ stick/3 ounces) unsalted butter, softened

1 packed tablespoon finely chopped grapefruit zest

1 packed teaspoon finely chopped lemon zest

1¾ teaspoons grapefruit juice

½ teaspoon vanilla extract

1 cup (4.5 ounces) confectioners' sugar, sifted

3 large pink grapefruits, peeled, segmented, and seeded

TO MAKE THE CAKE

› Position a rack in the center of the oven and heat the oven to 325°F. Coat the bottoms and sides of two 9-inch round cake pans with nonstick baking spray and line with parchment circles.

› Sift together the flour, sugar, baking powder, and salt into a medium bowl.

› Whisk together the water, oil, egg yolks, grapefruit zest, lemon zest, and grapefruit juice in a small bowl. Create a well in the center of the dry ingredients and pour in the wet mixture. Using a fork, slowly incorporate the dry ingredients into the wet, stirring until fully combined, about 3 minutes.

› In the bowl of a stand mixer fitted with the whisk attachment (or in a large bowl, using a handheld mixer), beat the egg whites and cream of tartar until the whites form stiff peaks. Fold the egg whites into the batter until just combined. Divide the batter between the prepared cake pans, spreading it evenly. Bake for 20 to 25 minutes, until the cakes are slightly golden and a toothpick inserted in the center comes out clean. Resist the urge to check on the cake layers until they have baked for at least 20 minutes; opening the oven door earlier may cause the centers to collapse. Let the cakes cool in the cake pans on a cooling rack for 30 to 45 minutes. Remove the cakes from the pans, peel off the parchment, and let the cakes cool completely on the rack. Wrap the cakes in plastic wrap and refrigerate until you are ready to assemble the cake.

TO MAKE THE ICING

› In the bowl of a stand mixer fitted with the whisk attachment (or in a large bowl, using a handheld mixer), beat the cream cheese at high speed until very smooth. Add the butter and beat until smooth. Add the zests, grapefruit juice, and vanilla and beat until completely incorporated, 2 to 3 minutes. Add the confectioners' sugar in three increments, mixing thoroughly after each addition.

TO ASSEMBLE THE CAKE

› Place one layer top side up on a cake stand. Slide strips of parchment or wax paper under the edges of the cake. Frost the top of the layer with a thin layer of icing, using approximately ½ cup. Cover with grapefruit segments, arranging them in concentric rings. Place the second cake layer top side down on the grapefruit layer and press gently to even the layers. Using a small offset spatula, frost the sides and top of the cake with the remaining icing.

› Arrange a circle of the remaining grapefruit segments around the top edge of the cake. Refrigerate for at least 1 hour before serving.

STORING

› This cake is best enjoyed the day it is assembled. Store it in a cake box or under a cake dome in the refrigerator.

Fruitcake Noir

Forget any preconceived notions of fruitcake—it can be fresh and delicious. After years of testing different fruitcake recipes, I stumbled upon a very straightforward recipe for a "dried fruit and nut cake" in Alice Medrich's *Pure Desserts*. I used her basic recipe as a starting point and created dark and light versions, thinking I could then choose between the two for a delicious holiday cake. No such luck—I liked them so much that we now make both cakes from mid-November through Christmas. Apparently I am not alone in my indecision, because we have many customers who get one of each. See page 46 for the light version. Note that the dried fruits and nuts must macerate overnight.

MAKES ONE 9¹/₂-INCH LOAF; SERVES 10 TO 12

FOR THE FRUIT AND NUTS

³/₄ cup (4.5 ounces) dark raisins

1 cup (4.75 ounces) dried Black Mission figs, julienned

¹/₂ cup (2.5 ounces) dried plums, pitted and julienned

¹/₂ cup (2.5 ounces) prunes, pitted and julienned

¹/₄ cup (2.75 ounces) dried cherries, julienned

2¹/₂ tablespoons chopped candied orange peel

2 cups (9 ounces) unblanched whole raw almonds

¹/₂ cup (4 ounces) port

FOR THE CAKE

²/₃ cup (3.33 ounces) all-purpose flour

¹/₄ teaspoon baking soda

¹/₄ teaspoon baking powder

1 teaspoon kosher salt

1 teaspoon Spice Mix (recipe follows)

2 teaspoons unsweetened cocoa powder

5 tablespoons (2.5 ounces) unsalted butter, softened

¹/₂ cup (3 ounces) light brown sugar

1 cup (8.25 ounces) almond paste, homemade (recipe follows) or store-bought

3 large eggs

1 teaspoon vanilla bean paste (see Resources, page 335)

TO PREPARE THE FRUIT AND NUTS

› Combine the dried fruits, almonds, and port in a medium bowl. Cover with plastic wrap and macerate for 24 to 48 hours at room temperature, stirring occasionally.

TO MAKE THE CAKE

› Sift together the flour, baking soda, baking powder, salt, spice mix, and cocoa powder into a medium bowl. Set aside.

› In the bowl of a stand mixer fitted with the paddle attachment (or in a large bowl, using a handheld mixer), cream the butter and sugar on medium speed until light and fluffy, about 3 minutes. With the mixer on low speed, gradually add the almond paste, mixing until thoroughly combined. Increase the speed to medium and add the eggs one at a time, mixing well after each addition. Add the vanilla paste and mix for 30 seconds. Scrape the bottom and sides of the bowl, then add the dry ingredients, beating just until the batter is smooth. Remove the bowl from the mixer stand.

› Pour the macerated fruits and nuts, with their liquid, into the bowl and mix with a rubber spatula until evenly distributed. Set the bowl aside for 30 minutes. (This resting time allows the batter to absorb the port.)

› Position a rack in the center of the oven and heat the oven to 300°F. Generously coat the bottom and sides of a 9¹/₂-by-5¹/₂-inch loaf pan with nonstick baking spray.

› Pour the batter into the prepared pan and smooth the top with a spatula. Bake for 30 minutes. Rotate the pan and bake for an additional 40 to 45 minutes, until the top of the cake is browned and a toothpick inserted in the center comes out clean. Put the loaf pan on a cooling rack and let the cake cool for 1 hour.

Continued ›

› Remove the cake from the pan and cool completely on the rack, about 2 hours.

STORING

› The cake can be stored, tightly wrapped in plastic wrap or parchment, at room temperature for up to 6 weeks.

Spice Mix

MAKES ABOUT 1 CUP

4 whole star anise

12 whole cloves

2 teaspoons whole white peppercorns

1/2 cup plus 2 tablespoons (2.5 ounces) ground cinnamon

1 tablespoon plus 1 teaspoon ground ginger

1 teaspoon ground mace

1 teaspoon freshly grated nutmeg

› Combine the star anise, cloves, and white peppercorns in a coffee or spice grinder and pulse to a fine powder, about 3 minutes. Pour the spices into a small bowl, add the ground cinnamon, ginger, mace, and nutmeg, and combine with a small whisk or a fork.

› Store in an airtight container for up to 3 months.

Almond Paste

MAKES ABOUT 3 CUPS

4 cups (14 ounces) raw almond flour (see Resources, page 335), toasted (see page 20)

1 cup (7 ounces) sugar

1/2 teaspoon kosher salt

4 to 6 tablespoons water

› Pour the toasted almond flour, sugar, and salt into the bowl of a food processor and pulse a few times until combined. Continue pulsing as you add water 1 tablespoon at a time until the paste comes together into a ball.

› Remove the almond paste from the processor, wrap tightly in plastic wrap, and store in the refrigerator for up to 2 months.

VARIATION

BLANCHED ALMOND PASTE: Replace the toasted almond flour with regular almond flour.

Fruitcake Blanc

If you are looking for an alternative to cookies for holiday gifts, try this cake or the noir version (on page 43). A sturdy cake like fruitcake is perfect for shipping across country, without any fear of breakage in transit. I also like to cut a couple of loaves into 2-inch slices, wrap them in parchment, and tie them with ribbon for small hostess gifts—it's very useful to have a few of these cakes on hand during the holidays. Note that the dried fruits and nuts must macerate overnight.

MAKES ONE 9¹/₂-INCH LOAF; SERVES 10 TO 12

FOR THE FRUIT AND NUTS

³/₄ cup (3.5 ounces) dried white figs

³/₄ cup (4.5 ounces) golden raisins

¹/₂ cup (2.25 ounces) dried pears, julienned

¹/₂ cup (1.25 ounces) dried apples, julienned

¹/₂ cup (2.5 ounces) dried apricots, julienned

2 cups (9 ounces) blanched whole almonds

¹/₂ cup (4 ounces) brandy

FOR THE CAKE

³/₄ cup (3.75 ounces) all-purpose flour

¹/₄ teaspoon baking soda

¹/₄ teaspoon baking powder

1 teaspoon kosher salt

5 tablespoons (2.5 ounces) butter, softened

¹/₂ cup (3.5 ounces) sugar

1 cup (8.25 ounces) Almond Paste (page 44), made with blanched almond flour (see page 20)

3 large eggs

1¹/₂ teaspoons vanilla bean paste (see Resources, page 335)

TO PREPARE THE FRUIT AND NUTS

▸ Combine the dried fruits, almonds, and brandy in a medium bowl. Cover with plastic wrap and macerate for 24 to 48 hours at room temperature, stirring occasionally.

TO MAKE THE CAKE

▸ Sift together the flour, baking soda, baking powder, and salt into a medium bowl. Set aside.

▸ In the bowl of a stand mixer fitted with the paddle attachment (or in a large bowl, using a handheld mixer), cream the butter and sugar on medium speed until light and fluffy, about 3 minutes. With the mixer on low speed, gradually add the almond paste, mixing until thoroughly combined. Increase the speed to medium and add the eggs one at a time, mixing well after each addition. Add the vanilla paste and mix for 30 seconds. Scrape the bottom and sides of the bowl, then add the dry ingredients, beating just until the batter is smooth. Remove the bowl from the mixer stand.

▸ Pour the macerated fruits and nuts, with their liquid, into the bowl and mix with a rubber spatula until evenly distributed. Set the bowl aside for 30 minutes. (This resting time allows the batter to absorb the brandy.)

▸ Position a rack in the center of the oven and heat the oven to 300°F. Generously coat the bottom and sides of a 9¹/₂-by-5¹/₂-inch loaf pan with nonstick baking spray.

▸ Pour the batter into the prepared pan and smooth the top with a spatula. Bake for 30 minutes. Rotate the pan and bake for an additional 40 to 45 minutes, until the top of the cake is golden brown and a toothpick inserted in the center comes out clean. Put the loaf pan on a cooling rack and let the cake cool for 1 hour.

▸ Remove the cake from the pan and cool completely on the rack, about 2 hours.

STORING

▸ The cake can be stored, tightly wrapped in plastic wrap or parchment, at room temperature for up to 6 weeks.

Pumpkin Cheesecake with Gingersnap Crust

The smell of pumpkin cheesecake baking is the perfect precursor to Thanksgiving dinner. This cheesecake is more delicate than you might expect: when I think cheesecake, I usually think of something very rich and dense, but this one has a surprising soufflé-like quality. It's also made in a tart pan, rather than a springform. Serve slightly chilled, with whipped cream if you like (see page 138).

MAKES ONE 11-INCH CHEESECAKE; SERVES 10 TO 14

FOR THE CRUST

1½ cups (6.5 ounces) finely ground gingersnap cookies

1 cup (3.5 ounces) raw almond flour

⅓ cup (1.66 ounces) all-purpose flour

¼ cup (1.5 ounces) light brown sugar

½ teaspoon ground ginger

4 tablespoons (½ stick/2 ounces) unsalted butter, melted

FOR THE FILLING

One 3- to 4-pound pumpkin, preferably Winter Luxury (see headnote, page 131)

1 pound cream cheese, softened

½ cup (3 ounces) light brown sugar

¼ cup (1.75 ounces) granulated sugar

¼ cup (2 ounces) sour cream or crème fraîche

2 large eggs

1 tablespoon all-purpose flour

1½ teaspoons Spice Mix (page 44)

1 tablespoon vanilla bean paste (see Resources, page 335)

TO MAKE THE CRUST

› Heat the oven to 350°F. Grease an 11-inch fluted tart pan with a removable bottom.

› Whisk together the ground cookies, flours, sugar, and ginger in a medium bowl. Pour the melted butter over the dry ingredients and mix thoroughly with a fork. Press the mixture evenly over the bottom of the prepared pan.

› Bake the crust for 12 minutes, or until slightly darker and set. Let cool completely on a cooling rack. (Leave the oven on.)

TO ROAST THE PUMPKIN

› Line a baking sheet with parchment paper. Using a heavy chef's knife, cut the pumpkin in half. Scoop out the seeds. Place the pumpkin halves cut side down on the baking sheet and roast for about 40 minutes, until the flesh is very soft. Pierce the pumpkin with a fork to check for doneness. Let the pumpkin cool completely. Reduce the oven temperature to 325°F.

› Scoop the pumpkin flesh out of the skin and puree in a food processor or blender, scraping down the sides once or twice. Reserve ¾ cup (6 ounces) of the puree for the filling. (The extra puree can be packed into a freezer Ziploc bag and frozen for up to 3 months.) Place a 9-inch pie or cake pan filled with 3 to 4 cups of water on the bottom rack of the oven (see Tip).

TO MAKE THE FILLING

› In the bowl of a stand mixer fitted with the paddle attachment (or in a large bowl, using a handheld mixer), beat the cream cheese on medium-high speed until very smooth. Scrape the bottom and sides of the bowl and beat for 1 minute. Add the sugars and beat on medium speed until light and fluffy, about 3 minutes. Add the pumpkin puree and sour cream and beat until thoroughly combined. Add the eggs one at a time, beating well after each addition. Add the flour, spice mix, and vanilla paste and beat on medium-high until creamy and fluffy.

› Pour the batter into the pan and spread it evenly on the gingersnap crust. Carefully pick up the tart pan and very gently tap it on the work surface to remove any air bubbles trapped in the batter. Bake for 1 hour and 10 minutes, or until the cheesecake puffs up like a soufflé and is firm around the edges. Carefully remove the cheesecake from the oven and cool completely on a cooling rack, about 3 hours. Cover with plastic wrap and refrigerate for at least 6 hours, or overnight, before serving.

› When ready to serve, remove the tart ring. Slide a hot offset spatula between the bottom of the pan and the cheesecake to release it and transfer to a serving platter.

STORING

› The cheesecake can be stored, covered, in the refrigerator for up to 3 days.

TIP: SOME RECIPES CALL FOR BAKING cheesecakes in a water bath, which reduces the chances of the cheesecake cracking. To reap the benefits of a steam water bath but avoid the possibility of water seeping into the cake, place a pan filled with water on the lowest oven rack, just below your cheesecake.

Goat-Cheese Cheesecake with Almond Crust

The idea for a goat-cheese cheesecake came to me when I was enjoying a bite of goat cheese with roasted almonds and gooey honeycomb . . . think of it as a cheese plate in dessert form. Serve it with candied nuts (see page 94) and chunks of fresh honeycomb (see Resources, page 335).

→ MAKES ONE 9-INCH CHEESECAKE; SERVES 12 TO 14 ←

FOR THE CRUST

6 tablespoons (¾ stick/3 ounces) unsalted butter, softened

¼ cup (1 ounce) confectioners' sugar, sifted

1 large egg

½ teaspoon vanilla extract

⅔ cup (3.33 ounces) all-purpose flour

½ cup plus 1 tablespoon (2 ounces) raw almond flour (see Resources, page 335), toasted (see page 20)

¼ teaspoon kosher salt

FOR THE FILLING

1 pound 5 ounces goat cheese, softened

1½ cups (12 ounces) mascarpone

¾ cup plus 1 tablespoon (5.75 ounces) sugar

2 tablespoons heavy cream

1½ teaspoons vanilla bean paste (see Resources, page 335)

1½ teaspoons grated lemon zest

3 large eggs

TO MAKE THE CRUST

› In the bowl of a stand mixer fitted with the paddle attachment (or in a large bowl, using a handheld mixer), beat the butter and sugar on medium speed until light and fluffy, about 3 minutes. Add the egg and vanilla and beat until well combined. Scrape the sides and bottom of the bowl and mix for 30 seconds. Add the flours and salt and beat until just combined. Shape the dough into a disk, wrap in plastic wrap or parchment paper, and chill for at least 2 hours.

› Heat the oven to 350°F. Coat the bottom and sides of a 9-inch spring-form pan with nonstick baking spray or butter. Line the pan with a parchment circle.

› Press the almond dough evenly over the bottom of the prepared pan.

› Bake for 25 minutes, or until the edges turn golden brown. Cool completely on a cooling rack, about 30 minutes, then wrap the bottom of the pan in aluminum foil to prevent leakage. Heat the oven to 350°F. Place a 9-inch pie or cake pan filled with 3 to 4 cups of water on the bottom rack of the oven (see Tip, opposite).

TO MAKE THE FILLING

› In the bowl of a stand mixer fitted with the paddle attachment (or in a large bowl, using a handheld mixer), beat the goat cheese on medium speed until smooth, about 3 minutes. Scrape the sides and bottom of the bowl and beat for 1 minute. Add the mascarpone and beat until fully combined. Add the sugar and beat until the mixture is light and fluffy, about 2 minutes. Reduce the speed to low and beat in the cream, vanilla paste, and zest. Scrape the sides and bottom of the bowl again. Increase the speed to medium and add the eggs one at a time, mixing well after each addition.

› Pour the batter into the prepared pan. Bake for 1 hour and 10 minutes, or until the edges appear firm but the center of the cheesecake is still a little jiggly when the pan is shaken gently. Carefully remove the cheesecake from the oven and cool completely on a cooling rack, about 4 hours. Cover with aluminum foil and refrigerate for at least 6 hours, or overnight, before serving.

Continued ›

› When ready to serve, run a hot knife or offset spatula around the sides of the cheesecake to release it from the pan; remove the sides of the pan. Line a baking sheet with parchment paper and invert the cake onto the parchment. Gently slide the bottom of the pan off the crust and peel off the round of parchment. Invert the cake onto a serving plate, so it is upright.

STORING

› The cheesecake can be stored, covered, in the refrigerator for up to 4 days.

White Chocolate Coconut Cake

Coconut cake makes me think of Christmas. The white-flocked cake looks so magnificent at the center of a holiday table that I can't help but save this recipe for December festivities. Instead of filling the cake with custard or coconut buttercream, I prefer the brightly acidic flavor of passion fruit here. The tart perfumed buttercream pairs particularly well with the sweetness of the white chocolate.

● MAKES ONE 9-INCH CAKE; SERVES 10 TO 14 ●

FOR THE CAKE

3¼ cups (16.25 ounces) all-purpose flour

1 tablespoon plus 1 teaspoon baking powder

2 teaspoons kosher salt

2½ sticks (10 ounces) unsalted butter, softened

2¼ cups (15.75 ounces) sugar

1 cup (3.75 ounces) sweetened shredded coconut, roughly chopped

8 large eggs

6.5 ounces 31% white chocolate, melted and cooled (see page 184)

1¼ cups (10 ounces) evaporated milk

FOR THE PASSION FRUIT BUTTERCREAM FILLING

2 sticks (8 ounces) unsalted butter, softened

¼ cup plus 2 tablespoons (1.68 ounces) confectioners' sugar, sifted

¼ cup (2 ounces) light corn syrup

½ cup (4 ounces) passion fruit puree (see Resources, page 335), at room temperature

4 ounces 31% white chocolate, melted and cooled (see page 184)

¼ teaspoon kosher salt

FOR THE WHITE CHOCOLATE BUTTERCREAM FROSTING

2 sticks (8 ounces) unsalted butter, softened

½ cup (2.25 ounces) confectioners' sugar, sifted

2 tablespoons light corn syrup

1 teaspoon vanilla extract

4 ounces 31% white chocolate, melted and cooled (see page 184)

¼ teaspoon kosher salt

3 cups (11.25 ounces) sweetened shredded coconut, for finishing

TO MAKE THE CAKE

› Position the racks in the upper and lower thirds of the oven and heat the oven to 325°F. Coat the bottom and sides of four 9-inch round cake pans with nonstick baking spray and line with parchment circles.

› Sift together the flour, baking powder, and salt into a medium bowl.

› In the bowl of a stand mixer fitted with the whisk attachment (or in a large bowl, using a handheld mixer), cream the butter and sugar on medium speed until light and fluffy, about 3 minutes. Sprinkle the coconut into the bowl and beat until well combined. Add the eggs one at a time, mixing well after each addition. Pour in the melted chocolate and mix well. Scrape the sides and bottom of the bowl and mix for about 15 seconds. Scrape the bowl once more. Alternately add the dry ingredients and evaporated milk in batches, beating until thoroughly combined.

› Divide the batter equally among the prepared cake pans, spreading it evenly. Place two pans on each oven rack and bake for 20 minutes. Rotate the pans and bake for 10 to 15 minutes, until the cakes are lightly golden and a toothpick inserted in the center comes out clean. Let the cakes cool for 10 minutes in the pans on cooling racks, then remove, peel off the parchment, and cool completely on the racks. Wrap the cakes in plastic wrap and refrigerate until you are ready to assemble the cake.

TO MAKE THE FILLING

› In the bowl of the stand mixer fitted with the paddle attachment (or in a large bowl, using a handheld mixer), beat the butter on medium speed until very soft and creamy, about 4 minutes. Scrape the sides and bottom of the bowl and beat for an additional minute. Add the confectioners' sugar and beat for 1 minute. Pour in the corn syrup and passion fruit puree and mix until thoroughly incorporated.

› Scrape the sides and bottom of the bowl and beat on low speed as you stream in the melted white chocolate. Add the salt and continue beating until the buttercream is light and fluffy, about 3 minutes. Scrape the bowl once more and beat for 30 seconds on medium-high speed. Set aside.

Continued ›

(The buttercream can be covered and stored in the refrigerator for up to 2 weeks; see instructions on page 102.)

TO MAKE THE FROSTING

› In the bowl of the stand mixer fitted with the paddle attachment (or in a large bowl, using a handheld mixer), beat the butter on medium speed until very soft and creamy, about 3 minutes. Scrape the sides and bottom of the bowl and beat for 1 minute. Add the confectioners' sugar and beat for 1 minute. Pour in the corn syrup and vanilla and mix until thoroughly incorporated.

› Scrape the sides and bottom of the bowl and beat on low speed as you stream in the melted white chocolate. Add the salt and continue beating until the buttercream is shiny and fluffy, about 3 minutes. Scrape the bowl once more and beat for 30 seconds on medium-high speed. (The buttercream can be covered and stored in the refrigerator for up to 2 weeks; see instructions on page 102.)

TO ASSEMBLE THE CAKE

› Place one layer top side up on a cake stand or turntable. Slide four strips of parchment under the edges of the cake to catch any stray frosting. Using an offset spatula, spread one-third of the passion fruit buttercream evenly over the surface. Repeat with 2 more cake layers and the remaining passion fruit buttercream. Place the fourth cake layer on top and refrigerate the cake, uncovered, for 15 minutes so the buttercream sets and the layers adhere to each other.

› Using an offset spatula, frost the sides and top of the cake with the white chocolate buttercream.

› Take a handful of coconut at a time and press onto the sides of the cake until the sides are covered. Sprinkle the remaining coconut on top of the cake. Chill for at least 30 minutes before serving.

STORING

› The cake can be stored, lightly covered, in the refrigerator for up to 2 days.

Scandia's Apple Cake

From 1946 to 1989, Scandia served a chic celebrity clientele at its Sunset Boulevard location. The design was distinctly midcentury, with a dramatic wood-paneled bar and bright red chairs. At its peak, Scandia had an award-winning wine list and served the best Scandinavian food in the country, with specialties like *kåldolmar* and lingonberry pudding. The flavor of this cake is reminiscent of an apple pie with whipped cream, but its dense layers have a far more complex texture.

● MAKES ONE 9-INCH CAKE; SERVES 8 TO 12 ●

FOR THE CAKE

15 medium baking apples, such as Pink Lady or Mutsu, peeled, cored, and sliced very thin

4 tablespoons (½ stick/2 ounces) unsalted butter, melted

½ cup (3 ounces) light brown sugar

Juice of 1 lemon

¼ cup (1.5 ounces) cornstarch

½ cup (4 ounces) currant jelly

1 cup (3.5 ounces) raw almond flour (see Resources, page 335), toasted (see page 20)

1 cup (2.5 ounces) Toasted Cake Crumbs (recipe follows)

12 almond macaroons (see Resources, page 335), roughly chopped

FOR THE TOPPING

1 cup (8 ounces) heavy cream

2 tablespoons sugar

½ cup (1.75 ounces) sliced blanched almonds, toasted

TO MAKE THE CAKE

❯ Position a rack in the center of the oven and heat the oven to 350°F.

❯ Put the sliced apples on a baking sheet and toss with 2 tablespoons of the melted butter, the brown sugar, and lemon juice. Spread the apples out and bake for 20 minutes, or until very tender when pierced with a fork.

❯ Remove the roasted apples from the oven and sprinkle with the cornstarch, tossing to coat. Set the pan on a cooling rack to cool completely.

❯ Heat the oven to 400°F.

❯ Pour the remaining 2 tablespoons melted butter into a 9-inch round cake pan and tilt the pan to coat the bottom evenly. Cover the bottom of the pan with apple slices, arranging them in concentric circles and overlapping them slightly, then repeat to make a second layer on top. Carefully spread the currant jelly over the apples, then sprinkle with the almond flour and ½ cup of the cake crumbs. Using a large spoon or spatula, press down on the top to compress the layers. Top the cake crumbs with a layer of the chopped macaroons and cover them with the remaining apples, arranging them in concentric circles.

❯ Cover with aluminum foil and bake for 30 minutes. Remove from the oven and reduce the temperature to 350°F. Remove the foil, sprinkle the remaining cake crumbs over the top of the cake, and bake for an additional 20 minutes, or until the top is golden brown. Let the cake cool for 1 hour on a cooling rack, then put in the refrigerator and chill completely, about 3 hours.

TO MAKE THE TOPPING

❯ In the bowl of a stand mixer fitted with the whisk attachment (or in a large bowl, using a handheld mixer), whip the cream with the sugar until it forms stiff peaks.

Continued ❯

TO ASSEMBLE THE CAKE

‣ Run a hot knife or offset spatula around the edges of the cake to loosen it from the pan. Invert the cake onto a cake stand or a serving plate. Spread the whipped cream on top and sprinkle with the almonds.

STORING

‣ The cake can be stored, in a cake box or under a cake dome, in the refrigerator for up to 2 days.

Toasted Cake Crumbs

MAKES ABOUT 4 CUPS

Vanilla Bean Cake (page 75)

‣ Heat the oven to 350°F. Line a 13-by-18-by-1-inch baking sheet with parchment paper or a silicone mat.

‣ Crumble the cake into little pieces on the prepared baking pan and spread them out. Bake for 15 minutes, or until the crumbs are golden brown. Let cool to room temperature, then store in an airtight container for up to 5 days; the crumbs can also be frozen for longer storage.

Carrot Cake with Cream Cheese Frosting

This recipe is the polar opposite of the rustic carrot cakes of the 1970s—
the cake is delicate and void of any chunky bits. I suppose it is a reaction
to the punishing "healthy" versions I ate during my childhood.

● MAKES ONE 9-INCH CAKE; SERVES 10 TO 14 ●

FOR THE CAKE

2¹/₂ cups (12.5 ounces) all-purpose flour

1 teaspoon baking powder

1 teaspoon baking soda

1 teaspoon kosher salt

1 tablespoon Spice Mix (page 44)

8 tablespoons (1 stick/4 ounces) unsalted
butter, softened

1¹/₄ cups (8.75 ounces) granulated sugar

³/₄ cup (4.5 ounces) light brown sugar

4 large eggs

¹/₂ cup (3.55 ounces) canola oil

1 teaspoon vanilla extract

3 packed cups (18 ounces) finely shredded
carrots (about 6 medium carrots)

FOR THE CREAM CHEESE FROSTING

11 ounces cream cheese, softened

6 tablespoons (³/₄ stick/3 ounces) unsalted
butter, softened

2 teaspoons grated lemon zest

1 teaspoon lemon juice

1 teaspoon vanilla extract

1 cup (4.5 ounces) confectioners' sugar, sifted

TO MAKE THE CAKE

▸ Position a rack in the center of the oven and heat the oven to 350°F. Coat the bottoms and sides of three 9-by-2-inch round cake pans with nonstick cooking spray or butter and line with parchment circles.

▸ Sift together the flour, baking powder, baking soda, salt, and spice mix into a medium bowl.

▸ In the bowl of a stand mixer fitted with the paddle attachment (or in a large bowl, using a handheld mixer), beat the butter and sugars on medium speed until light and fluffy, about 4 minutes.

▸ Whisk together the eggs, canola oil, and vanilla in a small bowl, pour the mixture into the creamed butter, and beat until smooth, 2 to 3 minutes. Scrape the bowl and beat for 1 minute. With the mixer on low speed, add the dry ingredients in two batches, mixing for 2 minutes after each addition. Scrape the bowl. Fold in the carrots and mix until incorporated, about 1 minute.

▸ Divide the batter among the prepared cake pans, spreading it evenly. Bake for 20 minutes. Rotate the cakes and bake for an additional 10 to 13 minutes, until the cakes appear firm and a toothpick inserted in the center comes out clean. Let the cakes cool for 10 minutes in the pans on cooling racks, then remove and cool completely on the racks. Wrap the cakes in plastic wrap and refrigerate until you are ready to assemble the cake.

TO MAKE THE FROSTING

▸ In the bowl of the stand mixer fitted with the paddle attachment (or in a large bowl, using a handheld mixer), beat the cream cheese on medium speed for about 3 minutes. Scrape the bowl and beat for 1 minute. Add the butter, lemon zest, juice, and vanilla and beat until smooth. Scrape the bowl. Reduce the mixer speed to low and slowly add the confectioners' sugar, mixing until combined.

TO ASSEMBLE THE CAKE

▸ Place one layer top side up on a cake stand or turntable. Using an offset spatula, spread one-third of the frosting over the top. Repeat with the remaining cake layers and frosting. Refrigerate the cake until ready to serve.

STORING

▸ The cake can be stored, in a cake box or under a cake dome, in the refrigerator for up to 2 days.

Butter Cake with Milk Chocolate Frosting

This is essentially a traditional birthday cake, with moist yellow cake layers and a thick coating of milk chocolate frosting. It's substantially sweeter than most of the cakes at Valerie Confections and much larger. Using a spoon when you frost the cake creates beautiful swirls of chocolaty frosting.

● MAKES ONE 9-INCH CAKE; SERVES 20 ●

FOR THE CAKE

4²/₃ cups (1 pound 7.33 ounces) all-purpose flour

1 tablespoon baking powder

1¹/₂ teaspoons salt

1¹/₄ pounds (5 sticks) unsalted butter, softened

3¹/₂ cups (24.5 ounces) sugar

¹/₂ cup (4 ounces) crème fraîche

8 large eggs

2 large egg whites

2 tablespoons vanilla extract

FOR THE MILK CHOCOLATE FROSTING

12 tablespoons (1¹/₂ sticks/6 ounces) unsalted butter, softened

6 cups (1¹/₂ pounds) confectioners' sugar, sifted

2 tablespoons vanilla extract

1 teaspoon kosher salt

14.5 ounces 38% milk chocolate, melted and cooled (see page 184)

9 ounces 61% bittersweet chocolate, melted and cooled (see page 184)

1 cup (8 ounces) whole milk

TO MAKE THE CAKE

› Position a rack in the center of the oven and heat the oven to 350°F. Coat the bottoms and sides of three 9-by-3-inch round cake pans with nonstick baking spray or butter and line with parchment circles.

› Sift together the flour, baking powder, and salt into a large bowl.

› In the bowl of a stand mixer fitted with the paddle attachment (or in a large bowl, using a handheld mixer), cream the butter and sugar on medium speed until light and fluffy, about 3 minutes.

› Whisk together the crème fraîche, eggs, egg whites, and vanilla in a medium bowl, then pour into the creamed butter and mix until smooth, 2 to 3 minutes. Scrape the bottom and sides of the bowl and mix for 1 minute. With the mixer on low speed, add the dry ingredients in three batches, mixing for 1 to 2 minutes after each addition. Scrape the bowl again and mix for 1 minute.

› Divide the batter among the prepared cake pans, smoothing the tops. Bake for 40 to 45 minutes, until the cakes are slightly golden at the edges and a toothpick inserted in the center comes out clean. Let the cakes cool for 15 minutes in the pans on cooling racks, then remove from the pans, peel off the parchment, and cool completely on the racks. Wrap the cakes in plastic wrap and refrigerate until you are ready to assemble the cake.

TO MAKE THE FROSTING

› In the bowl of the stand mixer fitted with the paddle attachment (or in a large bowl, using a handheld mixer), beat the butter on medium speed until light and fluffy, about 2 minutes. With the mixer on low speed, add the confectioners' sugar about ¹/₂ cup at a time, mixing until smooth. Scrape the sides and bottom of the bowl. Add the vanilla and salt and beat for 1 minute.

› If using a stand mixer, replace the paddle attachment with the whisk attachment. Gradually pour in the melted chocolates, mixing until well incorporated. Scrape the bowl again, then stream in the milk with the mixer on low speed and continue mixing until the frosting is creamy, smooth, and uniform in texture.

TO ASSEMBLE THE CAKE

‣ Place one cake layer top side up on a cake stand or turntable. Slide four strips of parchment under the edges of the cake to catch any stray frosting. Using an offset spatula, spread about 1½ cups of the frosting evenly over the top of the layer. Repeat with another cake layer and 1½ cups more frosting. Stack the third layer on top and press down gently to even the layers. Using an offset spatula, frost the sides and top of the cake with the remaining frosting. Then, with the back of a large spoon, create swirls in the frosting.

STORING

‣ The cake can be stored, lightly covered, at room temperature for up to 2 days.

A Cake for Alice

If you work in the California food industry long enough, you will probably be lucky enough to cross paths with Alice Waters. After seventeen years, Alice finally walked through my door. She was glowing and gracious and thrilled with the hand-touched nature of everything in the shop. She called a couple of days after her visit with a special request—would I make a dessert for her dinner party the following night? She and I talked through a couple of ideas—well, actually, she instructed me, under the guise of collaboration, to create a cake version of my mint mendiants. Of course I was thrilled to oblige.

● MAKES ONE 10-INCH CAKE; SERVES 12 TO 14 ●

FOR THE CAKE

3 cups (1 pound) 72% bittersweet chocolate fèves (see Resources, page 335) or
chopped 72% bittersweet chocolate

12 tablespoons (1½ sticks/6 ounces) unsalted
butter

7 large eggs, separated

1¼ cups (8.75 ounces) sugar

1 teaspoon kosher salt

2 teaspoons vanilla extract

1½ cups (5.25 ounces) raw almond flour
(see Resources, page 335), toasted
(see page 20)

FOR THE CHOCOLATE GLAZE

10 ounces 61% bittersweet chocolate,
chopped

7 tablespoons (3.5 ounces) unsalted butter,
cut into chunks

¼ cup (2.75 ounces) light corn syrup

12 to 14 Candied Mint Leaves (recipe follows)

TO MAKE THE CAKE

> Position a rack in the center of the oven and heat the oven to 325°F. Coat the bottom of a 10-inch springform pan with nonstick baking spray or butter and line the pan with a parchment circle.

> Melt the chocolate and butter in a double boiler or a heatproof bowl set over a pot of simmering water, stirring occasionally. Pour into a large bowl and set aside to cool for 5 minutes.

> In the bowl of a stand mixer fitted with the whisk attachment (or in a large bowl, using a handheld mixer), whip the egg whites, sugar, and salt until the whites form stiff peaks. Remove the bowl from the mixer stand.

> In a small bowl, whisk the egg yolks until they are broken up and smooth. Using a rubber spatula, fold the egg yolks into the egg whites. Fold the eggs into the melted chocolate until there are no visible signs of egg. Fold in the vanilla and almond flour until the batter is smooth, about 2 minutes.

> Pour the batter into the prepared cake pan. Bake for 1 hour, or until the cake looks set; a toothpick inserted in the center will come out with a few crumbs on it (do not bake until the toothpick comes out clean, or the cake will be dry). Let the cake cool completely in the pan on a cooling rack, about 1½ hours.

TO MAKE THE GLAZE

> Put the chocolate, butter, and corn syrup in the top of a double boiler or in a heatproof bowl set over a pot of simmering water and stir over medium-low heat until the chocolate and butter are melted and the glaze appears shiny, about 5 minutes. Pour the glaze into a 2-cup measuring cup or a small pitcher. Let cool to 90° to 95°F before using, using a candy or instant-read thermometer to monitor the temperature. (The glaze can be stored, covered, in the refrigerator for up to 3 weeks; reheat gently, stirring occasionally, before using.)

Continued ▸

TO FINISH THE CAKE

‣ Run a thin knife around the edges of the cake to release it from the pan. Remove the sides of the pan. Place a cooling rack on the top of the cake and invert the cake onto the rack. Using an offset spatula, remove the bottom of the cake pan and peel off the parchment paper. Set the rack (with the cake) on a baking sheet to catch the glaze drippings.

‣ Pour the chocolate glaze over the cake, starting at the edges and then moving to the center. Pick up the rack and bang it against the baking sheet to even out the glaze. Carefully arrange the candied mint leaves around the top edge of the cake. Allow the glaze to set completely before moving the cake; this can take 10 to 15 minutes. Or, if your kitchen is warm, put the cake, on the rack, in the refrigerator until the glaze is firm, just a few minutes.

‣ Run a hot offset spatula under the bottom of the cake to release it from the rack, and transfer to a cake stand or a serving plate.

STORING

‣ The cake can be stored, lightly covered, in the refrigerator for up to 3 days.

Candied Mint Leaves

MAKES 40

1 cup (7 ounces) sugar
40 uniform mint leaves, gently washed and dried
1 large egg white, beaten

‣ Pour the sugar onto a plate or into a baking pan. Using a very small brush or your fingertips, lightly coat a mint leaf with egg white on both sides, then place on the sugar. Using a teaspoon, sprinkle sugar over the leaf. Carefully flip the leaf and do the same on the other side, making sure the entire leaf is covered in sugar. Put the sugared leaf on a cooling rack. Repeat with the remaining leaves, and allow to set for 2 to 4 hours.

‣ Store in an airtight container for up to 3 months.

VARIATION

CANDIED ROSE PETALS: Substitute 40 large, uniform organic rose petals for the mint leaves.

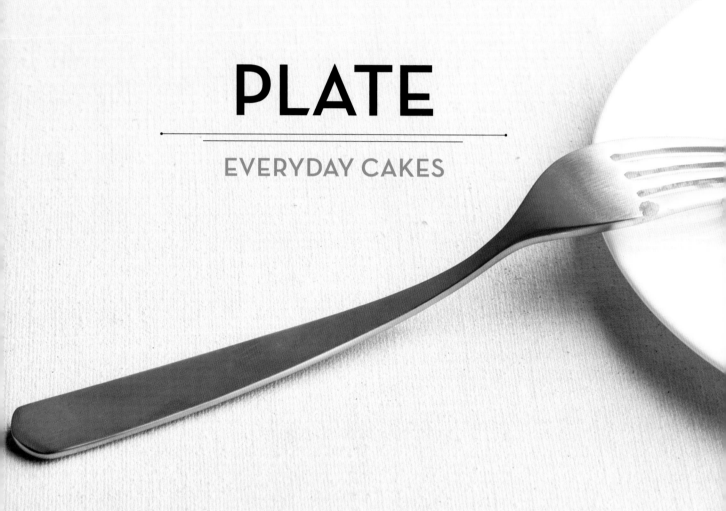

PLATE

EVERYDAY CAKES

FOR some occasions, we want a big, important cake with six layers served with flair on a cake stand, but at other times, a cake of smaller scale renders complete satisfaction. The recipes in this chapter are designed for the simple days; they are very personal to me and representative of how I usually like to eat dessert—simply and in moderation. But simplicity does not mean boring. Just like a perfect golden roasted chicken, a slice of moist vanilla-specked cake comforts the stomach and the soul. These everyday cakes come in flavors that go beyond the traditional chocolate and vanilla, shapes that range from a simple layer cake to precious petits fours, and colors from the darkest chocolate to sparkling gold.

Surely every home baker has made some version of the traditional 1-2-3-4 cake. This quintessential recipe creates a slightly fluffy cake that is great alone or embellished with different flavors and frostings. The Golden Butter Cake recipe (see page 77) is my 1-2-3-4; I used it as a base recipe for most of the other cakes in this chapter, and you can also vary it with lots of different flavors. My interpretation makes a cake that is substantially different in structure from the classic American butter cake. With lots of butter and a dose of crème fraîche, it is dense and rich, in a more European style. The cakes in this chapter are significantly shorter than most American layer cakes, averaging just two or three inches when built. The density of the cake layers also has a practical component: they are durable and easy to handle, resulting in less likelihood of tears or breaks when assembling the cake.

In keeping with the cherished simplicity of everyday cakes, the finishing methods given on these pages are very quick. No piping bags or fondants, just easy glazes and buttercreams. And the cake layers are baked in separate pans to facilitate stress-free cake building—no need for splitting layers horizontally or crumb coats. You just spread the filling and stack the layers to create pretty, modern desserts. The mini-cakes take a simple glaze or no coating at all, and while the petits fours might look complicated, they're easy to make.

This chapter also touches on my underlying culinary philosophy: make what you want to eat. You'll find my favorite cake recipes here, but you can customize them to make them your own. Take a look at Cake Compositions on page 110 for a few examples of how to combine cakes, fillings, and frostings, and then experiment. You can change a cake according to your mood or what fruit is at its peak. The strawberries on the Golden Butter Cake with Berries and Mascarpone Frosting (page 77), for example, could easily be replaced with figs, plums, or blood orange segments. The idea is to have fun and create your own signature desserts, defined only by your whim and the season.

Vanilla Bean Cake

A plain vanilla cake can be something remarkably elegant and satisfying.
Serve with spoonfuls of whipped cream if you like, but feel no obligation to
frost or fuss—a slice of this dense, moist cake can finish almost any meal.

● MAKES ONE 9-INCH CAKE; SERVES 6 TO 8 ●

1½ cups plus 2 tablespoons (8.12 ounces)
   all-purpose flour

⅓ teaspoon baking powder

⅓ teaspoon salt

1¾ sticks plus 1 tablespoon (7.5 ounces)
   unsalted butter, softened

1 tablespoon light corn syrup

1 cup (7 ounces) sugar

3 large eggs

2 tablespoons crème fraîche or sour cream

1 tablespoon vanilla bean paste
   (see Resources, page 335)

1 tablespoon vanilla extract

1 recipe Whipped Cream (optional; page 138)

‣ Position a rack in the center of the oven and heat the oven to 350°F.
Coat the bottom and sides of a 9-by-2-inch round cake pan with nonstick
baking spray or butter and line with a parchment circle.

‣ Sift together the flour, baking powder, and salt into a medium bowl.

‣ In the bowl of a stand mixer fitted with the paddle attachment (or in
a large bowl, using a handheld mixer), cream the butter, corn syrup, and
sugar on medium speed until light and fluffy, about 4 minutes.

‣ Whisk together the eggs, crème fraîche, vanilla paste, and vanilla in a
small bowl, then pour the mixture into the creamed butter and beat until
smooth. Scrape the bottom and sides of the bowl and the paddle and mix
for 30 seconds. With the mixer on low speed, add the dry ingredients
in three batches, mixing for 30 seconds after each addition. Scrape the
bowl again and mix for 15 seconds.

‣ Spread the batter evenly into the prepared cake pan. Bake for
15 minutes. Rotate the cake and bake for an additional 15 to 17 minutes
until the cake appears firm and has a matte finish; a toothpick inserted
in the center should come out clean. Let the cake cool completely in
the pan on a cooling rack. Run an offset spatula or a small knife around
the sides of the cake pan, then invert the cake onto a serving plate and
peel off the parchment paper. Serve dolloped with the whipped cream if
desired.

STORING

‣ The cake can be stored, covered, at room temperature for up to 3 days.
Or wrap tightly in plastic wrap and freeze for up to 2 months.

TIP: TOP THE CAKE WITH FRESH BERRIES
and confectioners' sugar and serve in lieu
of coffee cake or muffins for a summertime
brunch.

PLATE · 75

Golden Butter Cake with Berries and Mascarpone Frosting

Mascarpone frosting takes this butter cake to another level of satisfaction. Mascarpone is a double- or triple-cream cow's-milk cheese, originally from Italy. It is probably best known as an ingredient in tiramisu (see page 229), but it makes an exceptional addition to a simple cream-based frosting. Follow the instructions carefully; mascarpone can separate when overbeaten.

● MAKES ONE 9-INCH CAKE; SERVES 8 TO 12 ●

FOR THE CAKE

3¼ cups (16.25 ounces) all-purpose flour

¾ teaspoon baking powder

¾ teaspoon salt

3¾ sticks (15 ounces) unsalted butter, softened

2 tablespoons light corn syrup

2 cups (14 ounces) sugar

6 large eggs

⅓ cup (2.66 ounces) crème fraîche or sour cream

1½ tablespoons vanilla extract

FOR THE MASCARPONE FROSTING

1½ cups (12 ounces) mascarpone

½ cup (2.25 ounces) confectioners' sugar

1 teaspoon grated lemon zest

½ teaspoon vanilla bean paste (see Resources, page 335)

1 cup (8 ounces) heavy cream

5 cups (1 pound, 4 ounces) strawberries, half left whole, half hulled and sliced ½ inch thick

TO MAKE THE CAKE

▸ Position a rack in the center of the oven and heat the oven to 350°F. Coat the bottoms and sides of three 9-by-2-inch round cake pans with nonstick baking spray or butter and line with parchment circles.

▸ Sift together the flour, baking powder, and salt into a medium bowl.

▸ In the bowl of a stand mixer fitted with the paddle attachment (or in a large bowl, using a handheld mixer), cream the butter, corn syrup, and sugar on medium speed until light and fluffy, about 4 minutes.

▸ Whisk together the eggs, crème fraîche, and vanilla in a small bowl, then pour the mixture into the creamed butter and beat until smooth. Scrape the bottom and sides of the bowl and the paddle and mix for 30 seconds. With the mixer on low speed, add the dry ingredients in two batches, mixing for 30 seconds after each addition. Scrape the bowl again and mix for 15 seconds.

▸ Divide the batter among the prepared cake pans, spreading it evenly. Bake for 15 minutes. Rotate the cakes and bake for an additional 10 to 12 minutes, until the cakes appear firm and have a matte finish and a toothpick inserted in the center comes out clean. Let the cakes cool completely in the pans on cooling racks. Wrap the cakes in plastic wrap and refrigerate until you are ready to assemble the cake.

TO MAKE THE FROSTING

▸ In the bowl of the stand mixer fitted with the paddle attachment (or in a medium bowl, using a rubber spatula or whisk), mix the mascarpone, confectioners' sugar, lemon zest, and vanilla paste together, until thoroughly combined.

▸ In a large bowl, using a handheld mixer, whip the heavy cream until it forms soft peaks. Add the mascarpone mixture and beat until combined

PLATE · 77

and smooth; as soon as the frosting looks smooth, stop beating. If the frosting is overbeaten, it will become grainy.

TO ASSEMBLE THE CAKE

› Run an offset spatula or a small knife around the sides of the pans to release the layers and invert them onto cooling racks; peel off the parchment paper. Transfer one layer to a turntable or serving plate, top side down. Using an offset spatula, spread about one-third of the frosting (just under 1 cup) evenly over the top of the layer. Layer half the sliced strawberries over the frosting, without overlapping them, then spread about 2 tablespoons of frosting over the berries in the center of the cake. (This bit of frosting will help seal the layers together.)

› Place the second cake layer top side down on top of the berries and repeat the same pattern of frosting, berries, and frosting. Top with the last cake layer, top side down, and spread the remaining frosting evenly on top. Arrange the whole strawberries around the top of the cake. Refrigerate until ready to serve.

STORING

› The cake can be stored, in a cake box or under a cake dome, in the refrigerator for up to 2 days.

VARIATIONS

ORANGE CAKE: Make the batter, then add 2 tablespoons grated orange zest, 2 tablespoons orange juice, and 1 teaspoon orange oil (see Resources, page 335) and beat for 30 seconds.

LEMON CAKE: Make the batter, then add 1 tablespoon grated lemon zest and 2 tablespoons lemon juice and beat for 30 seconds.

TIPS: IF THE MASCARPONE SEPARATES, you can save it by whipping an additional cup of heavy cream and carefully mixing it into the frosting; this will give you extra frosting, but it's a better alternative to throwing out the whole batch.

It might sound curious, but a delicate drizzle of aged balsamic vinegar on top of the strawberries is a lovely way to accentuate the flavors in this cake. Don't add the vinegar until just before serving, or it will cause the berries to break down rapidly.

PLATE · 78

Chocolate Cake
with Chocolate Buttercream

I wasn't a fan of chocolate cake until I came across this recipe in an Australian magazine. (I subsequently lost the recipe, and I'm embarrassed by my inability to offer the chef credit.) Over the years, I've tweaked and perfected the recipe, but I am forever indebted to that very talented person who originated it. This recipe satisfies my craving for a chocolate cake that's moist and rich with an intense, almost overwhelming chocolaty flavor.

● MAKES ONE 9-INCH CAKE; SERVES 8 TO 12 ●

FOR THE CAKE

1¼ cups (6.75 ounces) 61% bittersweet chocolate chips or fèves (see Resources, page 335) or chopped 61% bittersweet chocolate

2 sticks (8 ounces) unsalted butter, cut into chunks

½ cup (4 ounces) strong brewed coffee, at room temperature

1¼ cups (6.25 ounces) all-purpose flour

1⅓ cups (8 ounces) light brown sugar

⅔ cup (4.66 ounces) granulated sugar

⅓ cup (1.3 ounces) Dutch-processed cocoa powder

1 teaspoon kosher salt

¼ teaspoon baking soda

3 large eggs

3 tablespoons sour cream

2 tablespoons heavy cream

3 cups (1 pound 2 ounces) Chocolate Buttercream (recipe follows), or more to taste

2 cups (10.8 ounces) Valrhona Crunchy Dark Chocolate Pearls (see Resources, page 335)

TO MAKE THE CAKE

▸ Position a rack in the center of the oven and heat the oven to 350°F. Coat the bottoms and sides of three 9-by-2-inch round cake pans with nonstick baking spray or butter and line with parchment circles.

▸ Melt the chocolate and butter in the top of a double boiler or in a heatproof bowl set over a pot of simmering water, stirring occasionally until smooth. Stir in the coffee, remove the top of the pan or the bowl, and set aside to cool for 10 minutes. Sift together the flour, sugars, cocoa powder, salt, and baking soda into a large bowl.

▸ In a medium bowl, whisk together the eggs, sour cream, and heavy cream until fully combined. Continue whisking as you stream in the chocolate mixture. Using a large rubber spatula, fold the chocolate mixture into the dry ingredients.

▸ Divide the batter among the prepared cake pans, spreading it evenly. Bake for 15 minutes. Rotate the cake pans and bake for an additional 12 to 15 minutes, until the cakes appear firm and a toothpick inserted in the center comes out clean. Let the cakes cool completely in the pans on cooling racks.

▸ Run an offset spatula or a small knife around the sides of the cake pans, invert the cakes onto cooling racks, and peel off the parchment paper. Wrap the cakes in plastic wrap and refrigerate until you are ready to assemble the cake.

TO ASSEMBLE THE CAKE

▸ Transfer one cake layer to a serving plate, top side down. Using an offset spatula, spread about ¾ cup of the buttercream evenly over the top of the layer. Place the second layer top side down on top of the buttercream and spread about ¾ cup of buttercream evenly over the top. Top with the third layer, top side down, and frost the top and sides of the cake with the remaining buttercream (or more to taste).

Continued ▸

PLATE · 79

▸ Take a handful of the Valrhona Pearls at a time and press onto the sides of the cake until the sides are covered. Cover any empty spots with more pearls. Chill the cake until the buttercream is firm and the pearls are set in place, at least 30 minutes. Remove from the refrigerator 30 minutes before serving.

STORING

▸ This cake can be stored, lightly covered, in the refrigerator for up to 3 days.

Chocolate Buttercream

MAKES JUST UNDER 5 CUPS

4 sticks (1 pound) unsalted butter, softened

1 cup (4.5 ounces) confectioners' sugar, sifted

2 teaspoons vanilla bean paste (see Resources, page 335)

¹/₄ cup (2 ounces) corn syrup

2 cups (11 ounces) 61% bittersweet chocolate chips or fèves (see Resources, page 335) or chopped 61% bittersweet chocolate, melted and cooled (see page 184)

³/₄ teaspoon kosher salt

▸ In the bowl of a stand mixer fitted with the paddle attachment (or in a large bowl, using a handheld mixer), beat the butter on medium speed until light and fluffy, about 2 minutes. Add the confectioners' sugar and continue beating until smooth. Add the vanilla paste and corn syrup and beat for 1 minute. Scrape the bottom and sides of the bowl and the paddle with a rubber spatula.

▸ With the mixer on low speed, slowly stream the melted chocolate into the bowl, mixing until the color is uniform and there are no ribbons of chocolate. Add the salt and beat for 30 seconds. The buttercream is ready to use. It can be stored, covered, in the refrigerator for up to 4 weeks; see instructions on page 102.

TIP: THE VALRHONA PEARLS USED AS DÉcor on this cake are made of tiny bits of toasted puffed cereal coated in bittersweet chocolate. Keep some on hand in your cupboard—they are a delicious snack and a great last-minute embellishment for myriad desserts, including puddings and ice creams.

PLATE · 81

Rose Petal Cake

Certain occasions call for an ultrafeminine dessert like this cake. Anniversaries, bridal showers, or dressy teas are all great excuses to indulge in a few candied rose petals. If you can't find organic rose petals to candy, use fresh roses as a nonedible garnish.

● MAKES ONE 8-INCH SQUARE CAKE; SERVES 8 TO 12 ●

FOR THE CAKE

3¼ cups (16.25 ounces) all-purpose flour

¾ teaspoon baking powder

¾ teaspoon salt

3¾ sticks (15 ounces) unsalted butter, softened

2 tablespoons light corn syrup

2 cups (14 ounces) sugar

6 large eggs

¼ cup (2 ounces) crème fraîche or sour cream

2 tablespoons vanilla bean paste (see Resources, page 335)

2 tablespoons vanilla extract

2 cups (16 ounces) Passion Fruit Buttercream Filling (page 55)

1½ cups (12.75 ounces) White-Chocolate Chambord Glaze (recipe follows)

20 to 30 Candied Rose Petals (page 68)

TO MAKE THE CAKE

▸ Position a rack in the center of the oven and heat the oven to 350°F. Coat the bottoms and sides of three 8-by-8-by-2-inch square baking pans with nonstick baking spray or butter and line the bottoms with parchment paper.

▸ Sift together the flour, baking powder, and salt into a medium bowl.

▸ In the bowl of a stand mixer fitted with the paddle attachment (or in a large bowl, using a handheld mixer), cream the butter, corn syrup, and sugar on medium speed until light and fluffy, about 4 minutes.

▸ Whisk together the eggs, crème fraîche, and vanillas in a small bowl, then pour into the creamed butter and beat until smooth. Scrape the bottom and sides of the bowl and the paddle and mix for 30 seconds. With the mixer on low speed, add the dry ingredients in three batches, mixing for 30 seconds after each addition. Scrape the bowl again and mix for 15 seconds.

▸ Divide the batter among the prepared cake pans, spreading it evenly. Bake for 15 minutes. Rotate the pans and bake for an additional 10 to 12 minutes, until the cakes appear firm and have a matte finish and a toothpick inserted in the center comes out clean. Let the cakes cool completely in the pans on cooling racks.

▸ Run an offset spatula or a small knife around the sides of the pans and invert the cakes onto cooling racks; remove the parchment paper. Wrap the cakes in plastic wrap and refrigerate until you are ready to assemble the cake.

TO ASSEMBLE THE CAKE

▸ Transfer one layer, top side down, to a serving plate. Using an offset spatula, spread about 1 cup of buttercream across the top of the layer. Place a second layer on top, top side down. Spread another cup of buttercream over the layer. Place the last inverted cake layer on top. Using your hands, press down gently to even the layers.

▸ Using an offset spatula, smooth the "seams" of the cake. You want the buttercream to completely fill the spaces between the layers; any concave areas will be very noticeable under the glaze. Refrigerate the cake, uncovered, until very cold, about 2 hours.

▸ Set the chilled cake on a cooling rack and set the rack on a baking sheet

PLATE • 83

to catch the glaze drippings. Pour the glaze over the top of the cake, starting at the edges and then moving to the center. Pick up the rack and bang it against the baking sheet to even out the glaze. If you missed a spot or two, move the rack with the cake aside and, using a bench scraper, collect the glaze from the pan and pour it back into the container. Place the rack back on the baking sheet and pour the glaze over the bare spots.

▸ Using your finger, touch the side of the cake. If the glaze feels very tacky and has visibly thickened and set, proceed with the décor. If it still feels very wet, place the whole pan in the refrigerator to set the glaze; check the cake every 2 to 3 minutes.

▸ While the glaze is still tacky, press the candied rose petals onto the sides of the cake (don't wait until the glaze is completely set, or the roses will fall off). Allow the glaze to set completely, 10 to 15 minutes, before moving the cake. Or, if your kitchen is warm, move the rack into the refrigerator until the glaze becomes firm, just a few minutes.

▸ Run a hot offset spatula under the bottom of the cake to release it from the rack and transfer to a serving plate. Serve at room temperature, or refrigerate and serve slightly chilled.

STORING

▸ This cake can be stored, in a cake box or under a cake dome, in the refrigerator for up to 3 days. (Wrapping the cake in plastic wrap would damage the glaze and crush the rose petals.)

White-Chocolate Chambord Glaze

MAKES ABOUT 2 CUPS

2^1/$_2$ cups (13.5 ounces) 31% white chocolate chips or fèves (see Resources, page 335) or chopped 31% white chocolate

^{2}/$_3$ cup (5.33 ounces) heavy cream

1 teaspoon light corn syrup

3^1/$_2$ tablespoons (1.75 ounces) unsalted butter, very soft

2 tablespoons Chambord

▸ Put the white chocolate into a medium bowl. Heat the heavy cream and corn syrup in a small saucepan over medium heat just until it boils. Pour the cream over the chocolate and let sit for 1 minute.

▸ Using a small rubber spatula, begin stirring the mixture in one direction, concentrating on the center, until it is smooth and glistening. Add the butter and stir until it is completely melted, about 1 minute. Whisk in the Chambord until just incorporated. Pour the glaze into a 2-cup measuring cup or a small pitcher. Let cool to 85° to 90°F before using; monitor the temperature with a candy or instant-read thermometer.

▸ Leftover glaze can be stored, covered, in the refrigerator for up to 2 weeks. This glaze does not reheat well; use chilled leftover glaze for fillings in sandwich cookies or meringues.

TIPS: THE SQUARE SHAPE OF THIS CAKE has greater impact with a perfectly flat top, so I like to leave the layers inverted and frost them that way.

Glaze cakes in the coolest part of your kitchen. If your kitchen is hot during the summer months, freeze the cake for 1 hour before glazing.

Pouring the glaze over the edges of the cake first and then moving to the center may sound backward, but I promise you, it works.

PLATE · 84

Champagne Cake

A traditional Champagne cake recipe includes Champagne in the cake batter in lieu of cream or water. The cake in this recipe isn't made with Champagne, but the ganache is. Make this festive dessert shine for a New Year's Eve or anniversary celebration by garnishing it with edible 23-karat gold décor.

● MAKES ONE 8-INCH SQUARE CAKE; SERVES 8 TO 12 ●

Batter for Golden Butter Cake (page 77)
½ recipe (1½ cups/13.5 ounces) Champagne Ganache (recipe follows)
1 recipe Milk Chocolate Glaze (page 89)
1 sheet 23-karat edible gold (optional; see Resources, page 335)

▸ Position a rack in the center of the oven and heat the oven to 350°F. Coat the bottoms and sides of three 9-by-3-inch round cake pans with nonstick baking spray or butter and line the bottoms with parchment paper.

▸ Divide the cake batter among the prepared cake pans, spreading it evenly. Bake for 15 minutes. Rotate the cakes and bake for an additional 10 to 12 minutes, until they appear firm and have a matte finish and a toothpick inserted in the center comes out clean. Let the cakes cool completely in the pans on cooling racks.

▸ Run an offset spatula or a small knife around the sides of the cake pans. Invert the cakes onto cooling racks and peel off the parchment paper. Wrap the cakes in plastic wrap and refrigerate until you are ready to assemble the cake.

▸ Transfer one cake layer, top side down, to a serving plate. Using an offset spatula, spread about ¾ cup of ganache over the top. Place the second cake layer on top, top side down, and spread another layer of ganache over it. Place the last inverted cake layer on top. Using your hands, press down gently to even the layers.

▸ Using an offset spatula, smooth the "seams" of the cake. You want the ganache to completely fill the spaces between the layers; concave areas will be very noticeable under the glaze. Refrigerate the cake, uncovered, until very cold, about 2 hours.

▸ Set the chilled cake on a cooling rack and set the rack on a baking sheet to catch the glaze drippings. Pour the glaze over the top of the cake, starting at the edges and then moving to the center. Pick up the rack and bang it against the baking sheet to even out the glaze. If you missed a spot or two, move the rack with the cake aside and, using a bench scraper, collect the glaze from the pan and pour it back into the measuring cup. Place the rack back on the baking sheet and pour the glaze over the bare spots.

▸ Allow the glaze to set completely, 10 to 15 minutes, before moving the cake. The glaze should be firm to the touch. Or, if your kitchen is warm, move the rack into the refrigerator until the glaze becomes firm, just a few minutes.

TIP: ALTHOUGH THE GOLD LEAF WOULD look more dramatic on the Bittersweet Chocolate Glaze (page 94) than on the milk chocolate glaze, the bittersweet chocolate would dominate the Champagne flavor of the cake. I don't recommend it.

Continued ▸

PLATE · 87

> Run a hot offset spatula under the bottom of the cake to release it from the rack and transfer to a serving plate.

> If you'd like to gild the lily, using a very small brush, lift a section of gold leaf off the sheet and gently lay it on the firm glaze. The gold will immediately stick to the glaze. Repeat with more gold leaf.

STORING

> The cake can be stored, in a cake box or under a cake dome, in the refrigerator for up to 3 days. (Wrapping the cake in plastic wrap would damage the glaze and the décor.)

Champagne Ganache

MAKES ABOUT 3 CUPS

1 tablespoon powdered gelatin

3 tablespoons cold water

$^2/_3$ cup (5.33 ounces) Champagne or sparkling wine (see Tip)

2 tablespoons Cognac or other brandy

$^1/_2$ teaspoon vanilla extract

2 cups (11 ounces) 38% milk chocolate chips or fèves (see Resources, page 335) or chopped 38% milk chocolate, melted (see page 184)

2 ounces 61% bittersweet chocolate, chopped and melted (see page 184)

$^1/_4$ cup (2 ounces) heavy cream

3 tablespoons light corn syrup

9 tablespoons (4.5 ounces) unsalted butter, softened

> Sprinkle the gelatin over the cold water in a small bowl. Let sit for 10 minutes, until the gelatin softens.

> Meanwhile, pour the Champagne, Cognac, and vanilla into a measuring cup.

> Combine the melted chocolates in a medium bowl. Pour the cream and corn syrup over the chocolates and, using a small silicone spatula, stir the mixture in one direction, concentrating on the center, until the ganache is smooth and glistening.

> Slowly pour the Champagne into the ganache, whisking constantly (if you add the Champagne too quickly, the ganache will separate). Add the butter and stir until it is completely melted, about 1 minute. Put the ganache in the coolest part of your kitchen and let set, stirring occasionally, until spreadable, for about 1 hour before using.

> Leftover ganache can be covered and refrigerated for up to 2 weeks; see instructions on page 102.

TIP: CHILL THE CHAMPAGNE BEFORE uncorking it. Opening a bottle of room-temperature Champagne is dangerous, as the cork is likely to explode out of the bottle.

PLATE · 88

Milk Chocolate Glaze

MAKES JUST UNDER 2 CUPS

1³/₄ cups (9.5 ounces) 38% milk chocolate chips or fèves (see Resources, page 335) or chopped
    38% milk chocolate
³/₄ cup (6 ounces) heavy cream
2 teaspoons corn syrup
4 tablespoons (¹/₂ stick/2 ounces) unsalted butter, diced and softened

‣ Put the milk chocolate into a medium bowl. Heat the heavy cream and corn syrup in a small saucepan over medium heat just until it boils. Pour the cream over the chocolate and let sit for 1 minute.

‣ Using a small spatula, begin stirring the mixture in one direction, concentrating on the center, until it is smooth and glistening. Add the butter and stir until it is completely melted, about 1 minute. Pour the glaze into a 2-cup measuring cup or a small pitcher. Let cool to 90° to 95°F before using, monitoring the temperature with a candy or instant-read thermometer.

‣ Leftover glaze can be stored, covered, in the refrigerator for up to 2 weeks (see Tip).

TIP: TO USE LEFTOVER CHILLED GLAZE, gently melt it in the top of a double boiler or in a heatproof bowl set over a pot of simmering water, stirring occasionally.

Why Corn Syrup?

Corn syrup is a controversial ingredient these days, and the prevailing health sentiment is one of abject negativity. The corn syrup we use for baking is not the high-fructose type found in many sodas, cereals, breads, and condiments, but either version has its detractors. I personally avoid beverages that contain high-fructose corn syrup—so why do I call for corn syrup in many of the cake and filling recipes in this chapter? The answer is twofold: First, there are flavor and textural benefits. Corn syrup enhances the flavor in a ganache, the shine of a glaze or buttercream, and the moisture in a cake. After multiple tests, I found these cakes had a better texture and superior moisture when made with corn syrup. Second, these are dessert recipes, not something people will eat in large quantities on a daily basis. A serving of one of these filled and frosted cakes includes approximately 12 grams of corn syrup. If you are truly opposed to corn syrup in your diet, just omit it from the ganaches, glazes, and buttercreams. If you remove it from the cake recipes, you'll need to increase the sugar and the crème fraîche by 1 tablespoon each.

PLATE · 89

Hazelnut Cake

Gianduja is an Italian confection made of hazelnut paste and milk chocolate. Most European chocolate shops offer gianduja bonbons, but gianduja is also available in brick form as an ingredient for desserts. The texture is wondrous, amazingly soft and smooth, and the flavor has the perfect balance of hazelnut and chocolate. Nutella is a mass-produced spreadable version of gianduja.

● MAKES ONE 9-BY-6-INCH CAKE; SERVES 8 TO 12 ●

FOR THE CAKE

2 cups (7 ounces) raw hazelnut flour (see Resources, page 335)

1³/₄ cups (8.75 ounces) all-purpose flour

2 teaspoons kosher salt

2 sticks plus 2 tablespoons (9 ounces) unsalted butter, softened

2 cups (14 ounces) sugar

1¹/₃ cups (11 ounces) hazelnut paste (see Resources, page 335)

6 large eggs

2 large egg yolks

1 teaspoon vanilla bean paste (see Resources, page 335)

3 cups (1 pound, 11 ounces) Gianduja Ganache (recipe follows)

1¹/₂ cups (4.25 ounces) Bittersweet Chocolate Glaze (page 94)

1 cup (7 ounces) Candied Hazelnuts (page 94)

TO MAKE THE CAKE

▸ Position a rack in the center of the oven and heat the oven to 350°F. Coat the bottoms and sides of four 9-by-6-by-1-inch rectangular baking pans with nonstick baking spray or butter and line the bottoms with parchment paper.

▸ Whisk together the hazelnut flour, flour, and salt in a medium bowl.

▸ In the bowl of a stand mixer fitted with the paddle attachment (or in a large bowl, using a handheld mixer), cream the butter and sugar on medium speed until light and fluffy, about 4 minutes. With the mixer on low speed, crumble in the hazelnut paste, then increase the speed to medium and beat until the paste has broken down to very small bits, 2 to 3 minutes.

▸ Whisk together the eggs, egg yolks, and vanilla paste in a small bowl, then add to the hazelnut mixture and beat until fully combined. Add the dry ingredients and beat until the batter appears smooth, with tiny dots of hazelnut paste.

▸ Divide the batter among the prepared cake pans, spreading it evenly. Bake for 12 minutes. Rotate the cakes and bake for an additional 8 to 10 minutes, until the cakes appear firm and have a matte finish and a toothpick inserted in the center comes out clean. Let the cakes cool completely in the pans on a cooling rack, then refrigerate, in the pans, for 30 minutes.

TO ASSEMBLE THE CAKE

▸ Run a knife around the sides of the cake pans and invert the cakes onto cooling racks; peel off the parchment. Place one of the layers top side down on another rack. Using an offset spatula, spread about 3/4 cup of the ganache over the top of the layer. Place a second cake layer on top, top side down, and spread another layer of ganache over the top. Repeat once more with the third cake layer, and then top with the last layer, top side down. Refrigerate the cake, uncovered, until very cold and firm, about 2 hours.

▸ Set the chilled cake, on the rack, on a baking sheet to catch the glaze drippings. Pour the chocolate glaze over the top of the cake, starting at

PLATE · 91

the edges and then moving to the center. Pick up the rack and bang it against the baking sheet to even out the glaze. If you missed a spot or two, move the rack with the cake aside and, using a bench scraper, collect the glaze from the pan and pour it back into the container. Place the rack back on the baking sheet and pour the glaze over the bare spots.

▸ When the glaze has started to set, gently run an offset spatula under the bottom of the cake to release it. Press the candied hazelnuts around the bottom of the cake. Allow the glaze to set completely, 10 to 15 minutes, before moving the cake. Or, if your kitchen is warm, move the rack into the refrigerator until the glaze becomes firm, just a few minutes.

▸ Run a hot offset spatula under the bottom of the cake to release it from the rack and transfer to a serving plate. Serve at room temperature, or refrigerate and serve slightly chilled.

STORING

▸ The cake can be stored, in a cake box or under a cake dome, in the refrigerator for up to 3 days. (Wrapping the cake in plastic wrap would damage the glaze and the décor.)

Gianduja Ganache

MAKES ABOUT 4 CUPS

1¼ cups (6.5 ounces) gianduja (see Resources, page 335), cut into small chunks
½ cup (2.5 ounces) 38% milk chocolate chips or fèves (see Resources, page 335) or chopped 38% milk chocolate
½ cup (2.5 ounces) 61% bittersweet chocolate chips or fèves (see Resources, page 335) or chopped 61% bittersweet chocolate
¾ cup plus 2 tablespoons (7 ounces) heavy cream
7 tablespoons (3.5 ounces) unsalted butter, softened
1½ tablespoons light rum
½ teaspoon kosher salt

▸ Put the gianduja and chocolates into a medium bowl. Heat the heavy cream in a small saucepan until it just boils. Pour the cream over the chocolate and let sit for 1 to 2 minutes.

▸ Using a small rubber spatula, begin stirring the mixture in one direction, concentrating on the center, until the ganache is smooth and glistening. Add the butter, rum, and salt and stir until the butter is completely melted, about 2 minutes. Put the ganache in the coolest part of your kitchen and let set, stirring occasionally, until spreadable, for about 1 hour before using.

▸ Leftover ganache can be covered and refrigerated for up to 2 weeks; see instructions on page 102.

TIP: TO MAKE CLEAN SLICES OF CAKE, heat a thin knife under hot water, wipe it dry, and then cut the cake; repeat before each cut. Do not use a serrated knife when cutting a glazed cake—it will result in jagged edges.

PLATE · 92

Bittersweet Chocolate Glaze

MAKES JUST UNDER 2 CUPS

2³/₄ cups (14.75 ounces) 61% bittersweet chocolate chips or fèves (see Resources, page 335)
8 tablespoons (1 stick/4 ounces) unsalted butter
¹/₄ cup (2 ounces) light corn syrup

▸ Combine the chocolate, butter, and corn syrup in the top of a double boiler or in a heatproof bowl set over a pot of simmering water, and stir over medium-low heat until the ingredients are completely melted and the glaze appears shiny, about 4 minutes. Pour the glaze into a 2-cup measuring cup or a small pitcher. Let cool to 90° to 95°F before using, using a candy or instant-read thermometer to monitor the temperature.

▸ Leftover glaze can be stored, covered, in the refrigerator for up to 4 weeks (see Tip).

TIP: TO USE LEFTOVER GLAZE, MELT IT again in a double boiler or a heatproof bowl over a pot of simmering water. You might want to make a double batch: this makes an incredible ice cream sauce.

Candied Nuts

MAKES 2 CUPS

³/₄ cup (5.25 ounces) sugar
¹/₃ cup (2.5 ounces) water
2 cups (9 ounces) nuts, such as almonds, cashews, halved hazelnuts, or pecans

▸ Lightly grease a marble slab, a stainless steel work surface, or a baking sheet.

▸ Attach a candy thermometer, preferably digital, to the side of a copper or heavy pot. Pour in the sugar and water and heat over medium-high heat until the temperature reaches 248°F. Immediately add the nuts, stirring with a wooden spoon. Reduce the heat to low and continue stirring. The sugar syrup will turn white and powdery, but as you continue stirring, it will slowly melt and form a clear coating.

▸ Pour the candied nuts onto the greased work surface. Using two forks, separate the nuts from each other as much as possible. Let cool completely. Store in an airtight container for up to 1 week.

PLATE · 94

HELPFUL HINTS FOR CAKE BUILDING

NOVICE AND EXPERIENCED BAKERS ALIKE can get nervous at the prospect of building, or assembling, a cake. A good way to relieve that anxiety is to define the process from a fresh perspective. Just think of cake building as layering ingredients—really, there is little difference between constructing a sandwich and constructing a cake. Here are a few suggestions that will make your cake building a little easier.

1. Coat the bottoms and sides of the cake pans with nonstick spray or butter and line the pans with parchment paper. These safeguards help ensure a clean release with the cake intact every time. The fat (spray or butter) anchors the parchment to the bottom of the pan; without fat, the parchment will move around as you spread the cake batter.

2. When constructing a layer cake, work with completely cooled or cold layers and room-temperature fillings. If you rush and try to unmold a hot cake or spread firm, cold ganache, you will get the same heartbreaking result: the cake will tear. Chill your cake layers before you build. A cold cake is sturdier than a room-temperature cake, and room-temperature ganache or buttercream spreads easily over the cold cake, creating a beautiful smooth finish.

3. When transferring a cake to a serving plate or a turntable, use the removable bottom of a cake or tart pan or a cardboard cake round. A large, stable surface makes it much easier to transfer a cake than using a narrow instrument, such as an offset spatula. Just slide the cake pan bottom or round under the cake layer, leaving a small overhang at the far edge. Gently tip the edge of the cake onto the serving plate, and pull the board out. After covering the cake layer with a layer of filling, repeat the process with another cake layer: tip the edge of the second layer onto the edge of the first one and withdraw the pan bottom or cardboard round, centering the two layers over each other.

4. Lay four strips of parchment paper under the edges of the first cake layer before building the cake. When you finish frosting the cake, slide the parchment out and discard. This will keep the serving platter clean.

5. If you will be transporting a layer cake, insert straws or small dowels into the cake to prevent shifting: think of them as temporary structural support. Before you frost or glaze the cake, insert a straw (or dowel) near the center of the layer cake. When you feel the straw make contact with the cake board or serving plate, gently withdraw it about 1/2 inch and cut the straw (or mark on the dowel, remove it, cut it, and slide it back into the cake). Push the trimmed straw back into the cake so it sits just under the surface. Repeat with a second straw 2 to 3 inches away from the original one. Then finish the cake.

6. To get a seamless finish for your frosting, cover the cake with the buttercream and then chill it for about 15 minutes. Fill a tall container with hot water, dip a large offset spatula into the hot water, shake off the excess liquid, and smooth the surface of the cake while spinning it on a cake turntable or a lazy Susan. The heat will melt the surface of the buttercream, giving it a smooth finish. Repeat as necessary. Using a hot spatula on room-temperature buttercream will create a rough, puckered effect, so make sure the buttercream is cold and firm to the touch before applying the hot spatula.

Lavender–Earl Grey Mini-Cakes with Lemon Ganache

Lavender has become a popular ingredient in desserts, and I like to use it in the spring and summer, when it's in peak season. However, it is important to use it in moderation; a heavy hand creates a flavor more akin to that of potpourri than dessert. The delicate, floral quality of lavender is balanced in this recipe by the dark, bergamot earthiness of Earl Grey tea, bringing out the best of both flavors.

● MAKES NINE 3-INCH ROUND MINI-CAKES ●

FOR THE CAKE

1 1/2 cups (7.5 ounces) all-purpose flour

1 1/2 tablespoons finely ground Earl Grey tea

3/4 teaspoon ground dried lavender (see Resources, page 335, and Tip)

1/3 teaspoon baking powder

1/3 teaspoon salt

1 3/4 sticks plus 1 tablespoon (7.5 ounces) unsalted butter, softened

1 tablespoon light corn syrup

1 cup (7 ounces) sugar

3 large eggs

3 tablespoons crème fraîche or sour cream

1 teaspoon vanilla extract

FOR THE LEMON GANACHE

2 teaspoons powdered gelatin

3 tablespoons cold water

11 ounces 31% white chocolate, chopped

1 cup (8 ounces) heavy cream

3 tablespoons light corn syrup

9 tablespoons (4.5 ounces) unsalted butter, softened

1 tablespoon grated lemon zest

1/2 cup (4 ounces) fresh lemon juice

FOR THE LEMON GLAZE

2 1/2 cups (13.5 ounces) 31% white chocolate chips or fèves (see Resources, page 335) or chopped 31% white chocolate

2/3 cup (5.5 ounces) heavy cream

1 teaspoon light corn syrup

3 1/2 tablespoons (1.75 ounces) unsalted butter, very soft

1/4 teaspoon lemon oil (see Resources, page 335)

Dried organic lavender for garnish

TO MAKE THE CAKE

› Position a rack in the center of the oven and heat the oven to 350°F. Coat the bottom and sides of a 13-by-18-by-1-inch baking sheet with non-stick spray or butter and line with parchment paper. Smooth the parchment, making sure there are no air bubbles.

› Sift together the flour, tea, lavender, baking powder, and salt into a medium bowl.

› In the bowl of a stand mixer fitted with the paddle attachment (or in a large bowl, using a handheld mixer), cream the butter, corn syrup, and sugar on medium speed until light and fluffy, about 3 minutes.

› Whisk together the eggs, crème fraîche, and vanilla in a small bowl, then pour into the creamed butter and beat until smooth. Scrape the bottom and sides of the bowl and the paddle and mix until smooth.

› With the mixer on low speed, add the dry ingredients in three batches, mixing for 1 to 2 minutes after each addition. Scrape the bowl again and mix for 15 seconds.

› Scrape the batter onto the prepared baking sheet, spreading it evenly with an offset spatula.

› Bake for 10 minutes. Rotate the pan and bake for an additional 3 to 4 minutes, until the cake appears firm and has a matte finish. Let the cake cool completely in the pan on a cooling rack. Chill the cake for a minimum of 10 to 15 minutes before building the mini-cakes.

TO MAKE THE GANACHE

› Sprinkle the gelatin over the cold water in a small bowl. Let sit for 10 minutes, until the gelatin softens.

› Put the chocolate into a medium bowl and set aside.

› Heat the heavy cream and corn syrup in a small saucepan just until it boils. Remove from the heat and stir in the gelatin until it is completely dissolved. Pour the cream over the chocolate. Using a small rubber

PLATE · 96

spatula, begin stirring the mixture in one direction, concentrating on the center, until the ganache is smooth and glistening. Add the butter and stir until it is completely melted, about 1 minute. Add the lemon zest and juice and stir. Put the ganache in the coolest part of your kitchen and let set, stirring occasionally, until spreadable, for about 1 hour before using. (The ganache can be covered and refrigerated for up to 2 weeks; see instructions on page 102.)

TO ASSEMBLE THE CAKES

▸ Line a baking sheet with parchment paper. Using a 3-inch round cookie cutter, cut out 27 rounds from the cake and set on a cooling rack.

▸ Place 9 cake rounds on the parchment-lined baking sheet. Using an offset spatula, spread approximately 2 tablespoons ganache over each one. Top each with a second round and 2 more tablespoons ganache; then top with a third layer of cake. Refrigerate for 1 hour, or until the ganache is firm.

TO MAKE THE GLAZE

▸ Put the white chocolate into a medium bowl. Heat the heavy cream and corn syrup in a small saucepan just until it boils. Pour the cream over the chocolate and let sit for 1 minute.

▸ Using a small rubber spatula, begin stirring the white chocolate mixture in one direction, concentrating on the center, until it is smooth and glistening. Add the butter and stir until it is completely melted, about 1 minute. Whisk in the lemon oil until just incorporated.

▸ Pour the glaze into a 2-cup measuring cup or a small pitcher. Let cool to 85° to 90°F before using, monitoring the temperature with a candy or instant-read thermometer.

TO GLAZE THE CAKES

▸ Set the cakes on a cooling rack and set the rack on a baking sheet to catch the glaze drippings. Pour about ¼ cup glaze onto the center of each cake. When all of the cakes are coated, pick up the baking rack and gently tap it to even out the glaze—use a delicate hand here, as the cakes are light and can topple over. If you missed a spot or two, using a bench scraper, collect the glaze from the pan and pour it back into the measuring cup. Place the rack back on the baking sheet and pour the glaze over the bare spots. Top each cake with a few pieces of dried lavender.

▸ Allow the glaze to set completely, 10 to 15 minutes, before moving the cakes. Or, if your kitchen is warm, move the rack into the refrigerator until the glaze becomes firm, just a few minutes.

▸ Run a hot offset spatula under the bottom of the cakes to release them from the rack and transfer the cakes to a serving platter. Refrigerate the cakes until slightly chilled before serving.

STORING

▸ The cakes can be stored, covered, in the refrigerator for up to 3 days.

TIP: GRIND THE TEA AND DRIED LAVENDER in a clean coffee or spice grinder. If your grinder has a strong coffee aroma, wipe the blade and interior with white vinegar and let dry completely, then wash the inside with soap and warm water.

PLATE · 97

Matcha Mini-Cakes
with Lemon Verbena Ganache

Lemon verbena is a perennial herb that imparts the bright flavor of lemon without the acidity. The combination of lemon and green tea tastes light, refreshing, and clean, making these cakes the perfect finish to a spicy meal. The tops and sides of the cakes are left unadorned for a minimalist look.

● MAKES EIGHT 3-INCH SQUARE MINI-CAKES ●

FOR THE CAKE

1½ cups (7.5 ounces) all-purpose flour

⅓ teaspoon baking powder

⅓ teaspoon salt

1½ sticks plus 2 tablespoons (7 ounces) unsalted butter, softened

1 cup (7 ounces) sugar

1½ tablespoons matcha tea (see Resources, page 335)

3 large eggs

3 tablespoons crème fraîche or sour cream

2½ teaspoons vanilla extract

FOR THE LEMON VERBENA GANACHE

1 cup (8 ounces) heavy cream

2 tablespoons light corn syrup

½ cup (4 grams) dried lemon verbena (see Resources, page 335)

2 teaspoons powdered gelatin

3 tablespoons cold water

1¾ cups (9.5 ounces) 31% white chocolate chips or fèves (see Resources, page 335) or chopped 31% white chocolate

8 tablespoons (1 stick/4 ounces) unsalted butter, softened

1 teaspoon grated lemon zest

1 tablespoon lemon juice

½ teaspoon ground dried lemon verbena (see Resources, page 335, and Tip, page 97)

TO MAKE THE CAKE

› Position a rack in the center of the oven and heat the oven to 325°F. Coat the bottom and sides of a 13-by-18-by-1-inch baking sheet with non-stick baking spray or butter and line with parchment paper. Smooth the parchment, making sure there are no air bubbles.

› Sift together the flour, baking powder, and salt into a medium bowl.

› In the bowl of a stand mixer fitted with the paddle attachment (or in a large bowl, using a handheld mixer), cream the butter and sugar on medium speed until light and fluffy, about 3 minutes. Add the matcha and beat for 30 seconds, or until the color of the butter mixture is uniform.

› Whisk together the eggs, crème fraîche, and vanilla in a small bowl, then pour into the creamed butter and beat until smooth. Scrape the bottom and sides of the bowl and the paddle and mix for 30 seconds.

› Beating on low speed, add the dry ingredients in three batches, mixing for 1 to 2 minutes after each addition. Scrape the bowl again and mix for 15 seconds.

› Pour the batter onto the prepared baking sheet, spreading it evenly with an offset spatula. Bake for 10 minutes. Rotate the pan and bake for an additional 3 to 4 minutes, until the cake appears firm and has a matte finish. Let the cake cool completely in the pan on a cooling rack. Chill the cake for a minimum of 10 to 15 minutes before building the mini-cakes.

TO MAKE THE GANACHE

› Put the cream, corn syrup, and ½ cup dried lemon verbena into a medium saucepan and bring to a boil over medium heat. Turn off the heat, cover the pan with aluminum foil, and poke a few holes into the top to allow steam to release. Let steep for 1 hour.

› Sprinkle the gelatin over the cold water in a small bowl. Let sit for 10 minutes, until the gelatin softens.

› Put the chocolate into a medium bowl and set aside.

› Strain the cream mixture and return it to the pan. Add the gelatin and

PLATE · 101

heat over medium-low heat, stirring until the gelatin is dissolved and the cream has almost come to a boil. Pour the cream over the chocolate and let sit for 1 minute.

▸ Using a small rubber spatula, begin stirring the white chocolate mixture in one direction, concentrating on the center, until smooth and glistening. Add the butter and stir until it is completely melted, about 1 minute. Add the lemon zest, lemon juice, and 1/2 teaspoon ground dried lemon verbena and stir until well incorporated. Put the ganache in the coolest part of your kitchen and let set, stirring occasionally, until spreadable, for about 1 hour before using. (The ganache can be covered and refrigerated for up to 2 weeks; see instructions below.)

TO ASSEMBLE THE CAKES

▸ Line a baking sheet with parchment paper. Using a ruler as a guide, score lines 3 inches apart, both vertically and horizontally, on the chilled sheet cake. Then cut into 24 squares with a very sharp knife.

▸ Place 8 cake squares on the parchment-lined baking sheet. Using an offset spatula, spread approximately 2 tablespoons ganache over each one. Top each with a second cake square and 2 tablespoons ganache, then top each with a third cake layer. Let stand until the ganache has set, then gently cover the tray pan with plastic wrap and refrigerate until serving.

STORING

▸ The cakes can be stored, covered, in the refrigerator for up to 3 days.

USING LEFTOVER (OR CHILLED) BUTTERCREAM AND GANACHE

LEFTOVER BUTTERCREAM OR GANACHE will keep in your refrigerator for up to 2 weeks, to be used for another dessert. And it will taste like fresh-made if you follow a few simple steps.

Chilled buttercream is very hard, so you need to let it come to room temperature and then aggressively whip it. Put the room-temperature buttercream in the bowl of a stand mixer fitted with the paddle attachment (or in a large bowl, and use a handheld mixer) and beat on low speed. As the buttercream starts to break up, increase the speed to medium. After about 1 minute, the buttercream will soften and separate. This may make you nervous, but just continue mixing, and

within another minute or so, the buttercream will come back together and appear brand-new.

Ganache is not as malleable as buttercream, and leftovers require a more delicate handling. Let the ganache come to room temperature (do not try to rush the process—firm chilled ganache is likely to separate and become grainy when beaten). Then put it in the bowl of a stand mixer fitted with the whisk attachment (or in a large bowl, and use a handheld mixer) and whip on medium-low speed until the ganache forms soft peaks. Chill for 10 to 15 minutes, then spread it with an offset spatula.

PLATE · 102

Rose Petal Petits Fours

These petits fours are impossibly charming, perfect little layered cakes dipped in white chocolate and topped with candied rose petals. Not only do they make an adorable dessert, petits fours transport well for gifting.

To make the prettiest petits fours, see Perfecting Petits Fours, page 109. You will need two dipping forks for coating the petits fours; see Resources, page 335.

● **MAKES THIRTY-FIVE 1½-INCH PETITS FOURS** ●

FOR THE CAKE
Batter for Vanilla Bean Cake (page 75)

FOR THE ROSE PETAL–PASSION FRUIT GANACHE
2½ teaspoons powdered gelatin

3 tablespoons cold water

2¼ cups (12 ounces) 31% white chocolate chips or fèves (see Resources, page 335) or chopped 31% white chocolate

¼ cup plus 2 tablespoons (3 ounces) crème fraîche or sour cream

¼ cup plus 2 tablespoons (3 ounces) heavy cream

½ cup (4 ounces) passion fruit puree (see Resources, page 335)

3 tablespoons light corn syrup

8 tablespoons (1 stick/4 ounces) unsalted butter, softened

1 tablespoon crushed dried rose petals (see Resources, page 335)

FOR THE COATING
2 tablespoons neutral oil, such as canola or grapeseed

2 pounds still-molten tempered 31% white chocolate (see page 175)

35 Candied Rose Petals (page 68)

TO MAKE THE CAKE

› Position a rack in the center of the oven and heat the oven to 350°F. Coat the bottoms and sides of three 9-by-13-by-2-inch baking pans with nonstick baking spray or butter and line with parchment paper. Smooth the parchment, making sure there are no air bubbles.

› Divide the batter among the prepared baking pans, spreading it evenly. Bake for 7 minutes. Rotate the pans and bake for an additional 3 to 4 minutes, until the cake appears firm and has a matte finish and a toothpick inserted into the center comes out clean. Let the cakes cool completely in the pans on cooling racks, then refrigerate, in the pans, for 30 minutes.

TO MAKE THE GANACHE

› Sprinkle the gelatin over the cold water in a small bowl. Let set for 10 minutes, until the gelatin softens.

› Put the chocolate into a medium bowl and set aside.

› Heat the crème fraîche, heavy cream, passion fruit puree, and corn syrup in a small saucepan until it just boils. Remove from the heat and stir in the gelatin until completely dissolved. Pour the cream over the chocolate and let sit for 1 minute.

› Using a small rubber spatula, begin stirring the white chocolate mixture in one direction, concentrating on the center, until smooth and glistening. Add the butter and stir until it is completely melted, about 1 minute. Add the rose petals and stir until evenly distributed.

› Put the ganache in the coolest part of your kitchen and let set, stirring occasionally, until spreadable, for about 1 hour before using. (The ganache can be covered and refrigerated for up to 2 weeks; see instructions opposite.)

TO ASSEMBLE THE PETITS FOURS

› Line a 9-by-13-by-2-inch baking pan with parchment paper. Run a knife around the sides of the cake pans and invert the cakes onto cooling racks. Lay one cake layer, top side down, in the pan and peel off the parchment paper. Using an offset spatula, spread about 1 cup of the

PLATE • 103

ganache evenly over the surface. Top with a second cake layer, top side down, and peel off the parchment paper. Spread with the remaining ganache and top with the third cake layer, top side down; do not remove the parchment paper from the last layer. Run a heavy rolling pin over the built petit four cake to press the layers together and flatten the surface. Wrap the pan in plastic wrap and freeze the cake for 3 hours, or until frozen solid.

TO COAT THE PETITS FOURS

› Line a baking sheet with parchment paper. Unwrap the baking pan and invert the cake onto a cutting board to remove it. Peel off the parchment paper and discard. Using a ruler as a guide, score the top of the cake with 4 horizontal lines and 6 vertical lines, both 1$\frac{1}{2}$ inches apart, giving you thirty-five 1$\frac{1}{2}$-inch squares. Using a sharp chef's knife, follow the score marks to cut out the squares. Place the petits fours on the lined baking sheet and refrigerate.

› Stir the oil into the tempered chocolate until it is fully incorporated and there are no streaks. (The oil thins the chocolate, making it easier to dip the petits fours.)

› Remove the petits fours from the refrigerator and place the baking pan next to the bowl of chocolate. Using dipping forks, dip one petit four into the chocolate, shake off the excess chocolate, and place the petit four back on the parchment-lined baking sheet. Top with a candied rose petal and continue with the remaining petits fours.

› Serve the petits fours in candy cups or on a small plate.

STORING

› The petits fours can be stored, covered, in the refrigerator for up to 2 weeks.

PLATE · 104

Ginger Petits Fours

Ginger has a sweet-spicy flavor that requires a strong counterpoint, like bittersweet chocolate. Use any bittersweet chocolate in the range of 61% to 72% for the most intense flavor combination here. See Perfecting Petits Fours, page 109. And note that you will need two dipping forks for coating the petits fours; see Resources, page 335.

MAKES THIRTY-FIVE 1¹/₂-INCH PETITS FOURS

FOR THE CAKE

1¹/₂ cups plus 2 tablespoons (8.12 ounces) all-purpose flour

³/₄ teaspoon ground ginger

¹/₃ teaspoon baking powder

¹/₃ teaspoon salt

¹/₄ teaspoon finely ground white pepper

1¹/₂ tablespoons finely chopped candied ginger (see Resources, page 335)

1³/₄ sticks plus 1 tablespoon (7.5 ounces) butter, softened

1 tablespoon light corn syrup

1 cup (7 ounces) sugar

3 large eggs

3 tablespoons crème fraîche or sour cream

¹/₂ teaspoon vanilla extract

FOR THE GINGER GANACHE

2¹/₂ teaspoons powdered gelatin

3 tablespoons cold water

2 cups (11 ounces) 31% white chocolate chips or fèves (see Resources, page 335) or chopped 31% white chocolate

1 cup plus 2 tablespoons (9 ounces) heavy cream

3 tablespoons light corn syrup

9 tablespoons (4.5 ounces) unsalted butter, softened

2 tablespoons ground ginger

FOR THE COATING

2 tablespoons neutral oil, such as canola or grapeseed

2 pounds still-molten tempered 61% to 72% bittersweet chocolate (see page 174)

34 small strips candied ginger (see Resources, page 335)

TO MAKE THE CAKE

▸ Position a rack in the center of the oven and heat the oven to 350°F. Coat the bottoms and sides of three 9-by-13-by-2-inch baking pans with nonstick baking spray or butter and line with parchment paper. Smooth the parchment, making sure there are no air bubbles.

▸ Sift together the flour, ground ginger, baking powder, salt, and white pepper into a medium bowl. Stir in the candied ginger.

▸ In the bowl of a stand mixer fitted with the paddle attachment (or in a large bowl, using a handheld mixer), cream the butter, corn syrup, and sugar on medium speed until light and fluffy, about 4 minutes.

▸ Whisk together the eggs, crème fraîche, and vanilla in a small bowl, then pour into the creamed butter and beat until smooth. Scrape the bottom and sides of the bowl and the paddle and mix for 30 seconds.

▸ Beating on low speed, add the dry ingredients in three batches, mixing for 30 seconds after each addition. Scrape the bowl again and mix for 15 seconds. Divide the batter among the prepared baking pans, spreading it evenly. Bake for 7 minutes. Rotate the pans and bake for an additional 3 to 4 minutes, until the cake appears firm and has a matte finish and a toothpick inserted in the center comes out clean. Let the cakes cool completely in the pans on cooling racks, then refrigerate, in the pans, for 30 minutes.

TO MAKE THE GANACHE

▸ Sprinkle the gelatin over the cold water in a small bowl. Let sit for 10 minutes, until the gelatin softens.

▸ Put the chocolate into a medium bowl and set aside.

▸ Heat the heavy cream and corn syrup in a small saucepan just until it boils. Remove from the heat and stir in the gelatin until completely dissolved. Pour the cream over the chocolate and let sit for 1 minute.

▸ Using a small rubber spatula, begin stirring the white chocolate mixture in one direction, concentrating on the center, until smooth and glistening. Add the butter and stir until it is completely melted, about 1 minute. Stir in the ginger.

PLATE · 105

Continued ▸

▸ Put the ganache in the coolest part of your kitchen and let set, stirring occasionally, until spreadable, for about 1 hour before using. (The ganache can be covered and refrigerated for up to 2 weeks; see instructions on page 102.)

TO ASSEMBLE THE PETITS FOURS

▸ Line a 9-by-13-by-2-inch baking pan with parchment paper. Run a knife around the sides of the cake pans and invert the cakes onto cooling racks. Lay a cake layer, top side down, in the prepared pan and peel off the parchment paper. Using an offset spatula, spread about 1 cup of the ganache evenly over the surface. Top with a second cake layer, top side down, and peel off the parchment paper. Spread with the remaining ganache and top with the third cake layer, top side down; do not remove the parchment paper. Run a heavy rolling pin over the built petit four cake to press the layers together and flatten the surface. Wrap the pan in plastic wrap and freeze the cake for 3 hours, or until frozen solid.

TO COAT THE PETITS FOURS

▸ Line a baking sheet with parchment paper. Unwrap the baking pan and invert the cake onto a cutting board. Peel off the parchment paper and discard. Using a ruler as a guide, score the top of the cake with 4 horizontal lines and 6 vertical lines, both 1½ inches apart, giving you thirty-five 1½-inch squares. Using a sharp chef's knife, follow the score marks to cut out the squares. Place the petits fours on the lined baking sheet and refrigerate.

▸ Stir the oil into the tempered chocolate until it is fully incorporated and there are no streaks. (The oil thins the chocolate, making it easier to dip the petits fours.)

▸ Remove the petits fours from the refrigerator and place the baking pan next to the bowl of chocolate. Using dipping forks, dip one petit four into the chocolate, shake off the excess chocolate, and place the petit four back on the parchment-lined baking sheet. Top with a strip of candied ginger and continue with the remaining petits fours.

▸ Serve the petits fours in candy cups or on a small plate.

STORING

▸ The petits fours can be stored, covered, in the refrigerator for up to 2 weeks.

TIP: WHEN ADDING A SOLID INGREDIENT like candied ginger to a cake batter, it is best to mix it into the dry ingredients first to coat and separate the bits. Adding the candied ginger directly to the batter toward the end of the mixing process would result in clumps of ginger instead of evenly distributed bits throughout the cake.

PLATE · 106

PERFECTING PETITS FOURS

PETITS FOURS ARE THE MOST POPULAR ITEM WE SELL AT VALERIE CONFECTIONS—everyone seems to love the tiny layer cakes dipped in chocolate. But making petits fours doesn't have to be a challenge; follow these tips for polished-looking petits fours. One of the best aspects of the petits fours is their shelf life; once coated in chocolate, they will keep well for up to 2 weeks refrigerated.

1. When preparing the baking pans, make sure to coat them well with nonstick baking spray or butter before lining them with parchment paper. Then smooth out the parchment paper; any bubbles or wrinkles will show in the thin cake layers.

2. When building petits fours, start with very cold cake. Not only is a cold, firm cake easier to handle than a room-temperature one, a cold cake will release fewer crumbs, resulting in a cleaner finish. If it is a hot day, freeze the cakes in the baking pans for 30 to 45 minutes before assembling the petits fours.

3. After spreading the first cake layer with ganache, crouch down to the level of the cake to get a clear horizontal view of the ganache. It should appear level. If the ganache looks wavy, smooth it with the offset spatula.

4. Run a heavy rolling pin over the built petit four cake to press the layers together and flatten the surface.

5. Freezing the cake beforehand helps maintain the shape of the individual squares when they are cut. If you don't freeze the built cake, the cake layers will shift substantially as you cut the cake and release more crumbs, and the ganache will ooze out, making it very difficult to coat the squares cleanly.

6. Use a very sharp knife to cut the petit four cake into squares; do not use a serrated knife, which would result in more crumbs and possibly tear the cake.

CAKE COMPOSITIONS

Create the cake of your dreams: this chapter is packed with enough components to make a hundred cake combinations. Here are a few suggestions, but you can follow your instincts to make your own signature cake.

- Lemon Cake (page 78) with Cassis Ganache (page 113) and White Chocolate Buttercream Frosting (page 55)
- Matcha Mini-Cakes (page 101) with Passion Fruit Buttercream Filling (page 55) and Whipped Cream (page 138)
- Vanilla Bean Cake (page 75) with Lemon Ganache (page 96) and Lemon Glaze (page 96)
- Chocolate Cake (page 79) with Milk Chocolate Ganache (page 113) and Bittersweet Chocolate Glaze (page 94)

CAKES

Chocolate (page 79)

Vanilla Bean (page 75)

Golden Butter (page 77)

Hazelnut (page 91)

Matcha (page 101)

Lemon (page 78)

Orange (page 78)

FILLINGS

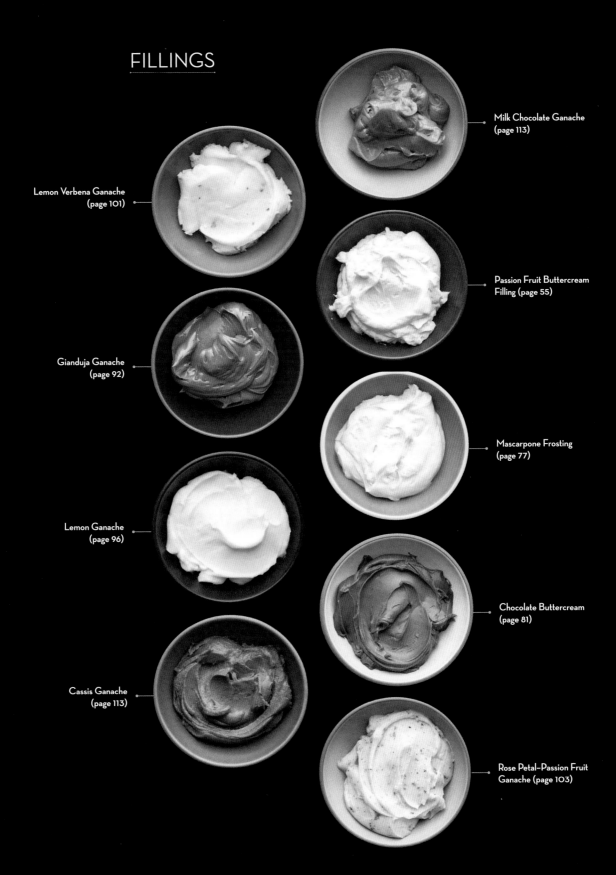

Milk Chocolate Ganache
(page 113)

Lemon Verbena Ganache
(page 101)

Passion Fruit Buttercream
Filling (page 55)

Gianduja Ganache
(page 92)

Mascarpone Frosting
(page 77)

Lemon Ganache
(page 96)

Chocolate Buttercream
(page 81)

Cassis Ganache
(page 113)

Rose Petal–Passion Fruit
Ganache (page 103)

COATINGS

White-Chocolate Chambord Glaze (page 84)

Lemon Glaze (page 96)

Bittersweet Chocolate Glaze (page 94)

Milk Chocolate Glaze (page 89)

Passion Fruit Buttercream (page 55)

Chocolate Buttercream (page 81)

White Chocolate Buttercream (page 55)

YIELDS

The cake batters, except for the Vanilla Bean Cake, yield three 9-inch round layers, three 8-inch square layers, or four 9-by-3-inch rectangular layers.

Half of any cake batter recipe, or one full Vanilla Bean Cake recipe, will yield three 9-by-13-inch sheet cakes for 35 petits fours, or one 13-by-18-inch sheet cake for 8 or 9 mini cakes.

A full recipe of any ganache will make enough filling for 35 petits fours, nine 3-layer round mini-cakes, or eight 3-layer square mini-cakes.

A full glaze recipe makes enough coating for a 3-layer 9-inch cake, a 3-layer 8-inch square cake, or a 4-layer 9-by-3-inch rectangular cake.

One and a half times a glaze recipe makes enough coating for nine 3-layer round mini-cakes or ten 3-layer square mini-cakes.

A full recipe of buttercream or frosting will fill and frost a 3-layer 9-inch cake, a 3-layer 8-inch square cake, a 4-layer 9-by-3-inch rectangular cake, nine 3-layer round mini-cakes, or ten 3-layer square mini-cakes.

Half a recipe of buttercream or frosting will fill and frost a 3-layer 9-inch cake, a 3-layer 8-inch square cake, a 4-layer 9-by-3-inch rectangular cake, nine 3-layer round mini-cakes, or eight 3-layer square mini-cakes.

Here are two additional ganache recipes for your repertoire. Refer to Cake Compositions, page 110, for pairing ideas.

Cassis Ganache

MAKES ABOUT 2¹/₂ CUPS

1 tablespoon powdered gelatin

3 tablespoons cold water

2 cups (11 ounces) 31% white chocolate chips or fèves (see Resources, page 335) or chopped 31% white chocolate

³/₄ cup (6 ounces) heavy cream

¹/₂ cup plus 1 tablespoon (4.5 ounces) cassis puree (see Resources, page 335)

3 tablespoons light corn syrup

1¹/₂ teaspoons lemon juice

9 tablespoons (4.5 ounces) unsalted butter, softened

› Sprinkle the gelatin over the cold water in a small bowl. Let sit for 10 minutes, until the gelatin softens.

› Put the chocolate into a medium bowl and set aside.

› Bring the heavy cream, cassis puree, corn syrup, and lemon juice just to a boil in a small saucepan. Remove from the heat and stir in the gelatin until it is completely dissolved. Pour the cream over the chocolate. Using a small rubber spatula, stir the mixture in one direction, concentrating on the center, until the ganache is smooth and glistening. Add the butter and stir until it is completely melted, about 1 minute. Put the ganache in the coolest part of your kitchen and let set, stirring occasionally, until spreadable, for about 1 hour before using (see sidebar on page 102).

Milk Chocolate Ganache

MAKES ABOUT 2¹/₂ CUPS

2¹/₃ cups (12.75 ounces) 38% milk chocolate chips or fèves (see Resources, page 335) or chopped 38% milk chocolate

³/₄ cup plus 2 tablespoons (7 ounces) heavy cream

10 tablespoons (1¹/₄ sticks/5 ounces) unsalted butter, softened

2 tablespoons light rum (optional)

¹/₂ teaspoon kosher salt

¹/₂ teaspoon vanilla extract

› Put the milk chocolate into a medium bowl. Heat the heavy cream in a small saucepan until it just boils. Pour the cream over the chocolate and let sit for 1 minute.

› Using a small rubber spatula, stir the chocolate mixture in one direction, concentrating on the center, until the ganache is smooth and glistening. Add the butter and stir until it is completely melted, about 1 minute. Add the rum, salt, and vanilla and stir until combined. Put the ganache in the coolest part of your kitchen and let set, stirring occasionally, until spreadable, for about 1 hour before using (see sidebar on page 102).

TIN

PIES AND TARTS

WHEN we started Valerie Confections in 2004, we spent a lot of time sourcing the finest ribbons and handcrafted boxes. Years later, with the growth of bakery items in our collection, I realized that packaging comes in many forms. By 2009, lattice strips and the flakiest, buttery piecrusts had captivated me just as ribbons and boxes had years earlier. A detailed crimp on a pie requires the same exacting care as tying the bows on our boxes of chocolate. The anticipation I experience when slicing into a pie holds the same seductive appeal as unveiling a box of chocolates. But I've realized that while my emotions relating to pies or tarts and boxed confections might feel similar, the material shift makes for drastically different results. No two pies are exactly the same—they change according to the temperature, where the fruit is grown, and whose fingers are pressing the dough. The unique qualities of each pie have created a sense of liberty in our kitchen: we can bake different flavors each week, and those gorgeous imperfections in the crusts and burst berries have given us a new perspective on "perfect" packaging.

Like the proliferation of preserves in the food world, pies and tarts have been given new life with the growth of local farmers' markets. Fifteen years ago, most home cooks might have made pies once or twice a year, and likely one of them was filled with canned pumpkin. The farmers' markets of today hold an embarrassment of riches, and now we have the ability to make fresh, delicious, seasonal fruit-filled packages year-round. It's no wonder pie shops have sprouted up around the country; it's a trend that has staying power because no one can seem to get enough of these homemade pies.

Pies and tarts are the perfect starting point for a novice baker. There is nothing complicated about the desserts in this chapter. Most recipes have just two simple components, crust and filling. Make a couple batches of dough and have some fun: get a feel for the way you like to roll dough or finish a crust (the ingredients are basically butter and flour, so the investment is minimal for a test run or two). The Pâte Sucrée (page 161) and Shortbread Crust (page 163) are essentially cookie doughs that you press into the tart tins, no rolling pin needed. The fruit fillings require little or no cooking; you simply sweeten the fruit to your satisfaction. Use this chapter to make your ideal pie. See Create Your Own Pies and Tarts, page 164, for more ideas, and then, when inspired, mix and match to your heart's content.

Quince and Pear Pie

The quince is a fabulous fruit that, sadly, is underused. Quinces have a curious look, yellow and fuzzy with an irregular bulbous shape. Genetically the quince is somewhere between pears and apples, but unlike its cousins, it is inedible in its raw state. However, when cooked, the astringent white flesh turns pink and sweet, with an intoxicating perfumed aroma. Serve this pie warm on a crisp autumn evening with a glass of Sauternes or another late-harvest dessert wine.

● MAKES ONE 9-INCH PIE; SERVES 6 TO 8 ●

1 pound quinces (2 to 3), peeled, cored, and sliced ½ inch thick

1 cup (6 ounces) light brown sugar

4 tablespoons (½ stick/2 ounces) unsalted butter, softened

1 pound Bartlett or d'Anjou pears (3 or 4), peeled, cored, and sliced ½ inch thick

¼ cup (1.5 ounces) raisins

2 teaspoons cornstarch

1 teaspoon kosher salt

½ teaspoon ground cinnamon

Pie Dough (recipe follows)

2 tablespoons Caramel Sauce (page 234)

1 egg, beaten

1 tablespoon sugar

▸ Position a rack in the center of the oven and heat the oven to 350°F.

▸ Toss the quinces with ½ cup of the brown sugar and the butter on a baking sheet, then spread out on the pan. Bake for 20 to 25 minutes; the quinces should be only partially baked, not soft or mushy. Use a fork to pierce a couple of slices; the flesh should resist the fork slightly. Turn the oven off.

▸ Stir the pear slices, the remaining ½ cup brown sugar, and the raisins into the quinces and bake for 5 minutes, or until the pears are softened. Remove the fruit from the oven and toss with the cornstarch, salt, and cinnamon. Let cool to room temperature.

▸ Meanwhile, remove one disk of dough from the refrigerator and place on a floured cool surface. Using a rolling pin, roll the dough out into a 13-inch circle: Start from the center of the dough and roll outward, rotating the dough 2 to 3 inches after each roll—this will help create a true circle. After every four to five rolls, run a large offset spatula under the dough to release it from the work surface. Add a little flour to the surface, rolling pin, and/or dough if the dough sticks or becomes difficult to roll.

▸ Roll the dough up onto the rolling pin, then unroll into a 9-inch pie pan, centering the round. Gently press the dough into the bottom of the pan and against the sides, making sure there are no air pockets. Press the dough against the upper edges of the pan so it extends about ½ inch beyond the edges, then trim any excess dough with kitchen shears. Chill the crust for 15 minutes, or until the dough is cool and firm.

▸ Roll out the second disk of dough into a 12-inch round. Slide onto a sheet pan and refrigerate until ready to use.

▸ Remove the pie pan from the refrigerator. Arrange half the slices of fruit in the bottom of the crust in concentric circles, starting from the outside and working toward the center, overlapping the fruit so there are no vacant spaces. Drizzle with the caramel sauce and continue building layers of fruit, mounding it higher in the center to create a domed effect.

▸ Roll the top crust up onto the rolling pin and drape the dough over the filling. Trim and crimp the edges of the double crust, following the

TIP: MARBLE, STAINLESS STEEL, AND wooden cutting boards with a finished surface are all great for rolling dough.

instructions on page 133. Refrigerate the pie until the crust is cold and firm to the touch, about 15 minutes.

› Heat the oven to 350°F.

› Brush the exposed surface of the pie with the beaten egg and then sprinkle with the sugar. Cut 4 to 6 slits in the top of the pie for steam vents.

› Place the pie on a baking sheet and bake for 30 minutes, or until the edges of the crust look golden brown. Remove the pie from the oven and cover the edges of the crust with a pie ring (see sidebar).

› Bake for an additional 35 to 45 minutes, until the crust is golden brown. Start checking the pie after 30 minutes, then continue baking, checking at 5-minute intervals, until the crust is golden, with no translucent areas. Remove the pie ring and bake for an additional 5 minutes or so, until the color of the crust is uniform. Transfer the pie to a cooling rack and serve warm or at room temperature.

STORING

› The pie can be stored at room temperature, covered, for up to 2 days.

Pie Dough

Given the choice between a piecrust made with butter and one made with shortening, I always choose butter. If you keep your dough cold at every step of the way, you can achieve the same flakiness that people attribute to shortening with the incomparable flavor of butter.

MAKES ENOUGH FOR ONE 9-INCH DOUBLE-CRUST PIE, TWO 9-INCH SINGLE-CRUST PIES, OR FIFTEEN 4-INCH HAND PIES

---

2 1/2 cups (12.5 ounces) all-purpose flour

2 teaspoons sugar

1 teaspoon salt

2 1/2 sticks (10 ounces) unsalted butter, cubed and chilled

1/4 to 1/3 cup (2 to 2.5 ounces) cold water

› To make the dough in a food processor: Put the flour, sugar, and salt in the processor bowl and pulse once or twice to combine. Drop the pieces of butter through the feed tube, continuing to pulse until the mixture resembles coarse crumbs. Slowly add 1/4 cup water as you continue pulsing a few more times, then add more water if necessary; stop when the dough just starts to come together.

› To make the dough by hand: Put the flour, sugar, and salt into a medium bowl and mix together with a fork or small whisk. Cut the butter into the dough using a pastry cutter or a large fork until the mixture resembles coarse crumbs. Drizzle 1/4 cup water directly over the dough, mixing with the pastry cutter or fork, then add more water if necessary, mixing until the dough just comes together.

› Remove the dough from the processor or bowl and form into 2 equal disks. Wrap each disk in plastic wrap and refrigerate for at least 2 hours, or up to 3 days. The dough can be frozen for up to 2 months; thaw in the refrigerator.

ENTERTAINING WITH DESSERT

BASED ON MY UNOFFICIAL RESEARCH (i.e., the requests we receive at Valerie Confections), the popularity of dessert buffets is growing. In generations past, a dessert table was ubiquitous at large gatherings, especially during the holidays, so it's exciting to see them return to fashion. When creating your table, remember that having desserts in a variety of flavors, shapes, and colors makes for the most dynamic setting. Buffets are popular because guests can experience a myriad of treats. It's decadent and, most important, sociable. A dessert table, like a bar, is a place for people to visit, share an experience, and relish a moment together. Here are a few suggestions for your next party.

Easter Dessert Buffet

‣ Lemon Shortbread (page 263)
‣ Lavender–Earl Grey Mini-Cakes with Lemon Ganache (page 96)
‣ Meyer Lemon Tea Cakes with Pomegranate Glaze (page 328)
‣ Blueberry–Vanilla Cream Hand Pies (page 147)
‣ Rose Petal Cake (page 83)
‣ Fruit and Cream Tart (page 163)

Mother's Day Tea

‣ Crème Fraîche Scones (page 323)
‣ Strawberry Rhubarb Jam (page 278)
‣ Strawberry–Vanilla Bean Jam (page 276)
‣ Rose Petal Petits Fours (page 103)
‣ Berry Mendiants (page 173)

‣ Golden Butter Cake with Berries and Mascarpone Frosting (page 77)
‣ Berry-Basket Galette (page 154)

Thanksgiving Dessert Buffet

‣ Winter Luxury Pumpkin Pie (page 131)
‣ Quince and Pear Pie (page 119)
‣ Goat-Cheese Cheesecake with Almond Crust (page 51)
‣ Carrot Cake with Cream Cheese Frosting (page 61)
‣ Upside-down Apple and Almond Cakes (page 331)
‣ Pumpkin Seed Toffee (page 189)
‣ Durango Bark (page 183)

Christmas Dessert Buffet

‣ A Cake for Alice (page 67)
‣ Tiramisu Trifle (page 229)
‣ White Chocolate Coconut Cake (page 55)
‣ Fruitcake Noir (page 43)
‣ Ginger Petits Fours (page 105)
‣ Snowballs (page 254)
‣ Almond Fleur de Sel Toffee (page 186)
‣ Peppermint Bark (page 181)

New Year's Eve Dessert Buffet

‣ Champagne Gelée (page 221)
‣ Rose Petal Petits Fours (page 103)
‣ Raspberry Truffles (page 203)
‣ Crème Fraîche Truffles (page 201)
‣ Meringues (page 208)
‣ Chocolate Marshmallows (page 211)

Lattice-Topped Berry Pie

This pie is bursting with berries—and little else. The result is a clean, refreshing dessert that pairs perfectly with picnic and barbecue foods. Serve at room temperature, alone or with a dollop of Whipped Cream (page 138).

● MAKES ONE 9-INCH PIE; SERVES 6 TO 8 ●

7 cups (1³/4 pounds) mixed berries, such as raspberries, blackberries, and blueberries

³/4 cup (5.25 ounces) sugar, or to taste

2 tablespoons (1 ounce) unsalted butter, melted

Grated zest of 1 lemon

¹/4 cup (1.5 ounces) cornstarch

Pie Dough (page 120)

1¹/2 teaspoons Pie Dust (recipe follows)

1 egg, beaten

1 tablespoon sugar

▸ Put 3 cups of the berries and the ³/4 cup sugar into a medium saucepan and cook over medium heat, stirring occasionally, until the fruit softens and releases some juices, about 5 minutes. Transfer to a medium bowl.

▸ Add the remaining berries to the cooked berries and toss. Taste the berries for sweetness: if you would like the pie a little sweeter, add more sugar to taste. Stir in the melted butter, lemon zest, and cornstarch and let cool to room temperature. (The filling can be covered and refrigerated for up to 3 days.)

▸ Meanwhile, remove one disk of dough from the refrigerator and place on a floured cool surface. Using a rolling pin, roll the dough out into a 13-inch circle: Start from the center of the dough and roll outward, rotating the dough 2 to 3 inches after each roll—this will help create a true circle. After every four to five rolls, run a large offset spatula under the dough to release it from the work surface. Add a little flour to the surface, rolling pin, and/or dough if the dough sticks or becomes difficult to roll.

▸ Roll the dough up onto the rolling pin, then unroll into a 9-inch pie pan, centering the round. Gently press the dough into the bottom of the pan and against the sides, making sure there are no air pockets. Press the dough against the upper edges of the pan so it extends about ¹/2 inch beyond the edges, then trim any excess dough with kitchen shears. Chill the crust for 15 minutes, or until the dough is cool and firm.

▸ Position a rack in the center of the oven and heat the oven to 350°F.

▸ Cover the bottom of the crust with the pie dust. Fill the crust with the berry filling. Roll out the second disk of dough into a 12-inch circle and follow the instructions on page 126 to make a lattice-topped pie. Using a pastry brush, paint the chilled lattice with the beaten egg, then sprinkle with the 1 tablespoon sugar.

▸ Place the pie on a baking sheet and bake for 30 minutes, or until the edges of the crust look golden brown. Remove the pie from the oven and cover the edges of the crust with a pie ring (see page 120).

▸ Bake for an additional 25 to 35 minutes, until the crust is golden brown. Start checking the pie after 20 minutes, then continue baking, checking at 5-minute intervals, until the crust is golden, with no translucent areas.

Continued ▸

Remove the pie ring and bake for an additional 5 minutes or so, until the color of the crust is uniform. Transfer the pie to a cooling rack to cool completely.

STORING

› The pie can be stored in the refrigerator, to serve cold, or at room temperature, covered, for up to 2 days.

Pie Dust

A scant sprinkling of this simple mixture prevents piecrusts from getting soggy on the bottom; I use it with all wet pie fillings.

MAKES ¹/₂ CUP

¹/₄ **cup (1.25 ounces) all-purpose flour**

¹/₄ **cup (1.75 ounces) sugar**

› Sift the flour and sugar together into a small bowl. The pie dust can be stored in an airtight container for up to 6 months.

HOW TO MAKE A LATTICE-TOPPED PIE

A CRISSCROSSED LATTICE TOPPING creates small windows into the colorful interior of a pie or tart. The openings also allow fruit juices to evaporate during the cooking process. A lattice is best used for berry and other fillings that are high in water content.

To create a lattice top, place the disk of chilled dough on a floured cool surface. Using a rolling pin, roll the dough into a 12-inch circle: Start from the center of the dough and roll outward, rotating the dough 2 to 3 inches after each roll—this will help create a true circle. After every four to five rolls, run a large offset spatula under the dough to release it. Add a little flour to the surface, rolling pin, and/or dough if the dough sticks or becomes difficult to roll.

Using a pastry wheel or a pizza cutter, cut the dough into 10 uniform strips approximately ³/₄ inch wide. (Feel free to make 8 wider strips or 12 narrower strips if you prefer.)

Lay 5 lattice strips vertically over the filling, starting in the center with the longest strip and working toward the edges using progressively shorter strips. Fold the second and fourth strips back to the top of the pie. Lay one of the remaining strips horizontally across the other three strips, then fold the second and fourth vertical strips back over it. Fold the first, third, and fifth strips back, lay another strip across the second and fourth strips, and then fold the first, third, and fifth strips back over it. Repeat this pattern with the remaining 3 lattice strips.

Trim the top crust to a ³/₄-inch overhang if necessary. Pinch the top and bottom crusts together around the entire edge and finish using one of the methods on page 133. Chill the pie for 15 minutes, or until the dough is cool and firm, before baking.

Cherry-Vanilla Bean Pie

Cold fresh cherries are sweet and deliciously satisfying during the first weeks of summer. Cooked cherries can be equally enjoyable, but they sometimes take on an unfortunate medicinal taste. Here a vanilla bean in the filling imparts a rich and aromatic quality to the cooked stone fruit. I suggest using Bing cherries or other dark red cherries for this recipe. Rainier cherries will taste fine, but they tend to turn brown in the cooking process.

● MAKES ONE 9-INCH PIE; SERVES 6 TO 8 ●

About 2 pounds Bing or other dark red cherries, rinsed and pitted (3½ cups)
¼ cup (1.5 ounces) light brown sugar
1 vanilla bean, split, seeds scraped out, seeds and bean reserved
½ cup (3.5 ounces) granulated sugar
¼ cup (1.5 ounces) cornstarch
Pie Dough (page 120)
1½ teaspoons Pie Dust (page 126)
2 tablespoons (1 ounce) unsalted butter

1 egg, beaten
1 tablespoon granulated sugar

▸ Combine half the cherries, the brown sugar, and the vanilla seeds and bean in a medium saucepan and cook over high heat, stirring frequently, for 15 minutes, until the cherries have released their juices and darkened in color.

▸ Meanwhile, toss the remaining cherries with the ½ cup granulated sugar and the cornstarch in a medium bowl.

▸ Pour the cooked cherries into the bowl and remove the vanilla bean. Stir the cherries and let cool to room temperature. (The filling can be covered and refrigerated for up to 3 days.)

▸ Meanwhile, remove one disk of dough from the refrigerator and place on a floured cool surface. Using a rolling pin, roll the dough out into a 13-inch circle: Start from the center of the dough and roll outward, rotating the dough 2 to 3 inches after each roll—this will help create a true circle. After every four to five rolls, run a large offset spatula under the dough to release it from the work surface. Add a little flour to the surface, rolling pin, and/or dough if the dough sticks or becomes difficult to roll.

▸ Roll the dough up onto the rolling pin, then unroll into a 9-inch pie pan, centering the round. Gently press the dough into the bottom of the pan and against the sides, making sure there are no air pockets. Press the dough against the upper edges of the pan so it extends about ½ inch beyond the edges, then trim any excess dough with kitchen shears. Chill the crust for 15 minutes, or until the dough is cool and firm.

▸ Position a rack in the center of the oven and heat the oven to 350°F.

▸ Cover the bottom of the crust with the pie dust. Pour in the cherry filling. Cut the butter into 4 pieces and place over the cherries. Roll out the second disk of dough into a 12-inch circle and follow the instructions on page 126 to make a lattice-topped pie. Using a pastry brush, paint the chilled lattice with the beaten egg, then sprinkle with the 1 tablespoon granulated sugar.

▸ Place the pie on a baking sheet and bake for 30 minutes, or until the edges of the crust look golden brown. Remove the pie from the oven and cover the edges of the crust with a pie ring (see page 120).

> Bake for an additional 25 to 35 minutes, until the crust is golden brown. Start checking the pie after 20 minutes, then continue baking, checking at 5-minute intervals, until the crust is golden, with no translucent areas. Remove the pie ring and bake for an additional 5 minutes or so, until the color of the crust is uniform. Transfer the pie to a cooling rack to cool completely.

STORING

> The pie can be stored in the refrigerator, to serve cold, or at room temperature, covered, for up to 2 days.

TIPS FOR WORKING WITH DOUGH

I REMEMBER BEING VERY INTIMIDATED THE FIRST TIME I made pie dough and, sadly, it wasn't very successful. After I'd practiced a few times, though, my comfort and skill level grew, and eventually making pie dough became very satisfying. Here are a few tips that will help make your doughs perfect from the get-go.

> Keep the dough as cold as possible when you are working with it. When dough is well chilled, the butter stays firm and that results in a flaky, tender crust that maintains its shape and crimp. Warm, shiny dough indicates that the butter has softened or melted and will result in a misshapen crust with a dense texture. Many of the recipes in this chapter call for repeated refrigeration of the dough; the chilling helps maintain the integrity of the crust.

> Overrolling dough also adversely affects its texture. Try to roll the dough out as quickly as possible; remember that each time you roll, the dough is becoming warmer and the butter is breaking down. Be efficient with your movements, and be discriminating with your use of flour to keep the texture at its best.

> You can reuse dough scraps—when making hand pies, for example—but wrap them together in plastic wrap and refrigerate until firm before rolling a second time.

Winter Luxury Pumpkin Pie

I know that roasting a whole pumpkin is a bigger time commitment than opening a can of pumpkin filling, but the flavor is absolutely incomparable. The wise farmers at Windrose Farms in Paso Robles, California, introduced me to the Winter Luxury variety of pumpkin at the Santa Monica Farmers' Market. A sign next to their pumpkins read, "Best Pumpkin Pie Ever!" They weren't lying; the pies I make with their pumpkins taste like roasted, caramelized pumpkin. The flavors are nuanced, the texture is silken, and it is an experience that will never be found in a can. Serve at room temperature with a large dollop of Vanilla Whipped Cream (page 138).

● MAKES ONE 9-INCH PIE; SERVES 6 TO 8 ●

One 3- to 4-pound pumpkin, preferably
   Winter Luxury

3/4 cup (4.5 ounces) light brown sugar

3 large eggs

1 teaspoon ground cinnamon

1/2 teaspoon ground ginger

1 teaspoon kosher salt

1/4 teaspoon ground cloves

1 tablespoon cornstarch

1/2 cup (4 ounces) crème fraîche or heavy
   cream, plus more if needed

1/2 recipe Pie Dough (page 120)

1 1/2 teaspoons Pie Dust (page 126)

1 egg, beaten

1 teaspoon granulated sugar

› Position a rack in the center of the oven and heat the oven to 350°F. Line a large baking sheet with parchment paper.

› Using a sharp chef's knife, cut the pumpkin in half. Scoop out the seeds. Place the pumpkin cut side down on the prepared baking sheet and roast for about 40 minutes, until the flesh is very soft. Pierce it with a fork to check for doneness. Let the pumpkin cool completely.

› Scoop the pumpkin flesh out of the skin and puree in a food processor or blender, scraping down the sides once or twice. Reserve 1 1/2 cups of the puree for the filling. (The extra puree can be packed into a Ziploc freezer bag and frozen for up to 3 months.)

› In the bowl of a stand mixer fitted with the paddle attachment (or in a large bowl, using a handheld mixer), beat the brown sugar and eggs on medium speed until blended, about 1 minute. Add the pumpkin puree and beat until smooth. Scrape the sides of the bowl, then add the cinnamon, ginger, salt, cloves, and cornstarch and beat until incorporated. Add the crème fraîche and beat until incorporated, about 30 seconds. If the filling looks stiff, add more crème fraîche 1 tablespoon at a time. (The filling can be stored, covered, in the refrigerator for up to 2 days.)

› Remove the dough from the refrigerator and place on a floured cool surface. Using a rolling pin, roll the dough out into a 13-inch circle: Start from the center of the dough and roll outward, rotating the dough 2 to 3 inches after each roll—this will help create a true circle. After every four to five rolls, run a large offset spatula under the dough to release it from the work surface. Add a little flour to the surface, rolling pin, and/or dough if the dough sticks or becomes difficult to roll.

› Roll the dough up onto the rolling pin, then unroll into a 9-inch pie pan, centering the round. Gently press the dough into the bottom of the pan and against the sides, making sure there are no air pockets. Press the dough against the upper edges of the pan so it extends about 1/2 inch beyond the edges, then trim any excess dough with kitchen shears. Crimp the dough, following the single-crust crimping instructions, opposite. Chill the crust for 15 minutes, or until the dough is cool and firm.

▶ Cover the bottom of the crust with the pie dust. Pour in the filling. Using a pastry brush, paint the crimped edge of the dough with the beaten eggs, then sprinkle with the granulated sugar.

▶ Place the pie on a baking sheet and bake for 30 minutes, or until the edges of the crust look golden brown. Remove the pie from the oven and cover the edges of the crust with a pie ring (see page 120).

▶ Bake for an additional 25 to 35 minutes, until the edges of the filling are set but the center jiggles slightly when the pan is gently shaken. Start checking the pie after 20 minutes, then continue baking, checking at 5-minute intervals. Remove the pie ring and bake for an additional 5 minutes, or until the pie is just set. (Do not bake the pie so long that it starts to brown on the top.) Transfer the pie to a cooling rack to cool completely.

STORING

▶ The pie can be stored in the refrigerator, covered, for up to 2 days.

CRIMPING A PIECRUST

CRUST DESIGN, OR CRIMPING, is a way to add a personal touch to your creations. Once you've mastered a few versions, try to do them more quickly without sacrificing precision; pie dough holds its shape best with minimal handling.

Forked Crimp

‣ FOR A SINGLE-CRUST PIE, using a fork dipped in flour, press the dough against the rim of the pie pan all around the pan, making sure you don't overlap the fork impressions. Chill the pie as directed in the recipe before proceeding.

‣ FOR LATTICE-TOPPED AND DOUBLE-CRUST PIES, trim the top crust to a ³/₄-inch overhang if necessary. Fold the edges of the top crust over the bottom crust and proceed as for a single crust.

Simple Crimp

‣ FOR A SINGLE-CRUST PIE, place your thumbs about ¼ inch apart on the edge of the crust and press them toward each other to create a crimp, then continue all around the edge of the pie. Chill as directed in the recipe before proceeding.

‣ FOR LATTICE-TOPPED AND DOUBLE-CRUST PIES, trim the top crust to a ³/₄-inch overhang if necessary. Fold the edges of the top crust over the bottom crust and proceed as for a single crust.

Fancy Crimp

‣ FOR A SINGLE-CRUST PIE, put your left index finger on the edge of the dough at a 30-degree angle. Using your right thumb, lift the edge of the dough just to the right of your index finger and press the dough between your index finger and thumb to create a crimp. Using your right thumb and index finger, press the dough together just to the right of the crimp, extending the dough down about ½ inch. Put your left index finger to the right of the established crimp and, with your right thumb, lift the extended dough up to your index finger, creating a second crimp. Continue all around the edge of the entire pie.

When the crimping is complete, pinch all the crimps one more time to give them more height and definition. Chill the crust as directed in the recipe before proceeding.

‣ FOR LATTICE-TOPPED AND DOUBLE-CRUST PIES, trim the top crust to a ³/₄-inch overhang if necessary. Pinch the top and bottom crusts together around the entire edge and proceed as for a single crust.

Blackberry–Mango Curd Pie

I chose the pairing of blackberries and mango in this pie partly for the amazing color combination, but raspberries, blueberries, and strawberries are equally pleasing flavors to pair with mango curd. Serve chilled or at room temperature, with Mango Cream (page 139).

● MAKES ONE 9-INCH PIE; SERVES 6 TO 8 ●

1 pint (about ½ pound) blackberries

⅓ cup (2.33 ounces) sugar

Pie Dough (page 120)

1½ teaspoons Pie Dust (page 126)

1¼ cups (10 ounces) Mango Curd (recipe follows)

1 egg, beaten

1 tablespoon sugar

› Pour the blackberries into a medium bowl and toss with the ⅓ cup sugar. Set aside.

› Remove one disk of dough from the refrigerator and place on a floured cool surface. Using a rolling pin, roll the dough out into a 13-inch circle: Start from the center of the dough and roll outward, rotating the dough 2 to 3 inches after each roll—this will help create a true circle. After every four to five rolls, run a large offset spatula under the dough to release it from the work surface. Add a little flour to the surface, rolling pin, and/or dough if the dough sticks or becomes difficult to roll.

› Roll the dough up onto the rolling pin, then unroll into a 9-inch pie pan, centering the round. Gently press the dough into the bottom of the pan and against the sides, making sure there are no air pockets. Press the dough against the upper edges of the pan so it extends about ½ inch beyond the edges, then trim any excess dough with kitchen shears. Chill the crust for 15 minutes, or until the dough is cool and firm.

› Position a rack in the center of the oven and heat the oven to 350°F.

› Cover the bottom of the crust with the pie dust. Fill the crust with the mango curd, spreading it evenly. Top the curd with the blackberries. Roll out the second disk of dough into a 12-inch circle and follow the instructions on page 126 to make a lattice-topped pie. Using a pastry brush, paint the chilled lattice with the beaten egg, then sprinkle with the 1 tablespoon sugar.

› Place the pie on a baking sheet and bake for 30 minutes, or until the edges of the crust look golden brown. Remove the pie from the oven and cover the edges of the crust with a pie ring (see page 120).

› Bake for an additional 25 to 35 minutes, until the crust is golden brown. Start checking the pie after 20 minutes, then continue baking, checking at 5-minute intervals, until the crust is golden with no translucent areas. Remove the pie ring and bake for an additional 5 minutes or so, until the color of the crust is uniform. Transfer the pie to a cooling rack to cool completely.

STORING

› The pie can be stored in the refrigerator, covered, for up to 2 days.

Mango Curd

MAKES 2$\frac{1}{2}$ CUPS

2 medium mangoes (1 pound), peeled, pitted, and cut into chunks

$\frac{1}{2}$ cup (3.5 ounces) sugar

$\frac{1}{4}$ cup (2 ounces) fresh lime juice

3 large egg yolks

5 tablespoons (2.5 ounces) unsalted butter, cut into chunks

> Set a double boiler over medium heat or fill a medium saucepan halfway with water and bring to a boil over medium heat.

> Combine the mango, sugar, and lime juice in the bowl of a food processor or blender and puree until smooth, about 1 minute. Add the egg yolks and blend for 30 seconds.

> Pour the mixture into the top of the double boiler or into a medium heatproof bowl set over the pan of water; lower the heat slightly. Stir the curd constantly as it slowly thickens, about 10 minutes. When the curd has reached 170°F on a candy or instant-read thermometer and coats the back of the spoon, remove it from the heat. Stir in the butter until it melts.

> Pour the curd through a fine-mesh sieve into a bowl or other container. Place plastic wrap directly on the surface of the curd to prevent a skin from forming and allow the curd to cool to room temperature, then refrigerate for at least 2 hours before using.

> The curd can be stored in the refrigerator, covered, for up to 5 days.

WHIPPED TOPPINGS

A GENEROUS DOLLOP OF BILLOWY WHIPPED CREAM is a wonderful way to garnish the fruit desserts in this chapter. Infusing another flavor into the whipped cream takes little time and allows for interesting variations.

Use a chilled bowl and very cold cream for the best results. I generally prefer lightly sweetened cream; use additional confectioners' sugar if you'd like it sweeter. It is best to make whipped cream right before serving, but, if necessary, it can be held in the refrigerator for up to 1 day; whisk it again before serving (the Lemon Cream and Mango Cream will keep for up to 2 days).

Whipped Cream

MAKES ABOUT $1^1/_2$ CUPS

1 cup (8 ounces) well-chilled heavy cream
1 tablespoon confectioners' sugar

› In the bowl of a stand mixer fitted with the whisk attachment (or in a medium bowl, using a handheld mixer), whip the heavy cream until it thickens. Add the confectioners' sugar and continue whipping until soft peaks form.

Vanilla Whipped Cream

MAKES ABOUT $1^1/_2$ CUPS

1 cup (8 ounces) well-chilled heavy cream
1 tablespoon plus 1 teaspoon confectioners' sugar
1 teaspoon vanilla bean paste (see Resources, page 335)

› In the bowl of a stand mixer fitted with the whisk attachment (or in a medium bowl, using a handheld mixer), whip the heavy cream until it thickens. Add the confectioners' sugar and vanilla paste and continue whipping until soft peaks form.

Chocolate Whipped Cream

MAKES ABOUT $1^1/_2$ CUPS

1 cup (8 ounces) well-chilled heavy cream
1 tablespoon atomized 69% bittersweet chocolate (see Resources, page 335)
1 teaspoon confectioners' sugar

› In the bowl of a stand mixer fitted with the whisk attachment (or in a medium bowl, using a handheld mixer), whip the heavy cream until it thickens. Add the atomized chocolate and confectioners' sugar and continue whipping until soft peaks form.

Tangy Whipped Cream

MAKES ABOUT 1^1/$_2$ CUPS

^{1}/$_2$ cup (4 ounces) well-chilled crème fraîche
^{1}/$_2$ cup (4 ounces) well-chilled heavy cream
1 tablespoon confectioners' sugar

› In the bowl of a stand mixer fitted with the whisk attachment (or in a medium bowl, using a handheld mixer), whip the crème fraîche and heavy cream until they thicken. Add the confectioners' sugar and continue whipping until medium peaks form.

Raspberry Whipped Cream

MAKES ABOUT 1^1/$_2$ CUPS

1 cup (8 ounces) well-chilled heavy cream
1 tablespoon confectioners' sugar
2 teaspoons freeze-dried raspberry powder (see Resources, page 335)

› In the bowl of a stand mixer fitted with the whisk attachment (or in a medium bowl, using a handheld mixer), whip the heavy cream until it thickens. Add the confectioners' sugar and raspberry powder and continue whipping until medium peaks form.

Lemon Cream

MAKES ABOUT 1^1/$_3$ CUPS

^{1}/$_2$ cup (4 ounces) well-chilled heavy cream
^{1}/$_2$ cup (4 ounces) Lemon Curd (page 154)
^{1}/$_4$ teaspoon grated lemon zest

› In the bowl of a stand mixer fitted with the whisk attachment (or in a medium bowl, using a handheld mixer), whip the heavy cream until it thickens. Add the lemon curd and lemon zest and continue whipping until medium peaks form.

Mango Cream

MAKES ABOUT 1^1/$_3$ CUPS

^{1}/$_2$ cup (4 ounces) well-chilled heavy cream
^{1}/$_2$ cup (4 ounces) Mango Curd (page 137)

› In the bowl of a stand mixer fitted with the whisk attachment (or in a medium bowl, using a handheld mixer), whip the heavy cream until it thickens. Add the mango curd and continue whipping until medium peaks form.

Plum and Marzipan Crumble Pie

Although plums are available throughout the summer, I always think of making this pie in the fall. Deep purple plums, like late-season Angelinos, are the best complement to the crunchy sweetness of the marzipan crumble. If you are inspired to use a golden summer plum for this pie, be conservative with the sugar, since the recipe was designed for tart-skinned plums. Serve at room temperature, with Tangy Whipped Cream (page 139).

● MAKES ONE 9-INCH PIE; SERVES 6 TO 8 ●

2 pounds (8 to 12 medium) purple plums, pitted and cut into 1/2-inch-thick slices

1 1/2 to 2 cups (10.5 to 14 ounces) sugar

1/4 cup (1.5 ounces) cornstarch

1/2 recipe Pie Dough (page 120)

1 1/2 teaspoons Pie Dust (page 126)

1 egg, beaten

1 teaspoon sugar

3/4 cup (3.75 ounces) Marzipan Crumble (recipe follows)

› Put half of the plums and 3/4 cup of the sugar into a medium saucepan and cook, stirring frequently, over medium heat until the fruit softens and releases some juices, about 10 minutes. Transfer to a medium bowl.

› Add the raw plums to the cooked plums and stir in another 3/4 cup sugar. Taste the plums for sweetness. If you would like the pie a little sweeter, add up to 1/2 cup more sugar. Stir in the cornstarch and let the filling cool to room temperature.

› Remove the dough from the refrigerator and place on a floured cool surface. Using a rolling pin, roll the dough out into a 13-inch circle: Start from the center of the dough and roll outward, rotating the dough 2 to 3 inches after each roll—this will help create a true circle. After every four to five rolls, run a large offset spatula under the dough to release it from the work surface. Add a little flour to the surface, rolling pin, and/or dough if the dough sticks or becomes difficult to roll.

› Roll the dough up onto the rolling pin, then unroll into a 9-inch pie pan, centering the round. Gently press the dough into the bottom of the pan and against the sides, making sure there are no air pockets. Press the dough against the upper edges of the pan so it extends about 1/2 inch beyond the edges, then trim any excess dough with kitchen shears. Crimp the dough, following the single-crust crimping instructions on page 133. Chill the crust for 15 minutes, or until the dough is cool and firm.

› Position a rack in the center of the oven and heat the oven to 350°F.

› Cover the bottom of the crust with the pie dust. If the plum filling appears very watery, drain off some of the liquid. Fill the crust with the filling. Using a pastry brush, paint the crimped edge of the dough with the beaten egg, then sprinkle with the 1 teaspoon sugar.

› Place the pie on a baking sheet and bake for 30 minutes, or until the edges of the crust look golden brown. Remove the pie from the oven and sprinkle the plum filling with the marzipan crumble. Cover the edges of the crust with a pie ring (see page 120).

› Bake for an additional 35 to 45 minutes, until the marzipan is golden and crunchy. Start checking the pie after 30 minutes, then continue baking, checking at 5-minute intervals, until the marzipan topping is golden. Remove the pie ring. If the crust is too pale or is translucent in any spots, bake for an additional 5 minutes, or until it is golden brown. Transfer the pie to a cooling rack to cool completely.

STORING

‣ The pie can be stored in the refrigerator, to serve cold, or at room temperature, covered, for up to 2 days.

Marzipan Crumble

MAKES 1¹/₂ CUPS

1 cup (10 ounces) marzipan

¹/₃ cup (1 ounce) raw almond flour (see Resources, page 335), toasted (see page 20)

2 tablespoons (1 ounce) cold unsalted butter, diced

2 tablespoons sugar

TO MAKE THE CRUMBLE IN A FOOD PROCESSOR

‣ Break the marzipan into small pieces and place in the bowl of the food processor. Pulse a few times, and then add the almond flour through the feed tube, pulsing to blend. Continue pulsing as you add the butter and sugar. Do not let the mixture get smooth—stop pulsing when the crumble is in pea-sized pieces.

TO MAKE THE CRUMBLE BY HAND

‣ Break the marzipan into small pieces and put in a medium bowl. Cut in the almond flour, butter, and sugar, using a pastry blender or large fork, until the mixture is in pea-sized crumbs.

‣ Use the crumble immediately, or store in an airtight container in the refrigerator for up to 3 weeks.

Valentine's Pie

There is nothing wrong with giving a box of chocolates on Valentine's Day (of course!), but sometimes an alternative can be refreshing. Consider this heartwarming crimson fruit pie. Serve a slice to your Valentine, perhaps accompanied by a glass of rosé Champagne.

12 ounces (about 10 medium stalks) rhubarb, rinsed, trimmed, and sliced into ½-inch pieces (3 cups)

1 cup (7 ounces) sugar, or more to taste

3 cups (12 ounces) strawberries, rinsed, hulled, and sliced

2 cups (8 ounces) raspberries, rinsed and dried

2 tablespoons cornstarch

20 to 25 organic rose petals (see Resources, page 335), rinsed and dried

Pie Dough (page 120)

1½ teaspoons Pie Dust (page 126)

1 egg, beaten

> Put the rhubarb and sugar into a medium saucepan and cook over medium heat, stirring periodically, until the fruit softens, about 5 minutes. Add the strawberries and continue cooking for 5 minutes, stirring frequently.

> Remove the pan from the heat and stir in the raspberries. Taste the mixture, and if you would like the pie a little sweeter, add more sugar. Stir in the cornstarch and rose petals and let the filling cool to room temperature. (The filling can be stored, covered, in the refrigerator for up to 2 days.)

> Position a rack in the center of the oven and heat the oven to 350°F.

> Remove one disk of dough from the refrigerator and place on a floured cool surface. Using a rolling pin, roll the dough out into a 13-inch circle: Start from the center of the dough and roll outward, rotating the dough 2 to 3 inches after each roll—this will help create a true circle. After every four to five rolls, run a large offset spatula under the dough to release it from the work surface. Add a little flour to the surface, rolling pin, and/or dough if the dough sticks or becomes difficult to roll.

> Roll the dough up onto the rolling pin, then unroll into a 9-inch pie pan, centering the round. Gently press the dough into the bottom of the pan and against the sides, making sure there are no air pockets. Press the dough against the upper edges of the pan so it extends about ½ inch beyond the edges, then trim any excess dough with kitchen shears. Chill the crust for 15 minutes, or until the dough is cool and firm.

> Meanwhile, roll out the second disk of dough into a 12-inch circle. Using a 2-inch heart-shaped cookie cutter, cut a shape in the center of the pie round and remove it. (See Tip.)

> Cover the bottom of the crust with the pie dust. Fill the crust with the filling. Using a pastry brush, paint the beaten egg around the edges of the crust.

> Roll the top crust up onto the rolling pin and drape the dough over the filling. Trim and crimp the edges of the double crust, following the

instructions on page 133. Refrigerate the pie until the crust is cold and firm to the touch, about 15 minutes.

▸ Place the pie on a baking sheet and bake for 30 minutes, or until the edges of the crust look golden brown. Remove the pie from the oven and cover the edges of the crust with a pie ring (see page 120).

▸ Bake for an additional 35 to 45 minutes, until the crust is golden brown. Start checking the pie after 30 minutes, then continue baking, checking at 5-minute intervals, until the crust is golden, with no translucent areas. Remove the pie ring and bake for an additional 5 minutes or so, until the crust is golden brown. Transfer the pie to a cooling rack to cool completely.

STORING

▸ The pie can be stored in the refrigerator, to serve cold, or at room temperature, covered, for up to 2 days.

TIP: IF YOU LIKE, BRUSH THE HEART-shaped cutout with beaten egg, sprinkle with sugar, and bake on the baking sheet beside the pie for 20 to 25 minutes, until golden. Serve with a dollop of jam for a mini-pie treat.

Strawberry Hand Pies

Individual hand pies are a great alternative to a full-sized pie when you want a dessert "to go." They're perfect for picnics or lunch boxes or any occasion where plates and forks would seem cumbersome. When you first make a hand pie, you might be surprised at how little fruit it can hold— I always find myself trying to stuff in another berry, only to remove it when the pie won't close. If you do want to overstuff your pies, let the dough soften before wrapping it around the fruit so it will stretch a little—as long as the edges seal, the pie should stay together.

● MAKES 15 HAND PIES ●

2¹/₂ cups (10 ounces) strawberries, rinsed, hulled, and sliced about ¹/₃ inch thick

¹/₄ cup (1.75 ounces) sugar, plus more for sprinkling

¹/₂ teaspoon cornstarch

Pie Dough (page 120)

1 egg, beaten

› Toss the strawberry slices with the sugar and cornstarch in a medium bowl. Let sit for 10 to 15 minutes, until the berries soften and release some juice.

› Position the racks in the upper and lower thirds of the oven and heat the oven to 350°F. Line two 13-by-18-by-1-inch baking sheets with parchment paper or silicone liners.

› Remove the dough from the refrigerator and place one disk on a floured cool surface. Using a rolling pin, roll the dough out approximately ¹/₈ inch thick. Start from the center of the dough and roll outward, rotating the dough 2 to 3 inches after each roll. After every four to five rolls, run a large offset spatula under the dough to release it from the work surface. Add a little flour to the surface, rolling pin, and/or dough if the dough sticks or becomes difficult to roll.

› Using a 4-inch ring mold, cut out rounds and place on one of the lined baking sheets; reserve the scraps. Refrigerate until ready to use. Repeat the rolling process with the second disk of dough. If you have fewer than 15 rounds, pile the dough scraps together, wrap in plastic, and chill until firm, then roll out and cut out more rounds.

› Remove the first sheet of dough from the refrigerator. Spoon about 2 tablespoons of strawberries onto one half of one round, leaving a border. Using a pastry brush, brush the beaten egg around the edges of the dough. Lift the empty side of the round over the filling and slowly drape the dough over the fruit so the two edges meet. (If you force the dough, it may crack or tear; gently cajoling the dough will help it soften and yield.) Gently press the edges of the dough together and then, using a fork, crimp the edges to seal them. Repeat with the remaining rounds, then repeat with the second sheet of rounds. Refrigerate the pies until the crusts are cold and firm to the touch, about 15 minutes. (Reserve the remaining beaten egg.)

Continued ›

› Brush the top and edge of each pie with beaten egg and sprinkle with a little sugar. Slash the top of each pie once or twice with a paring knife to create a steam vent.

› Bake for 20 minutes. Rotate the pans and bake for an additional 15 minutes, or until the pies are golden brown and oozing strawberry juices. Let the pies cool completely on the baking sheets on cooling racks, then remove with an offset spatula.

STORING

› The pies can be stored, covered, at room temperature for up to 2 days.

Blueberry–Vanilla Cream Hand Pies

Bright, tart berry flavors are deliciously enhanced when juxtaposed with
sweet vanilla-specked cream. The flavors and textures of pie à la mode
are paired inside these delicious hand pies. Serve at room temperature,
or reheat for 5 minutes in a 300°F oven.

◆ MAKES 15 HAND PIES ◆

Pie Dough (page 120)

1 cup (8 ounces) Vanilla Cream (recipe
    follows)

3 cups (12 ounces) blueberries, rinsed and
    dried

1 egg, beaten

Sugar for dusting

› Position the racks in the upper and lower thirds of the oven and heat
the oven to 350°F. Line two 13-by-18-by-1-inch baking sheets with parchment or silicone liners.

› Remove the dough from the refrigerator and place one disk on a floured
cool surface. Using a rolling pin, roll the dough out approximately 1/8 inch
thick: Start from the center of the dough and roll outward, rotating the
dough 2 to 3 inches after each roll. After every four to five rolls, run a
large offset spatula under the dough to release it from the work surface.
Add a little flour to the surface, rolling pin, and/or dough if the dough
sticks or becomes difficult to roll.

› Using a 4-inch ring mold, cut out rounds and place on one of the lined
baking sheets; reserve the scraps. Refrigerate until ready to use. Repeat
the rolling process with the second disk of dough. If you have fewer than
15 rounds, pile the dough scraps together, wrap in plastic, and chill until
firm, then roll out and cut out more rounds.

› Remove the first sheet of dough from the refrigerator. Spoon 1 tablespoon vanilla cream, leaving a border, and then 4 to 6 blueberries onto
one half of one round. Using a pastry brush, brush the beaten egg around
the edges of the dough. Lift the empty side of the round over the filling
and slowly drape the dough over the fruit so the two edges meet. (If you
force the dough, it may crack or tear; gently cajoling the dough will help it
soften and yield.) Gently press the edges of the dough together and then,
using a fork, crimp the edges to seal them. Repeat with the remaining
rounds, then repeat with the second sheet of rounds. Refrigerate the pies
until the crusts are cold and firm to the touch, about 15 minutes. (Reserve
the remaining beaten egg.)

› Brush the top and edge of each pie with beaten egg and dust with a
little sugar. Slash the top of each pie once or twice with a paring knife to
create a steam vent.

› Bake for 20 minutes. Rotate the pans and bake for an additional
15 minutes, or until the pies are golden brown and oozing juices. Cool
completely on the baking sheets, then remove with an offset spatula.

STORING

› The pies can be stored, covered, at room temperature for up to 2 days.

Continued ›

Vanilla Cream

MAKES ABOUT 1¹/₂ CUPS

³/₄ cup (6 ounces) whole milk

¹/₄ cup (1.75 ounces) granulated sugar

1 tablespoon light brown sugar

¹/₂ vanilla bean, slit, seeds scraped out, seeds and bean reserved, or 1 teaspoon vanilla bean paste (see Resources, page 335)

¹/₄ cup (2 ounces) heavy cream

2 large egg yolks

2 tablespoons cornstarch

2 tablespoons (1 ounce) unsalted butter, cut into small chunks

› Combine the milk, granulated sugar, brown sugar, and vanilla seeds and bean in a medium saucepan and bring just to a simmer over medium-low heat, stirring constantly. Turn off the heat and remove the vanilla bean.

› Whisk together the heavy cream, egg yolks, and cornstarch in a medium bowl. Continue whisking as you slowly stream in the hot milk mixture. (Put a dish towel underneath the bowl so it stays still while you're whisking.) Pour the vanilla cream back into the pan and cook over medium-low heat, whisking constantly, until the cream thickens. Remove from the heat and stir in the butter until melted.

› Pour the cream through a fine-mesh sieve into a medium bowl. Cover the surface of the cream with plastic wrap so it doesn't form a skin, and refrigerate until cold, about 2 hours.

› The cream can be stored in an airtight container, refrigerated, for up to 1 week.

Apricot–Basil Cream Galettes

The pairing of apricot and basil sounds like an unlikely match, but as the old saying goes, "What grows together goes together." You can replace the apricots with nectarines, peaches, or just about any fruit that is in season. Serve chilled or at room temperature with Blenheim Apricot Ice Cream (page 237).

• MAKES 8 INDIVIDUAL GALETTES •

FOR THE BASIL CREAM

1 cup (8 ounces) whole milk

1/3 cup (2.33 ounces) granulated sugar

12 to 15 large basil leaves

2 large egg yolks

1/4 cup (2 ounces) heavy cream

2 1/2 tablespoons cornstarch

2 tablespoons (1 ounce) unsalted butter, cut into small chunks

Galette Dough (recipe follows)

3 tablespoons Pie Dust (page 126)

1 1/2 pounds (12 to 16 medium) apricots, rinsed, pitted, and sliced into 6 wedges each

About 3 tablespoons light brown sugar

1 egg, beaten

Granulated sugar for dusting

ADD A LITTLE FLOUR TO THE SURFACE, rolling pin, and/or dough if the dough sticks or becomes difficult to roll.

› To make the basil cream: Combine the milk, granulated sugar, and basil in a medium saucepan and bring just to a simmer over low heat, stirring constantly. Remove from the heat and muddle (crush) the basil with a wooden spoon until the milk takes on a pale green color. Cover the pan with aluminum foil and poke a few holes into the top to allow steam to escape. Let steep for 30 minutes.

› Remove the aluminum foil and strain the cream, discarding the basil, then return the cream to the pan and bring to a simmer.

› Meanwhile, whisk the yolks, heavy cream, and cornstarch in a medium bowl, until combined. Continue whisking as you slowly stream in the hot milk mixture. (Put a dish towel underneath the mixing bowl so it stays still while you're whisking.) Pour the basil cream back into the pan and cook over medium-low heat, whisking constantly, until the cream thickens and comes to a boil. Turn off the heat and stir in the butter until melted.

› Pour the cream through a fine-mesh sieve into a medium bowl. Cover the surface of the cream with plastic wrap so it doesn't form a skin, and refrigerate until cold, about 2 hours.

› Position the racks in the upper and lower thirds of the oven and heat the oven to 350°F. Line two 13-by-18-by-1-inch baking sheets with parchment or silicone liners.

› Remove the dough from the refrigerator and place one disk on a floured surface. Using a rolling pin, roll the dough out approximately 1/8 inch thick: Start from the center of the dough and roll outward, rotating the dough 2 to 3 inches after each roll. After every four to five rolls, run an offset spatula under the dough to release it from the work surface. Using a 6-inch ring mold, cut out rounds and place on the lined baking sheets; reserve the scraps. Refrigerate until ready to use. Repeat the rolling process with the second disk. If you have fewer than 8 rounds, pile the dough scraps together, wrap in plastic, and chill until firm, then roll out and cut out more rounds.

› Sprinkle approximately 1 teaspoon of pie dust over a 5-inch-square area in the center of each galette round. Scoop 3 tablespoons of basil cream into the center of each circle and, using an offset spatula, spread it into a 3- to 4-inch square, so the corners almost touch the edges of the dough. Arrange one-eighth of the apricot slices side by side in a diagonal strip

over the cream on each dough round and sprinkle 1 teaspoon brown sugar over the apricots.

▸ Using a pastry brush, brush the edges of the dough with the beaten egg (reserve the remaining egg). Using your thumb and forefinger, pinch the upper-right-hand portion of one dough round together, framing the apricots and basil cream. Pinch the remaining three corners in the same fashion, creating a square. Repeat with the remaining galettes. Refrigerate the galettes until the dough is cold and firm to the touch, about 15 minutes.

▸ Brush the "frames" of dough with beaten egg and dust with a little sugar.

▸ Bake the galettes, rotating the pans halfway through, for 35 to 40 minutes, until the crust is golden brown. Let the galettes cool completely on the baking sheets, then remove with an offset spatula.

STORING

▸ The galettes can be stored, covered, at room temperature for up to 2 days.

Galette Dough

A galette is a tart made without a tin. This recipe makes enough dough for two large galettes—you can halve the recipe easily to make just one crust, but it's handy to have the dough in the freezer for an extra crust.

MAKES ENOUGH FOR TWO 9-INCH SQUARE GALETTES OR EIGHT 4-INCH INDIVIDUAL GALETTES

3 cups (15 ounces) all-purpose flour

1 tablespoon sugar

3/4 teaspoon salt

2 sticks plus 1 tablespoon (8.5 ounces) unsalted butter, cubed and chilled

1/2 teaspoon vanilla extract

1/4 to 1/3 cup (2 to 2.5 ounces) cold water

TO MAKE THE DOUGH IN A FOOD PROCESSOR

▸ Pulse the flour, sugar, and salt in the bowl of the processor once or twice to combine. Drop the pieces of butter through the feed tube, continuing to pulse until the mixture resembles coarse crumbs. Pour the vanilla through the tube. Slowly add 1/4 cup water as you continue pulsing a few more times, then add more water if necessary; stop when the dough just starts to come together.

TO MAKE THE DOUGH BY HAND

▸ Put the flour, sugar, and salt into a medium bowl and mix together with a fork or small whisk. Cut in the butter, using a pastry blender or large fork, until the mixture resembles coarse crumbs. Drizzle in the vanilla.

▸ Drizzle 1/4 cup water over the dough, mixing with the pastry cutter or fork, then add more water if necessary, mixing until the dough just comes together.

▸ Remove the dough from the processor or bowl and form it into 2 disks. Wrap each disk in plastic wrap and refrigerate for at least 2 hours, or up to 3 days. The dough can be frozen for up to 2 months; thaw in the refrigerator.

Berry-Basket Galette

The combination of berries in this recipe is just a suggestion; you can substitute whatever berries you find at your local market. Golden raspberries, boysenberries, and Persian mulberries would be a unique and delicious mix, or try blueberries, marionberries, and raspberries. Serve at room temperature topped with Raspberry Whipped Cream (page 139).

MAKES ONE 9-INCH SQUARE GALETTE; SERVES 6 TO 8

FOR THE LEMON CURD

1 tablespoon grated lemon zest

2/3 cup (5.33 ounces) fresh lemon juice

8 tablespoons (1 stick/4 ounces) unsalted butter

1 cup (7 ounces) sugar

2 large eggs

2 large egg yolks

1/2 recipe Galette Dough (page 152)

1 teaspoon Pie Dust (page 126)

1 cup (5 ounces) sliced strawberries

3/4 cup (3 ounces) blueberries, rinsed and dried

3/4 cup (3 ounces) raspberries, rinsed and dried

3/4 cup (3 ounces) blackberries, rinsed and dried

2 tablespoons sugar, plus more for finishing

1 egg, beaten

▸ To make the lemon curd: Heat the lemon zest, juice, 6 tablespoons of the butter, and 3/4 cup of the sugar in a small saucepan over medium heat until the mixture gently simmers.

▸ Meanwhile, in the bowl of a stand mixer fitted with the whisk attachment (or in a large bowl, using a handheld mixer), beat the eggs, yolks, and the remaining 1/4 cup sugar until pale and light, about 2 minutes. Slowly stream in the warm juice mixture and continue beating until incorporated.

▸ Set a double boiler over medium heat or fill a medium saucepan halfway with water and bring to a boil over medium heat. Pour the lemon mixture into the top of the double boiler or into a medium heatproof bowl set over the pan of water; lower the heat slightly. Stir the curd constantly as it slowly thickens, about 10 minutes. When the curd has reached 170°F on a candy or instant-read thermometer and coats the back of the spoon, remove it from the heat. Stir the remaining 2 tablespoons butter into the curd until it melts.

▸ Pour the curd through a fine-mesh sieve into a bowl or other container. Place plastic wrap directly on the surface of the curd to prevent a skin from forming and allow the curd to cool to room temperature, then refrigerate for at least 2 hours before using. (The curd can be refrigerated, covered, for up to 2 weeks.)

▸ Position a rack in the center of the oven and heat the oven to 350°F. Line a baking sheet with parchment or a silicone liner.

▸ Remove the dough from the refrigerator and place on a floured cool surface. Using a rolling pin, roll the dough out into a 13-inch circle: Start from the center of the dough and roll outward, rotating the dough 2 to 3 inches after each roll—this will help create a true circle. After every four to five rolls, run a large offset spatula under the dough to release it from the work surface. Add a little flour to the surface, rolling pin, and/or dough if the dough sticks or becomes difficult to roll.

▸ Place the round on the lined baking sheet. Sprinkle the pie dust over the center of the circle. Using an offset spatula, spread the lemon curd over the round into an 8- to 9-inch square, so the corners almost touch the edges of the dough. Arrange the berries in diagonal rows on the curd. You may use slightly less fruit than the recipe specifies, depending on the size of the berries. Sprinkle the 2 tablespoons sugar over the berries.

› Using a pastry brush, brush the edges of the dough with the beaten egg (reserve the remaining egg). Using your thumb and forefinger, pinch the upper-right-hand portion of the dough together, framing the berries and lemon curd. The "seam" of sealed dough should be 2 to 2½ inches wide. Pinch the remaining three corners in the same fashion, creating a square. Refrigerate the galette until the dough is cold and firm to the touch, about 15 minutes.

› Brush the "frame" of dough with beaten egg and dust with sugar. Bake for 55 to 60 minutes, or until the crust is golden brown. Let the galette cool completely on the baking sheet, then, with a large offset spatula, transfer to a serving plate.

STORING

› The galette can be stored, covered, at room temperature for up to 2 days.

Apple-and-Caramel Aged Gouda Crostata

Apple pie with Cheddar cheese is an old-time favorite in diners and coffee shops. Here is an updated version that highlights the surprisingly satisfying combination of apples and a savory cheese. Aged Gouda is a Dutch cow's-milk cheese that has notes of butterscotch intermingled with sharp, salty characteristics.

MAKES ONE 9-INCH CROSTATA; SERVES 6 TO 8

5 medium Granny Smith or Pink Lady apples (1¹/₂ pounds), peeled, cored, and thinly sliced

¹/₂ cup (3 ounces) light brown sugar

¹/₂ recipe Aged Gouda Cornmeal Crust (recipe follows)

¹/₂ cup Caramel Sauce (page 234)

1 egg, beaten

¹/₂ teaspoon fleur de sel

› Line a 13-by-18-by-1-inch baking sheet with parchment or a silicone liner. Mix the apple slices with the brown sugar in a medium bowl.

› Remove one disk of dough from the refrigerator and place on a floured cool surface. Using a rolling pin, roll the dough out into a 13-inch circle: Start from the center of the dough and roll outward, rotating the dough 2 to 3 inches after each roll—this will help create a true circle. After every four to five rolls, run a large offset spatula under the dough to release it from the work surface. Add a little flour to the surface, rolling pin, and/or dough if the dough sticks or becomes difficult to roll. Transfer the dough to the lined baking sheet and refrigerate for 15 minutes.

› Position a rack in the center of the oven and heat the oven to 325°F. Arrange the apples on the dough, leaving a 2-inch border all around: overlap the apple slices as you arrange them in concentric circles, working from the outside in until you reach the center. Drizzle the caramel sauce over the apples.

› Lift one side of the dough over the apples and press it down over the fruit, making 5 or 6 large pleat folds. Then continue around the crostata, pressing the pleats so they adhere. Refrigerate the crostata until the crust is cold and firm to the touch, about 15 minutes.

› Using a pastry brush, brush the edges of the dough with the beaten egg. Sprinkle the fleur de sel over the fruit. Bake for 45 to 55 minutes, or until the crust is golden. Let the crostata cool completely on the baking sheet, then, using an offset spatula, transfer to a serving platter.

STORING

› The crostata can be stored, covered, at room temperature for up to 2 days.

Aged Gouda Cornmeal Crust

Aged Gouda cheese gives this crust its addictively salty, savory quality, but it's the cornmeal that adds an unexpected crunch. If Aged Gouda isn't available, substitute an aged Cheddar or Parmesan.

MAKES ENOUGH FOR TWO 9-INCH CROSTATAS

1⅓ cups (6.65 ounces) all-purpose flour

¼ cup (1.5 ounces) stone-ground yellow cornmeal (see Resources, page 335)

3 tablespoons sugar

1 cup (3 ounces) grated Aged Gouda (see Resources, page 335), chilled

1¾ sticks (7 ounces) unsalted butter, cubed and chilled

2 to 4 tablespoons ice water

TO MAKE THE DOUGH IN A FOOD PROCESSOR

› Pulse the flour, cornmeal, and sugar in the processor bowl a few times to combine. Add the grated Gouda through the feed tube, continuing to pulse, then drop the pieces of butter through the feed tube, pulsing until the mixture resembles pea-sized crumbs. Slowly add 2 tablespoons water as you continue pulsing a few more times, then add more water if necessary; stop when the dough just starts to come together.

TO MAKE THE DOUGH BY HAND

› Put the flour, cornmeal, and sugar into a medium bowl and mix together with a fork or small whisk. Add the Gouda and mix until combined. Cut in the butter using a pastry blender or large fork until the mixture resembles pea-sized crumbs. Drizzle 2 tablespoons water over the dough, mixing with the pastry cutter or fork, then add more water if necessary, mixing until the dough just comes together.

› Remove the dough from the processor or bowl and form it into 2 equal disks. Wrap each disk in plastic wrap and refrigerate for at least 2 hours.

› The dough can be refrigerated for up to 2 days or frozen for up to 1 month; thaw in the refrigerator.

Cherry Frangipane Tart

Frangipane, or almond cream, is a traditional component of French tarts and other desserts. It pairs beautifully with a litany of fruits, including apricots, figs, and, most frequently, pears. Serve this after a bistro-inspired dinner, with Tangy Whipped Cream (page 139).

● MAKES ONE 9-INCH TART; SERVES 6 TO 8 ●

Pâte Sucrée (recipe follows)

2 cups (1 pound, 1 ounce) Frangipane (page 162)

1 cup (7.5 ounces) Stewed Cherries (page 162)

› Remove the dough from the refrigerator and place on a floured cool surface. Using a rolling pin, roll the dough out into a 12-inch circle: Start from the center of the dough and roll outward, rotating the dough 2 to 3 inches after each roll—this will help create a true circle. After four to five rolls, run a large offset spatula under the dough to release it. Add a little flour to the surface, rolling pin, and/or dough if the dough sticks or becomes difficult to roll.

› Roll the dough up onto the rolling pin, then unroll into a 9-inch fluted pan with a removable bottom. Use your fingers to fit the dough into the pan. If any dough extends over the top of the pan, carefully roll the rolling pin over the edges of the pan to cut off the excess. Chill the tart shell until cold and firm, about 30 minutes.

› Position a rack in the center of the oven and heat the oven to 350°F.

› Dock, or prick, the bottom and the sides of the dough all over with a fork. (Docking allows steam to escape during baking and results in a flat tart shell.) Lay a large piece of parchment paper or aluminum foil in the tart shell and fill it with pie weights or dried beans. Place the tart shell on a baking sheet and bake for 15 to 20 minutes, until the edges have a hint of golden color. Transfer the tart pan to a cooling rack to cool completely. (Leave the oven on.)

› Spread the frangipane over the bottom of the tart shell. Drain the cherries well and arrange on the frangipane. Place the tart on the baking sheet and bake for 40 to 45 minutes, until the frangipane has darkened around the edges, puffed slightly, and formed a crust. Transfer to a cooling rack to cool completely.

STORING

› The tart can be stored, covered, at room temperature for up to 2 days.

Pâte Sucrée (Sweet Tart Dough)

This traditional French tart crust is crunchy and crisp with a subtle sweetness. Be careful not to overmix the dough, or it will become tough and lose its wonderful texture.

MAKES ENOUGH FOR ONE 9-INCH TART SHELL

1¼ cups plus 2 tablespoons (7 ounces) all-purpose flour

½ cup (2.25 ounces) confectioners' sugar

½ teaspoon salt

Continued ›

4½ tablespoons (2.25 ounces) unsalted butter, cubed and chilled

1 medium egg, beaten

TO MAKE THE DOUGH IN A FOOD PROCESSOR

▸ Pulse the flour, sugar, and salt in the processor bowl once or twice to combine. Drop the pieces of butter through the feed tube, continuing to pulse until the mixture resembles coarse crumbs. Slowly pour the egg through the feed tube, pulsing just until the dough comes together, 10 to 15 seconds; do not overprocess the dough.

TO MAKE THE DOUGH BY HAND

▸ Put the flour, sugar, and salt into a medium bowl and mix together with a fork or small whisk. Cut in the butter using a pastry blender or large fork, until the mixture resembles coarse crumbs. Drizzle the egg over the dough and knead the dough just a few times until the egg is incorporated.

▸ Remove the dough from the processor or bowl and form it into a disk. Wrap in plastic wrap and refrigerate for at least 2 hours.

▸ The dough can be refrigerated for up to 3 days or frozen for up to 2 months; thaw in the refrigerator.

Frangipane

MAKES 2½ CUPS

2½ cups (8.75 ounces) almond flour (see Resources, page 335), toasted (see page 20)

⅔ cup (4.66 ounces) sugar

3 large eggs

2 teaspoons vanilla extract

½ teaspoon salt

2 tablespoons (1 ounce) unsalted butter, melted

▸ In the bowl of a stand mixer fitted with the paddle attachment (or in a large bowl, using a handheld mixer), beat all of the ingredients together until fully combined, about 1 minute.

▸ The frangipane can be stored, covered, in the refrigerator for up to 5 days. Bring to room temperature before using.

Stewed Cherries

MAKES ABOUT 1⅔ CUPS

1½ pounds Bing or dark red cherries, rinsed and pitted (2 cups)

⅓ cup (2.25 ounces) sugar

▸ Put the cherries and sugar into a medium saucepan and cook over medium heat, stirring frequently, for 5 minutes, or until the cherries begin to release their juices. Remove from the heat and let cool completely.

▸ The cherries can be stored in an airtight container in the refrigerator for up to 2 weeks.

Fruit and Cream Tart

This is a great tart to make with children: the shortbread dough is completely hands-on. My five-year-old loves pressing the dough into the tart shell.

Shortbread Crust (recipe follows)

1/2 cup (4.5 ounces) Strawberry–Vanilla Bean Jam (page 276) or store-bought strawberry jam

2 cups (6.5 ounces) Whipped Cream (page 138)

2 cups (10 ounces) strawberries, rinsed and hulled

› Put the disk of dough in the center of a 9-inch fluted tart pan with a removable bottom. Using your fingers, press the dough evenly over the bottom of the pan. Chill the dough until it is firm and cold, about 30 minutes.

› Position a rack in the center of the oven and heat the oven to 350°F.

› Place the tart shell on a baking sheet and bake for 20 to 25 minutes, until the edges have a hint of golden color. Transfer the tart pan to a cooling rack to cool completely.

› Remove the sides of the tart pan and slide the tart crust onto a serving plate. Spread the jam over the tart crust. Spread the whipped cream over the jam and top with the strawberries. Refrigerate until ready to serve.

STORING

› The tart is best served within a few hours of constructing it, but leftover tart can be lightly covered and refrigerated for up to 1 day.

Shortbread Crust

There is no need to worry about properly chilling anything; this is a simple cookie dough that is pressed into the tart tin. Tender and buttery, it is the perfect complement to fruits and creamy fillings.

MAKES ENOUGH FOR ONE 9-INCH TART SHELL

8 tablespoons (1 stick/4 ounces) unsalted butter, softened

1/4 cup (1.75 ounces) sugar

1 cup (5 ounces) all-purpose flour

3/8 teaspoon salt

1 teaspoon vanilla bean paste (see Resources, page 335)

› In the bowl of a stand mixer fitted with the paddle attachment (or in a large bowl, using a handheld mixer), beat the butter on medium speed until light and fluffy, about 2 minutes. Add the sugar and beat until thoroughly mixed.

› Using a fork or a small whisk, mix the flour, salt, and vanilla paste in a small bowl. Add to the butter mixture in two batches, mixing thoroughly after each addition. Remove the dough from the bowl and shape into a disk.

› The dough is ready to use. Wrap tightly in plastic wrap and refrigerate for up to 1 week or freeze for up to 2 months; thaw in the refrigerator.

CREATE YOUR OWN PIES AND TARTS

Mix and match to create a signature pie of your own. I have never tried pumpkin pie filling with the Aged Gouda Cornmeal Crust (page 158), but it sounds divine—even better when topped with Whipped Cream (page 138). Here are some other suggestions to give you a start.

- Frangipane and Poached Apricot Galette
- Vanilla Cream and Stewed Cherries Galette
- Basil Cream, White Peach, and Candied Basil Tart
- Mango Curd and Whipped Cream in the Shortbread Crust
- Poached Pears and Marzipan Crumble in the Aged Gouda Cornmeal Crust
- Lemon Curd, Lemon Cream, and Candied Lemon Verbena in a Shortbread Crust

CRUST

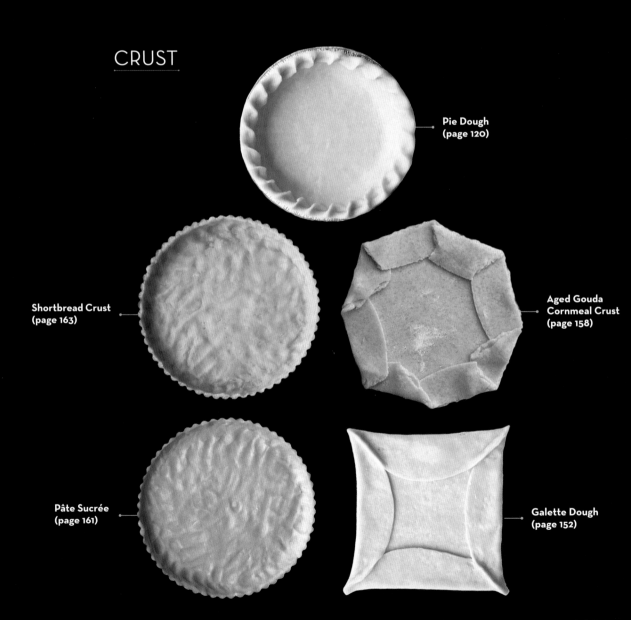

Pie Dough
(page 120)

Shortbread Crust
(page 163)

Aged Gouda
Cornmeal Crust
(page 158)

Pâte Sucrée
(page 161)

Galette Dough
(page 152)

FILLINGS

Lemon Cream
(page 139)

Lemon Curd
(page 154)

Basil Cream
(page 150)

Mango Curd
(page 137)

Frangipane
(page 162)

Stewed Cherries
(page 162)

Caramel Sauce
(page 234)

Vanilla Cream
(page 149)

Chocolate Ganache
(page 194)

Sliced fruit
(any kind)

TOPPINGS

Candied Herbs (opposite)
Marzipan Crumble (page 141)
Poached Quinces or Pears (below)
Poached Apricots (opposite)
Whipped Cream (page 138)
Vanilla Whipped Cream (page 138)
Chocolate Whipped Cream (page 138)
Tangy Whipped Cream (page 139)
Raspberry Whipped Cream (page 139)
Lemon Cream (page 139)
Mango Cream (page 139)

Here are two recipes for poached fruits, which make delicious and versatile fillings for tarts and pies.

Poached Quinces or Pears

MAKES ABOUT 2 CUPS

4 cups (32 ounces) water

1 cup (7 ounces) sugar

1 vanilla bean, split

Juice of 1 lemon

4 quinces or pears (about 2 pounds), peeled, quartered, and cored

› Put the water and sugar into a medium nonreactive pot and set over medium heat. Scrape the seeds from the vanilla bean into the pot, then add the vanilla pod and lemon juice and heat until the liquid starts to simmer. Gently place the quinces or pears in the poaching liquid and reduce the heat to low. Cut a round of parchment paper the size of the inner circumference of the pot and cut a golf-ball-sized hole out of the center. Place the paper directly on the fruit and simmer the quinces for about an hour, the pears for about 15 minutes, until the fruit yields when pierced with a fork.

› Remove the vanilla bean and pour the fruit and poaching liquid into a bowl and let cool to room temperature. The fruit can be stored, covered, in the refrigerator for up to 2 days.

Poached Apricots

MAKES ABOUT 3 CUPS

1¹/₂ cups (12 ounces) water

³/₄ cup (5.25 ounces) sugar

1 vanilla bean, split

2 teaspoons lemon juice

1¹/₄ pounds apricots (12 to 15), rinsed, halved, and pitted

› Put the water and sugar into a medium saucepan and set over medium-high heat. Scrape the seeds from the vanilla bean into the pan, then add the vanilla pod and lemon juice and bring to a boil. Add the apricots, then reduce the heat and poach at a bare simmer, turning the apricots once, until the fruit is tender but still holds its shape and the skins are still intact, 2 to 6 minutes, depending on the ripeness of the fruit.

› Remove the vanilla pod and pour the apricots and poaching syrup into a bowl and let cool to room temperature. The fruit can be stored, covered, in the refrigerator for 1 to 2 days; the apricots will soften and brown somewhat but will still taste good.

Edible botanicals are beautiful décor for tarts and pies.

Candied Herbs

MAKES ABOUT 40 PIECES

2 cups (14 ounces) sugar

10 to 15 stems or small clusters of thyme, basil, lemon verbena, bay, or mint leaves, rinsed and dried

2 egg whites, beaten

› Pour the sugar onto a plate or into a baking pan. Using a very small brush or your fingertips, gently coat herb leaves or sprigs with egg white on both sides, then place on the sugar. Using a teaspoon, sprinkle sugar over the leaf. Carefully flip the leaf and do the same on the other side, making sure the entire leaf is covered in sugar. Put the sugared leaf on a cooling rack. Repeat with the remaining leaves and allow 2 to 4 hours to set. Store the herbs in an airtight container for up to 2 months.

BOX

CHOCOLATES AND CONFECTIONS

THE first time I made caramel and tempered some chocolate, I felt a little intimidated, but very excited. I remember those early explorations into the world of confections and chocolate so clearly. There were many stumbles along the way as I turned sugar into caramel, or cautiously heated and cooled chocolate until I finally found myself a proficient candy maker. The transformation didn't happen overnight; many of the techniques required more practice and patience than I was accustomed to in the kitchen. But with each new technique I learned, or recipe I tried, there was one constant teacher at my side: cookbooks.

My natural instinct with food is to experiment, and I frequently use recipes as merely guidelines for making something more appealing to my palate. In hindsight, this inclination toward recipe interpretation caused many unnecessary setbacks with my early batches of chocolate and confections. Precise temperature, timing, and measurements are all integral to successful candy making. So commit to specificity—it's the only shortcut at your disposal.

When prepping fruit for jam, I am a chatterbox. While frosting a cake or making a batter, I am selectively conversational. But when making chocolates, I work in silence. I plan my chocolate and candy sessions in advance, adhere to my tested recipes, and focus on creating beautiful, flawless confections. Although the recipes in this chapter list both volume and weight, as elsewhere, for this chapter I urge you to follow the weight measurements for consistent results. Many of them are two-day projects and require advance planning.

There is a lot of science involved in tempering chocolate, which can occasionally make it a challenge. I have attempted to simplify the process as much as possible (see pages 174-75), and really the only fundamental bit of science you need for successful chocolate making is reading a temperature correctly. So invest in a digital candy thermometer—the single most important tool for chocolate and candy making. And if it's a hot, sunny day, take a pass on working with chocolate—you will have a frustrating time in the kitchen. Make a sorbet or a batch of cookies instead of truffles.

Within this chapter, you will find a few basic recipes, such as mendiants, meringues, and barks, as well as elaborate recipes, like hand-dipped infused truffles and elegant toffees. This is an exciting time to experiment with chocolate, as the scope of chocolate production has expanded exponentially over the last fifteen years. Chocolates with a huge range of cocoa percentages are now available for our use, allowing greater dimension and expression of flavors. All of the recipes in this chapter include cocoa percentages for the chocolates I use (see Chocolate Percentages, page 200).

Berry Mendiants

Mendiants are a traditional French confection, disks of chocolate topped with dried fruits and nuts. This fresh variation is delicious in the late spring and summer, when berries are abundant at the market; I particularly like blueberries and raspberries for these. I serve them as a light dessert or with afternoon tea. The other mendiants in this chapter are better for gift-giving, as fresh berries spoil quickly at room temperature.

● MAKES ABOUT 50 MENDIANTS ●

1 pound still-molten tempered 61% to 68% bittersweet chocolate (see page 174)

1 cup (5 to 6 ounces) fresh berries, rinsed and dried

¼ cup (1 ounce) freeze-dried berry powder (see Tip and Resources, page 335)

> TIP: FREEZE-DRIED BERRIES ARE NOT THE same thing as dried berries. Regular dried berries can have a gummy, fibrous texture, but freeze-drying berries makes them crisp and accentuates their tart sweetness.

› Line two 13-by-18-by-1-inch baking sheets with parchment paper or silicone mats.

› Pour the tempered chocolate into a depositor. (If you do not have a depositor, leave the tempered chocolate in the bowl and use a tablespoon to portion the chocolate.) Holding the depositor about 6 inches above one of the baking sheets, release the chocolate in short bursts, creating 2-inch disks and leaving 1½ inches of space between them, as the chocolate will continue to spread a bit. After making one row of disks, top each one with a fresh berry and a sprinkle of berry powder. Continue making and topping the mendiants one row at a time. Allow the chocolate to set at room temperature, about 2 hours.

STORING

› The mendiants can be stored, in candy cups and lightly covered, in the refrigerator for up to 3 days.

BOX · 173

TEMPERING CHOCOLATE

— · —

TEMPERING CHOCOLATE IS THE PROCESS of breaking down chocolate's elements so it can be used in a different form. For instance, if you have a perfect, shiny block of chocolate and you want to transform it into chocolate bark, you'll need to melt the chocolate and then resolidify it in a different shape. In order to perform this magic, first you melt 75 percent of the chocolate and heat it to a specific temperature. Then the remaining 25 percent, the "seed" chocolate, is added to the molten chocolate, which cools down the larger mass while stabilizing the total structure. When the chocolate reaches the specified temperature, it is successfully tempered.

The elements that separate in the melting process are cocoa butter, cocoa liquor, and sugar. If those components are left to cool and solidify on their own, the result will be a white-streaked, dull, chalky mass. Careful monitoring of temperature and continuous movement of the chocolate are necessary for successful tempering.

When you temper chocolate, the room temperature should be between 60° and 68°F. If your kitchen is more than a couple of degrees outside of that range, postpone your chocolate work for another day: If the room is too cold, the tempered chocolate will set thick very quickly—possibly too rapidly for you to use it. If the room is too hot, the chocolate will bloom or not set.

Pour any leftover chocolate onto parchment. After it solidifies, break it into pieces and store in a Ziploc bag or an airtight container for future use.

Tempered Bittersweet Chocolate

MAKES 1 POUND

12 ounces 61% to 75% bittersweet chocolate, finely chopped

4 ounces 61% to 75% bittersweet chocolate chips or fèves (see Resources, page 335) or solid bar chocolate
  if you prefer

› Melt the finely chopped chocolate according to the instructions on page 184, then continue heating it until the chocolate reaches 120°F on an instant-read thermometer.

› Add the seed chocolate a few pieces at a time, stirring the chocolate constantly with a small silicone spatula. Be sure each addition melts completely before you add more. The chocolate will be in temper when it reaches 88° to 90°F; check the temperature frequently. To test for temper, dip a small offset spatula in the chocolate and put the spatula on your work surface. If the chocolate sets within 2 to 3 minutes and looks shiny and smooth, it is in temper. If the chocolate looks streaky or spotted or doesn't set, it is not in temper. Continue stirring and then test the chocolate again—sometimes the components need a little extra agitation before they can unify.

› Once the chocolate is tempered, work efficiently; the temper will hold for about 20 minutes.

› For 1$\frac{1}{2}$ pounds tempered chocolate: Use 18 ounces bittersweet chocolate, finely chopped, and 6 ounces bittersweet chocolate chips or fèves.

› For 2 pounds tempered chocolate: Use 1$\frac{1}{2}$ pounds bittersweet chocolate, finely chopped, and 8 ounces bittersweet chocolate chips or fèves.

Tempered Milk or White Chocolate

MAKES 1 POUND

12 ounces 34% to 40% milk or 31% white chocolate, finely chopped

4 ounces 34% to 40% milk or 31% white chocolate chips or fèves (see Resources, page 335)

› Melt the finely chopped chocolate according to the instructions on page 184, then continue heating it until the chocolate reaches 112°F on an instant-read thermometer.

› Add the seed chocolate a few pieces at a time, stirring the chocolate constantly with a small silicone spatula. Be sure each addition melts completely before you add more. The chocolate will be in temper when it reaches 86° to 88°F; check the temperature frequently. To test for temper, dip a small offset spatula in the chocolate and put the spatula on your work surface. If the chocolate sets within 2 to 3 minutes and looks shiny and smooth, it is in temper. If the chocolate looks streaky or spotted or doesn't set, it is not in temper. Continue stirring and then test the chocolate again—sometimes the components need a little extra agitation before they can unify.

› Once the chocolate is tempered, work efficiently; the temper will hold for about 20 minutes.

› For 1 1/2 pounds tempered chocolate: Use 18 ounces milk or white chocolate, finely chopped, and 6 ounces milk or white chocolate chips or fèves.

› For 2 pounds tempered chocolate: Use 1 1/2 pounds milk or white chocolate, finely chopped, and 8 ounces milk or white chocolate chips or fèves.

Tempered Dark Milk Chocolate (44%)

MAKES 1 POUND

9 ounces 38% milk chocolate, finely chopped

3 ounces 61% bittersweet chocolate, finely chopped

3 ounces 38% milk chocolate chips or fèves (see Resources, page 335)

1 ounce 61% bittersweet chocolate chips or fèves (see Resources, page 335)

› Melt the finely chopped chocolate according to the instructions on page 184, then continue heating it until the chocolate reaches 112°F on an instant-read candy thermometer.

› Add the seed chocolate a few pieces at a time, stirring the chocolate constantly with a small silicone spatula. Be sure each addition melts completely before you add more. The chocolate will be in temper when it reaches 86° to 88°F; check the temperature frequently. To test for temper, dip a small offset spatula in the chocolate and put the spatula on your work surface. If the chocolate sets within 2 to 3 minutes and looks shiny and smooth, it is in temper. If the chocolate looks streaky or spotted or doesn't set, it is not in temper. Continue stirring and then test the chocolate again; sometimes the components need a little extra agitation before they can unify.

› Once the chocolate is tempered, work efficiently; the temper will hold for about 20 minutes.

› For 1 1/2 pounds tempered chocolate: Use 13.5 ounces milk chocolate, finely chopped, 4.5 ounces bittersweet chocolate, finely chopped, plus 4.5 ounces milk chocolate chips or fèves and 1.5 ounces bittersweet chocolate chips or fèves.

› For 2 pounds tempered chocolate: Use 18 ounces milk chocolate, finely chopped, 6 ounces bittersweet chocolate, finely chopped, 6 ounces milk chocolate chips or fèves, and 2 ounces bittersweet chocolate chips or fèves.

Raspberry, Black Sesame, and Matcha Mendiants

A disk of chocolate can be the perfect template for exploring flavors and colors. With this mendiant, I started with flavorings of raspberry and matcha because green tea and berries complement each other well. From there, I tasted bittersweet chocolate with those flavors, but I found the chocolate overpowering and opted for the smooth sweetness of dark milk chocolate instead. Sesame seeds have a subtle nuttiness, but the color of white sesame seeds looked flat next to the green tea and bright pink raspberry—black sesame seeds result in the perfect balance of color and flavor.

● MAKES ABOUT 50 MENDIANTS ●

1 pound still-molten tempered 44% dark milk chocolate (see page 175)

1 tablespoon freeze-dried raspberry powder (see Resources, page 335)

1 tablespoon black sesame seeds (see Resources, page 335)

1 tablespoon matcha tea (see Resources, page 335)

› Line two 13-by-18-by-1-inch baking sheets with parchment paper or silicone mats.

› Pour the tempered chocolate into a depositor. (If you do not have a depositor, leave the tempered chocolate in the bowl and use a tablespoon to portion the chocolate.) Holding the depositor about 6 inches above one of the baking sheets, release the chocolate in short bursts, creating 2-inch disks and leaving 1½ inches of space between them, as the chocolate will continue to spread a bit. After making one row of disks, top each one with a sprinkle each of raspberry powder, black sesame, and matcha, creating three stripes. Continue making and topping the mendiants one row at a time. Allow the chocolate to set at room temperature, about 2 hours.

STORING

› The mendiants can be stored in an airtight container in a cool, dry area for up to 2 months.

BOX • 176

Almond, Black Fig, and Urfa Biber Mendiants

Urfa biber is a dried Turkish pepper; it has a beautiful dark purple color and a subtle smoky, roasted aroma. It gives this mendiant warming but not overwhelming heat.

● **MAKES ABOUT 50 MENDIANTS** ●

1 pound still-molten tempered 68% to 72% bittersweet chocolate (see page 174)

1 tablespoon urfa biber flakes (see Resources, page 335)

1½ cups (7 ounces) halved dried figs

⅓ cup (1.5 ounces) roasted almonds

› Line two 13-by-18-by-1-inch baking sheets with parchment paper or silicone mats.

› Pour the tempered chocolate into a depositor. (If you do not have a depositor, leave the tempered chocolate in the bowl and use a tablespoon to portion the chocolate.) Holding the depositor about 6 inches above one of the baking sheets, release the chocolate in short bursts, creating 2-inch disks and leaving 1½ inches of space between them, as the chocolate will continue to spread a bit. After making one row of disks, sprinkle a pinch of urfa biber on each one and then top with a fig and an almond. Continue making and topping the mendiants one row at a time. Allow the chocolate to set at room temperature, about 2 hours.

STORING

› The mendiants can be stored in an airtight container in a cool, dry area for up to 2 months.

VARIATION

DARK RAISIN, SMOKED PAPRIKA, AND DURANGO SALT MENDIANTS: Omit the pepper, figs, and almonds and top each mendiant instead with 1 raisin and a sprinkle of sweet smoked paprika and Durango salt (see Resources, page 335).

BOX · 178

SAFETY FIRST

MAKING CANDY AT HOME IS INCREDIBLY GRATIFYING. Whether the treats are for you and your family or for gift-giving, making a homemade confection feels like an accomplishment. It takes patience, skill, and a bit of science to make any caramel or hard candy—and it also means following necessary safety precautions to produce candy without incident. When making confections such as toffee, never forget that you are dealing with a pot of boiling fat and sugar. Here are a few tips to help you stay injury-free in your candy kitchen.

▸ Always wear a long-sleeved shirt and a heat-resistant oven mitt when stirring hot candy.

▸ Use a long heatproof silicone spatula or wooden spoon for candy making so your hand is well outside the pot.

▸ Making candy with a group of friends sounds like fun, but, unfortunately, it's not advisable. It's too easy to become distracted with a group, especially if children are present.

▸ Do not talk on the phone while making candy; again, the distraction can easily lead to injury. Early in my candy-making career, I dropped a cell phone into a boiling pot of toffee. Luckily, the toffee didn't splash into my face. Typically, I was more upset at the loss of toffee than the loss of the phone!

▸ Many of the recipes in this chapter call for pouring hot candy onto a marble slab. Consider the location of the marble before you start cooking—you want it on a stable surface as close to your stove as possible, which might necessitate moving a table. Avoid having to cross a room with a hot pot of candy.

▸ Keep your body a good 8 to 12 inches away from the stove; you want to be able to stir the candy comfortably, but you never want your body too close to the heat. Consider your candy pot as you would a deep fryer, and maintain a safe buffer zone, as a boiling candy mixture can pop without notice.

▸ And, finally, invest in a tube of antibiotic ointment and burn spray and keep them in a first-aid kit in your kitchen.

Peppermint Bark

Just about every specialty food catalog offers some version of peppermint bark during the holiday season, and for good reason: the combination of crunchy mint candy, creamy white chocolate, and bold bittersweet chocolate is addictive. Your friends and family will adore receiving this homemade version.

• MAKES ABOUT 2 POUNDS 6 OUNCES •

1 pound still-molten tempered 61% bittersweet chocolate (see page 174)

1 teaspoon chopped dried mint

1 pound still-molten tempered 31% white chocolate (see page 175)

1 cup (6 ounces) chopped Peppermint Candy (recipe follows)

> Spray a 13-by-18-by-1-inch baking sheet with nonstick baking spray. Line with a sheet of parchment paper.

> Pour the tempered bittersweet chocolate onto the baking sheet and use a large offset spatula to spread it evenly. Sprinkle the dried mint over the chocolate. Refrigerate on a level surface for 4 to 5 minutes, or until the chocolate has set and pulled away from the edges of the pan.

> Let the bittersweet chocolate layer come to room temperature, then spread the tempered white chocolate evenly over it. (Do not spread the white chocolate while the chocolate layer is still cold, or the white chocolate will set too quickly and the bark will be uneven.) Sprinkle with the chopped peppermint candy. Allow the chocolate to set at room temperature, about 2 hours, then break it into 2- to 3-inch pieces.

STORING

> The bark can be stored in an airtight container for up to 1 month.

Peppermint Candy

MAKES ABOUT 1¹⁄₂ CUPS

1¹⁄₂ cups plus 1 tablespoon (10.72 ounces) sugar

3 tablespoons water

¹⁄₄ cup plus 2 tablespoons (3 ounces) corn syrup

2 teaspoons peppermint oil (see Resources, page 335)

3 to 4 drops red food coloring (see Resources, page 335)

> Combine the sugar and water in a 2-quart copper or heavy stainless steel saucepan, stir in the corn syrup, and attach a candy thermometer to the side of the pan. Set the pan over medium-high heat—do not stir the mixture again—and cook until the mixture reaches 310°F.

> Meanwhile, spray a slab of marble with nonstick cooking spray or coat lightly with a neutral oil, such as canola or grapeseed. Put the peppermint oil and food coloring next to the marble.

Continued ›

BOX · 181

TIP: THIS BARK IS A HANDY STAPLE TO have on hand during the month of December, when you might want to quickly add a holiday feel to everyday desserts. Here are a couple of suggestions: Chop the bark and stir into vanilla ice cream for a festive frozen treat, or use the bark as a seasonal replacement for the Valrhona Pearl décor on Chocolate Cake with Chocolate Buttercream (page 79).

› As soon as the syrup reaches 310°F, pour it onto the center of the marble slab. Quickly pour the peppermint oil and a few drops of red food coloring onto the candy. Using two offset spatulas, spread the candy out with one spatula while folding it over with the second one. Continue this pattern over and over, reversing the movement with each pass. You are creating thin layers in the cooked sugar that will result in a pleasing crunchy texture once the candy sets. The candy will become more difficult to move as it hardens—that's a sign that you are finished folding and "pulling" the candy. Let cool until hard to the touch, about 10 minutes.

› With a cleaver or sharp chef's knife, chop the candy into small pieces.

› The peppermint candy can be stored in an airtight container for up to 2 months.

Durango Bark

Durango salt is a Pacific sea salt smoked with hickory wood, creating an intensely aromatic flavor. I first tasted this addictive salt at Spice Station, a fantastic spice and tea apothecary in the Silverlake area of Los Angeles. I recall that the sales-clerk suggested sprinkling it on ribs, but I think chocolate is the better application, and this bark was created specifically as a vehicle for Durango salt.

● MAKES ABOUT 2 POUNDS 6 OUNCES ●

2 pounds still-molten tempered 44% dark milk chocolate (see page 175)

1 teaspoon Durango salt (see Resources, page 335)

1 cup (4 ounces) chopped roasted almonds

⅓ cup plus 1 tablespoon (1.5 ounces) cocoa nibs (see Resources, page 335)

› Line a 13-by-18-by-1-inch baking sheet with parchment paper or a silicone mat.

› Pour the tempered chocolate onto the baking sheet and use a large offset spatula to spread it evenly in the pan. Sprinkle the salt over the chocolate, followed by the almonds and cocoa nibs. Bang the pan a couple of times on your work surface to ensure the almonds and nibs settle into the chocolate. Refrigerate on a level surface for about 10 minutes, until the chocolate has set and pulled away from the edges of the pan.

› Allow the chocolate to come to room temperature, then break it into 2-inch pieces.

STORING

› The bark can be stored in an airtight container for up to 2 months.

BOX · 183

MELTING CHOCOLATE

MELTING CHOCOLATE IS A VERY SIMPLE PROCESS as long as you monitor the temperature and watch the chocolate closely. There are three methods of melting chocolate: in the top of a double boiler, in a heatproof bowl set over a pot of simmering water, or in a microwave. Here are a few basic rules to follow regardless of which method you choose.

› Finely chop the chocolate for quick and even melting.

› Use glass, ceramic, or stainless steel bowls; avoid porous materials like plastic, which can harbor residual odors and flavors.

› Melt chocolate delicately; if using a double boiler or a bowl set over simmering water, keep the heat low and stir the chocolate as it melts. If using a microwave, heat the chocolate in a microwave-safe bowl for 10- to 15-second intervals, stirring after each interval to prevent the chocolate from overheating.

› Do not let chocolate come into contact with water; it will cause it to seize, rendering it unusable. Likewise, never melt chocolate over boiling water; that will produce high amounts of steam and likely introduce moisture into the chocolate. Also make sure that your equipment is completely dry.

› Monitor the temperature with a digital or instant-read thermometer when you are melting chocolate. Bittersweet chocolate should not be heated to over 120°F; dark milk, milk, and white chocolate should not be heated to over 112°F.

› Keep an eye on the chocolate to make sure it doesn't overheat. Scorched chocolate will become grainy and coarse, and there is no way to repair chocolate in this state.

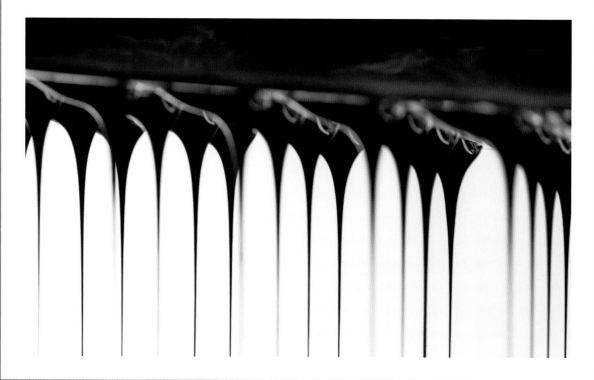

Chocolate-Dipped Coffee Crunch

When you're surrounded by melted chocolate most of the time, you find yourself dipping everything in it. Some things work better than others, but this marriage is a natural: the crunchy coffee-infused honeycomb candy from the Blum's Coffee Crunch Cake (page 31) dipped in tempered milk chocolate. But please stray from this combination and dip your favorite candy, cookie, or dried fruit in tempered chocolate whenever you feel the urge.

MAKES ABOUT 30 PIECES

1 recipe Coffee Crunch (page 31), cooled and chopped into irregular 1½- to 2-inch pieces

1 pound still-molten tempered 38% milk chocolate (see page 175)

› Line two 13-by-18-by-1-inch baking sheets with parchment paper or silicone mats.

› Dip the crunch in the chocolate following the two-fork method (see page 190). When dipping the crunch, be sure to check each piece for complete chocolate coverage before setting it down on the parchment to dry. Any exposed areas of crunch will result in a soft, tacky texture, adversely affecting the longevity of the candy.

STORING

› The candy can be stored in an airtight container for up to 1 month.

BOX · 185

Almond Fleur de Sel Toffee

My sister, Marina, shared an almond toffee recipe with me years ago that quickly became the most popular item in my repertoire. This is a version of that recipe that we used to transform into Valerie Confections all those years ago. It is a basic toffee recipe that I enhance by coating the individual pieces in 61% Valrhona chocolate and then sprinkling them with fleur de sel. At the time, I feared that salt and chocolate might be a passing trend and was hesitant to use it on more than one type of toffee. Almost a decade later, we know the combination is as perennial as toffee itself.

• MAKES ABOUT 40 PIECES •

FOR THE TOFFEE

2 sticks (8 ounces) unsalted butter

1 teaspoon kosher salt

1 cup (7 ounces) sugar

3/4 cup (3 ounces) chopped raw almonds

2 teaspoons vanilla extract

1 1/2 pounds still-molten tempered 61% bittersweet chocolate (see page 174)

2 tablespoons fleur de sel

› To make the toffee: Lightly coat a marble slab with cold butter. Using confectionery bars, make a 9-by-12-inch rectangle in the middle of the marble (or make the toffee in a 9-by-13-by-2-inch baking pan).

› Put the butter and salt into a 3-quart copper or heavy stainless steel saucepan and set over medium-low heat. When the butter is half melted, gradually add the sugar, stirring with a heatproof silicone spatula, then continue stirring until the mixture becomes a thick yellow paste. Attach a digital candy thermometer to the side of the pan, increase the heat to medium-high, and stir the toffee occasionally as the temperature rises. When it reaches 252°F, add the chopped almonds and stir until fully incorporated. Continue stirring occasionally until the temperature reaches 290°F, at which point you should begin to stir more frequently to prevent burning. When the temperature reaches 300°F, stir constantly until it reaches 310°F.

› Remove the pan from the heat and quickly stir in the vanilla, then pour the toffee onto the marble (or into the baking pan). Using a buttered offset spatula, spread the toffee evenly to fill the confectionery frame. Let the toffee set for 1 to 3 minutes, until it is no longer fluid.

› Pull one of the frames away from the toffee: If the toffee moves, return the frame to its original position; if the toffee is set, remove the frames.

› Using a buttered pizza cutter, cut the toffee lengthwise into 1 1/4-inch-wide strips, then cut crosswise into 1 1/4-inch squares. Let the toffee sit for 30 seconds to a minute, then retrace the cuts with the pizza cutter. Let the toffee cool completely, about 10 minutes.

› Using a cleaver or other heavy knife, loosen the toffee pieces from the marble by placing the knife along the cut delineating the top row of toffee squares and gently press the toffee away from you; this will release the toffee in a clean fashion, resulting in perfect squares. After separating the top row, work your way down to the bottom of the slab of toffee, then separate the individual squares.

BOX · 186

› Pick up each piece of toffee, brush off any shards or little bits of toffee, and put on a parchment-lined baking sheet. Cover with plastic wrap until you are ready to dip the toffee in chocolate. (The toffee can be prepared to this point up to 2 days ahead.)

› Dip the toffee in the tempered chocolate, following the directions for the two-fork method on page 190. Sprinkle fleur de sel on each piece before the chocolate sets.

STORING

› The toffee can be stored in an airtight container for up to 2 months.

Pumpkin Seed Toffee

Halloween has been transformed into an all-ages holiday. While the kids are trick-or-treating, indulge in a few pieces of this sweet-and-savory autumn treat with the other adults.

FOR THE TOFFEE

2 sticks (8 ounces) unsalted butter

1 teaspoon kosher salt

1 cup (7 ounces) sugar

1 cup (5.25 ounces) raw pumpkin seeds

4 teaspoons sweet smoked paprika (see Resources, page 335)

1½ pounds still-molten tempered 61% bittersweet chocolate (see page 174)

1 tablespoon Durango salt (see Resources, page 335)

▸ To make the toffee: Lightly coat a marble slab with cold butter. Using confectionery bars, make a 9-by-12-inch rectangle in the middle of the marble (or make the toffee in a 9-by-13-by-2-inch baking pan).

▸ Put the butter and salt into a 3-quart copper or heavy stainless steel saucepan and set over medium-low heat. When the butter is half melted, gradually add the sugar, stirring with a heatproof silicone spatula, then continue stirring until the mixture becomes a thick yellow paste. Attach a digital candy thermometer to the side of the pan, increase the heat to medium-high, and stir the toffee occasionally as the temperature rises. When it reaches 245°F, add the pumpkin seeds and stir until fully incorporated. Continue stirring occasionally until the temperature reaches 290°F, at which point stir more frequently to prevent burning. When the temperature reaches 300°F, stir constantly until it reaches 310°F.

▸ Remove the pan from the heat and quickly stir in 1 tablespoon of the smoked paprika, then pour the toffee onto the marble (or into the baking pan). Using a buttered offset spatula, spread the toffee evenly to fill the confectionery frame. Let the toffee set for 1 to 3 minutes, until it is no longer fluid.

▸ Pull one of the frames away from the toffee: If the toffee moves, return the frame to its original position; if the toffee is set, remove the frames.

▸ Using a buttered pizza cutter, cut the toffee lengthwise into 1¼-inch-wide strips, then cut crosswise into 1¼-inch squares. Let the toffee sit for 30 seconds to a minute, then retrace the cuts with the pizza cutter. Let the toffee cool completely, about 10 minutes.

▸ Using a cleaver or other heavy knife, loosen the toffee pieces by placing the knife along the cut delineating the top row of toffee squares and gently press the toffee away from you; this will release the toffee. Repeat with the remaining rows, then separate the individual squares.

▸ Brush off any shards and place each toffee on a parchment-lined baking sheet. Cover with plastic wrap until you are ready to dip the toffee in chocolate. (The toffee can be prepared to this point up to 2 days ahead.)

▸ Dip the toffee in the tempered chocolate, following the directions for the two-fork method on page 190. Sprinkle a pinch each of smoked paprika and Durango salt on each piece of toffee before the chocolate sets.

STORING

▸ The toffee can be stored in an airtight container for up to 2 months.

BOX · 189

DIPPING CHOCOLATE

— • —

THE FIRST STEP IN DIPPING CHOCOLATES is making sure your kitchen is cool enough. Set a thermometer in your work space. If the temperature is over 72°F, you are likely to have problems both tempering and dipping chocolate and should wait for a cooler day.

If your kitchen is between 60° and 68°F, it is in the ideal temperature range for chocolate dipping. If the temperature is between 69° and 72°F, a fan set behind your receiving pan will lower the temperature to allow the chocolate to set properly.

Time is also an important factor. The longer you work with tempered chocolate, the cooler and thicker it becomes, which can affect both the ease of dipping and the uniformity of your finished work. Therefore, it is important to be organized before the chocolate is dipped. *Mise en place,* a French phrase used in professional kitchens, means "everything in place." Setting up your *mise en place* includes laying out all necessary ingredients and tools exactly where you will need them.

Begin with a clear work space in the coolest area of your kitchen. Work left to right if you are right-handed (or set everything up the opposite way if you are left-handed). Set the tray of truffles or toffee for dipping on the left. Leave space in front of you for the bowl of tempered chocolate, and put one or two dipping forks and an offset spatula on one side. Put the bowl of cocoa or nuts for rolling to the right, and put a parchment-lined baking sheet to the far right for receiving. (If your recipe doesn't call for a coating of cocoa or nuts, replace with your décor ingredient.)

The following are slight variations on the basic chocolate-dipping technique, for the assorted chocolates in this chapter.

One-Fork Method (for truffles and toffee that will be rolled in cocoa or nuts)

Using a dipping fork, submerge the truffle or toffee in the tempered chocolate, then lift it up and tap the fork against the edge of the bowl so excess chocolate drips back into the bowl. Place the chocolate on the coating and wait for about 20 seconds before covering it with the coating.

Let the chocolate sit for 5 minutes to set before moving to a parchment-lined baking sheet.

Two-Fork Method (for truffles and toffee with décor)

This method requires a little extra effort but results in a clean finish. Using a dipping fork, submerge the truffle or toffee in the tempered chocolate. Pick up a dipping fork with each hand and lift the coated center out with one fork, then intertwine the tines of the forks and tilt the center so the excess chocolate runs off. Move the dipped center onto the right fork and run the left fork underneath to wipe off the dripping chocolate, then repeat on the opposite side, transfer the chocolate back to the right fork once more, and tap the fork with the left fork. Wipe the bottom one last time and gently slide the chocolate onto a parchment-lined baking sheet. Wait for about 20 seconds and then sprinkle or place the décor on top of the chocolate.

Marking with the Two-Fork Method (for truffles and toffee)

Follow the two-fork method above, but instead of placing décor on top of the chocolate, press the dipping fork against the chocolate and then quickly pull it away, leaving a mark in its place.

Finishing the Chocolates

"Feet" is a term that refers to the extra chocolate that spreads out at the bottom of a chocolate after dipping. Use the edge of an offset spatula to trim away the feet before the chocolate has completely set.

After dipping chocolates, let them set on the parchment paper for 1 hour before moving them.

Moving chocolates with bare hands will leave fingerprints on them. Either put on a nonpowdered latex glove or use an offset spatula to move chocolates from the receiving tray to candy cups or boxes.

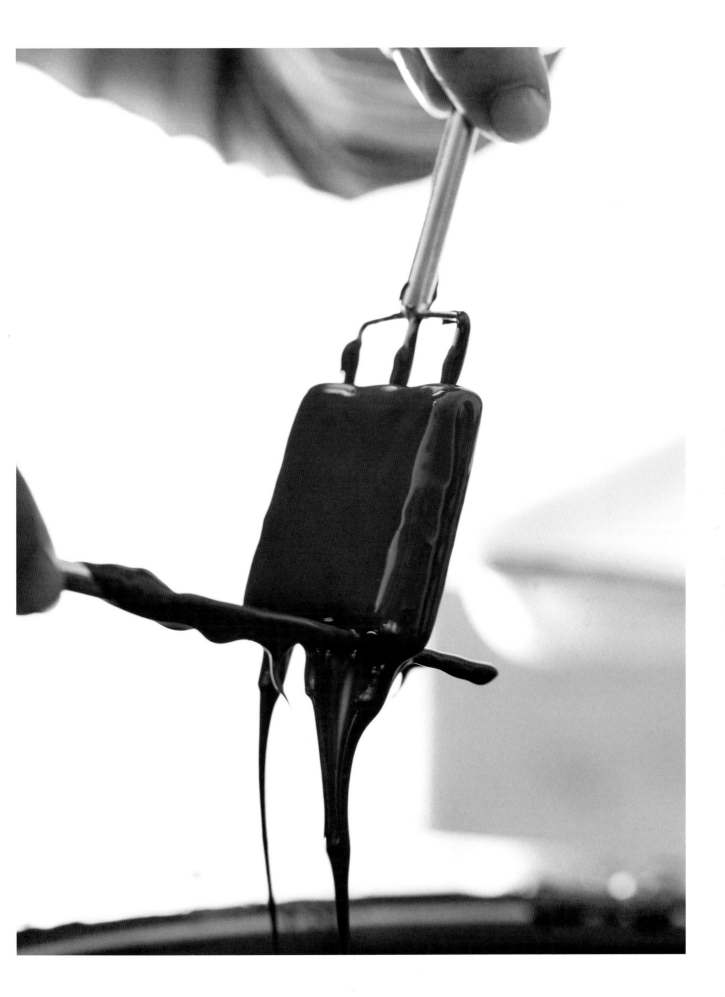

Mint Toffee

In this updated version of the classic after-dinner mint, dried mint imparts a refreshingly clean herbaceous quality, making the toffee a kind of confectionery digestif.

● MAKES ABOUT 48 PIECES ●

FOR THE TOFFEE

2 sticks (8 ounces) unsalted butter

1 teaspoon kosher salt

1 cup (7 ounces) sugar

2 teaspoons chopped dried mint (see Resources, page 335)

1½ teaspoons vanilla extract

1½ pounds still-molten tempered 61% bittersweet chocolate (see page 174)

▸ To make the toffee: Lightly coat a marble slab with cold butter. Using confectionery bars, make a 9-by-12-inch rectangle in the middle of the marble (or make the toffee in a 9-by-13-by-2-inch baking pan).

▸ Put the butter and salt into a 3-quart copper or heavy stainless steel saucepan and set over medium-low heat. When the butter is half melted, add the sugar, stirring with a heatproof silicone spatula, then stir until the mixture becomes a thick yellow paste. Attach a digital candy thermometer to the side of the pan and increase the heat to medium-high, and continue stirring occasionally until the temperature reaches 290°F, at which point you should begin to stir more frequently to prevent burning. When the temperature reaches 300°F, stir constantly until it reaches 310°F.

▸ Remove the pan from the heat and stir in the mint and vanilla, then pour the toffee onto the marble (or into the baking pan). Using a buttered offset spatula, spread the toffee evenly to fill the confectionery frame. Let the toffee set for 1 to 3 minutes, until it is no longer fluid.

▸ Pull one of the frames away from the toffee: If the toffee moves, return the frame to its original position; if the toffee is set, remove the frames.

▸ Using a buttered pizza cutter, cut the toffee lengthwise into 1¼-inch-wide strips, then cut crosswise into 1¼-inch squares. Let the toffee sit for 30 seconds to a minute, then retrace the cuts with the pizza cutter. Let the toffee cool completely, about 10 minutes.

▸ Using a cleaver or other heavy knife, loosen the toffee pieces by placing the knife along the cut delineating the top row of toffee squares and gently press the toffee away from you; this will release the toffee in a clean fashion. After separating the top row, work your way down to the bottom of the slab of toffee, then separate the individual squares.

▸ Pick up each piece of toffee, brush off any shards or little bits of toffee, and put on a parchment-lined baking sheet. Cover with plastic wrap until you are ready to dip the toffee in chocolate. (The toffee can be prepared to this point up to 2 days ahead.)

▸ Dip the toffee in the tempered chocolate, following the directions for the two-fork method and marking each chocolate with a dipping fork (see page 190) before the chocolate sets.

STORING

▸ The toffee can be stored in an airtight container for up to 2 months.

BOX · 193

Fleur de Sel Truffles

Ganache is a combination of chocolate and hot cream. When the two ingredients are blended properly, they form an emulsion, resulting in the creamy texture of good truffles. "Slabbing" is a process in truffle making where the ganache is poured into a confectionery frame, resulting in truffles of uniform size and thickness. At home, a baking pan can effectively achieve the same effect. This recipe calls for tempered chocolate, which creates a firm yet incredibly smooth ganache that is easy to cut and handle when dipping.

● MAKES ABOUT 60 TRUFFLES ●

FOR THE GANACHE

1 cup (8 ounces) heavy cream

2 tablespoons corn syrup

12 ounces still-molten tempered 61% bittersweet chocolate (see page 174)

2¹/₂ tablespoons (1.25 ounces) unsalted butter, softened

¹/₄ teaspoon kosher salt

1 tablespoon vodka (optional; see Tip)

1 teaspoon vanilla extract

1 teaspoon neutral-flavored oil, such as canola or grapeseed

3 ounces 61% bittersweet chocolate, melted (see page 184)

1¹/₂ pounds still-molten tempered 61% bittersweet chocolate (see page 174)

2 to 3 tablespoons fleur de sel

TIP: I INCLUDE SMALL AMOUNTS OF VODKA in all of my truffle recipes that do not contain another type of alcohol. The alcohol extends the shelf life of truffles without affecting the flavor. If you choose to omit the vodka, the truffles can be stored for up to 10 days.

› To make the ganache: Pour the heavy cream and corn syrup into a small saucepan and bring to a boil over medium heat. Remove from the heat and set aside to cool to 105°F, about 20 minutes; monitor the temperature with an instant-read thermometer.

› Line a 9-by-13-by-2-inch baking sheet with plastic wrap, leaving a 7-inch overhang on both short ends.

› When the cream is at 105°F, pour it into the bowl of tempered chocolate. Using a small silicone spatula, aggressively stir the cream and chocolate together in one direction, concentrating on the center of the mixture, until smooth and glistening, about 2 minutes. Add the butter and salt and quickly incorporate, then stir in the vodka, if using, and vanilla.

› Pour the ganache into the prepared baking pan. Level the surface with an offset spatula and bang the pan a couple of times on the work surface. Fold the excess plastic wrap over the ganache and let stand in a cool, dry place overnight.

› The following day, stir the oil into the melted chocolate.

› Pull back the plastic wrap and, using a pastry brush, paint the top of the ganache with a very thin layer of the melted chocolate; this process, called bottoming or precoating, will prevent the dipping forks from sticking to the ganache. Let the chocolate set, about 1 minute.

› Line a baking sheet with parchment paper.

› When the precoat has hardened, invert the ganache onto the lined pan and remove the plastic wrap. With a very sharp thin knife, using a ruler as a guide, cut the ganache lengthwise into 1¹/₄-inch-wide strips, then cut crosswise into 1¹/₄-inch squares. Separate the squares and set aside until you are ready to dip the truffles.

BOX · 194

› Dip the truffles in the tempered chocolate, following the directions for the two-fork method on page 190. Sprinkle a pinch of fleur de sel on each truffle before the chocolate sets.

STORING

› The truffles can be stored in an airtight container for up to 3 weeks.

Bloom?

Bloom is the dull white coating or grainy streaks you sometimes see on chocolate; there are two types, fat and sugar. Fat bloom appears as a white coating and occurs when tempered chocolate is exposed to excessive heat. The components separate, and the cocoa butter floats to the surface of the chocolate. Sugar bloom results in a granular surface or gray and white streaks; it occurs when tempered chocolate is stored in a moist environment, like a refrigerator. To avoid fat or sugar bloom, always store chocolate in a cool, dry environment, preferably between 60° and 70°F.

BOX · 195

Black Pepper Truffles

When you take a bite, the black pepper infusion in this truffle creates a unique warming sensation in your mouth. The mild spiciness pairs exceptionally well with big, full-bodied wines, such as Amarone or a Petite Syrah.

• MAKES ABOUT 60 TRUFFLES •

FOR THE GANACHE

1 cup plus 2 tablespoons (9 ounces) heavy cream

3 tablespoons light corn syrup

2 tablespoons coarsely ground black pepper

11.5 ounces still-molten tempered 61% bitter-sweet chocolate (see page 174)

2 tablespoons (1 ounce) unsalted butter, softened

1/2 teaspoon kosher salt

1/4 teaspoon finely ground black pepper

1 tablespoon vodka (optional; see Tip, page 194)

1 teaspoon neutral-flavored oil, such as canola or grapeseed

3 ounces 61% bittersweet chocolate, melted (see page 184)

1 1/2 pounds still-molten tempered 61% bitter-sweet chocolate (see page 174)

Finely ground black pepper

› To make the ganache: Put the cream, corn syrup, and coarsely ground pepper into a medium saucepan and bring to a boil over medium heat. Turn off the heat, cover the pan with aluminum foil, and poke a few holes into the foil to allow steam to release. Let steep for 1 hour.

› Line a 9-by-13-by-2-inch baking sheet with plastic wrap, leaving a 7-inch overhang on both short ends.

› Line a fine-mesh sieve with a piece of cheesecloth and strain the infused cream into a small bowl. If the temperature has dropped below 105°F, pour the cream back into the saucepan and warm over low heat.

› Pour the cream into the bowl of tempered chocolate. Using a small silicone spatula, aggressively stir the cream and chocolate together in one direction, concentrating on the center of the mixture until smooth and glistening, about 2 minutes. Add the butter, salt, and finely ground pepper and quickly incorporate, then stir in the vodka, if using.

› Pour the ganache into the prepared baking pan. Level the surface with an offset spatula and bang the pan a couple of times on the work surface. Fold the excess plastic wrap over the ganache and let stand in a cool, dry place overnight.

› The following day, stir the oil into the melted chocolate.

› Pull back the wrap and, using a pastry brush, paint the top of the ganache with a thin layer of the melted chocolate; this process will prevent the dipping forks from sticking to the ganache. Let the chocolate set, about 1 minute.

› Line a baking sheet with parchment paper.

› When the precoat has hardened, invert the ganache onto the lined pan and remove the plastic wrap. With a very sharp thin knife, using a ruler as a guide, cut the ganache lengthwise into 1 1/4-inch-wide strips, then cut crosswise into 1 1/4-inch squares. Separate the squares and set aside until you are ready to dip the truffles.

› Dip the truffles in the tempered chocolate, following the directions for the two-fork method on page 190. Sprinkle a pinch of pepper on each truffle before the chocolate sets.

STORING

› The truffles can be stored in an airtight container for up to 3 weeks.

TIP: FRESHLY GROUND PEPPER WILL HAVE a more robust pepper taste and aroma than preground pepper. A small coffee grinder is the perfect tool for grinding large amounts of pepper.

BOX · 197

Single-Malt-Scotch Truffles

After being surrounded by rose petals, passion fruit, and delicate tea cakes for a few years, my tolerant partner, Stan, craved something more masculine. One day he pleaded, "Can we make something with Scotch?" The following Valentine's Day, I presented him with his gift: this bittersweet truffle, brimming with peaty, twelve-year-old single-malt Scotch, accompanied by a bottle of Macallan.

● MAKES ABOUT 60 TRUFFLES ●

FOR THE GANACHE

1 cup plus 2 tablespoons (9 ounces) heavy cream

2 tablespoons corn syrup

11 ounces still-molten tempered 61% bittersweet chocolate (see page 174)

3 tablespoons (1.5 ounces) unsalted butter

1/2 teaspoon kosher salt

1/4 cup (2 ounces) single-malt Scotch, such as Macallan, Lagavulin, or Glenfiddich

1 teaspoon neutral-flavored oil, such as canola or grapeseed

3 ounces 61% bittersweet chocolate, melted (see page 184)

1 1/2 pounds still-molten tempered 61% to 72% bittersweet chocolate (see page 174)

TIP: THE SCOTCH CAN BE REPLACED WITH rum, whiskey, tequila, brandy, Calvados, or Cognac if your taste leans toward a different spirit.

› To make the ganache: Pour the cream and corn syrup into a medium saucepan and bring to a boil over medium heat. Remove from the heat and let cool to 105°F.

› Line a 9-by-13-by-2-inch baking sheet with plastic wrap, leaving a 7-inch overhang on both short ends.

› When the cream is at 105°F, pour it into the bowl of tempered chocolate. Using a small silicone spatula, aggressively stir the cream and chocolate together in one direction, concentrating on the center of the mixture, until smooth and glistening, about 2 minutes. Add the butter and salt and quickly incorporate, then stir in the Scotch.

› Pour the ganache into the prepared baking pan. Level the surface with an offset spatula and bang the pan a couple of times on the work surface. Fold the excess plastic wrap over the ganache and let stand in a cool, dry place overnight.

› The following day, stir the oil into the melted chocolate.

› Pull back the plastic wrap and, using a pastry brush, paint the top of the ganache with a very thin layer of the melted chocolate; this process, called bottoming or precoating, will prevent the dipping forks from sticking to the ganache. Let the chocolate set, about 1 minute.

› Line a baking sheet with parchment paper.

› When the precoat has hardened, invert the ganache onto the lined pan and remove the plastic wrap. With a very sharp thin knife, using a ruler as a guide, cut the ganache lengthwise into 1 1/4-inch-wide strips, then cut crosswise into 1 1/4-inch squares. Separate the squares and set aside until you are ready to dip the truffles.

› Dip the truffles in the tempered chocolate, following the directions for the two-fork method and marking each truffle with a dipping fork (see page 190) before the chocolate sets.

STORING

› The truffles can be stored in an airtight container for up to 3 weeks.

BOX · 198

CHOCOLATE PERCENTAGES

IT SEEMS AS IF ALMOST EVERY CHOCOLATE BAR has a number and a percentage sign somewhere on the label these days. The numbers you see represent the percentage of cocoa solids in the chocolate; the higher the number, the stronger the chocolate flavor—at least in most cases. The percentage is no reflection on the quality of the chocolate, roasting methods, or a number of other variables that greatly affect the flavor and experience. The exact percentage necessary for a chocolate to be labeled bittersweet, dark, or milk is not regulated, so you may see labels with seemingly contradictory information, but I do find the following numbers to be accurate for home chocolatier purposes. As with any ingredient, taste a few chocolates to determine which ones you most enjoy eating and using in desserts and to make chocolates.

› 76% to 90% = extra bittersweet chocolate

› 61% to 75% = bittersweet chocolate

› 34% to 40% = milk chocolate

› 28% to 31% = white chocolate

In this chapter, you will see tempered dark milk chocolate called for in a number of recipes. This hybrid chocolate is a blend of milk chocolate and bittersweet chocolate, which gives the milk chocolate a deeper flavor and color while maintaining its smooth mouthfeel and creamy taste.

Crème Fraîche Truffles

The tangy flavor of crème fraîche brightens the bittersweet chocolate in this delicate truffle and imparts a velvety texture to the ganache. The smooth truffle center is complemented by the coating of atomized chocolate—powdered and sweetened 69% chocolate.

● MAKES ABOUT 50 TRUFFLES ●

FOR THE GANACHE

11 ounces 61% bittersweet chocolate, finely chopped

¾ cup plus 2 tablespoons (7 ounces) crème fraîche

3 tablespoons (1.5 ounces) unsalted butter, softened

1 cup (4 ounces) atomized 69% bittersweet chocolate (see Resources, page 335)

1½ pounds still-molten tempered 61% to 68% bittersweet chocolate (see page 174)

> To make the ganache: Line a 9-by-13-by-2-inch baking pan with parchment paper. Set a large bowl on a dish towel and add the chopped chocolate (see Tip).

> Spoon the crème fraîche into a small saucepan and bring just to a boil over medium heat. Pour the crème fraîche over the chocolate and let sit for 1 minute.

> Using a small rubber spatula, stir the cream and chocolate together in one direction, concentrating on the center of the mixture, until smooth and glistening, about 2 minutes. Add the butter and stir until it is completely melted, about 1 minute.

> Pour the ganache into the prepared baking pan. Cover the ganache with a second piece of parchment paper. Place the pan in the coolest part of the kitchen and let set, 4 to 6 hours.

> Line a baking sheet with parchment paper. Using a melon baller or teaspoon measure, scoop small balls of the ganache onto the lined pan. Let stand at room temperature for 1 to 2 hours. The truffles will develop a thin crust, which will make dipping them substantially easier.

> Spread the atomized chocolate in a baking pan. Dip the truffles in the tempered chocolate, following the directions for the single-fork method on page 190, then roll in the atomized chocolate.

STORING

> The truffles can be stored in an airtight container in the refrigerator for up to 1 week.

TIP: PLACING A DISH TOWEL UNDERNEATH a mixing bowl will stop the bowl from moving when you are stirring ingredients together. This technique is particularly helpful when mixing ganache because of the urgent pace necessary to emulsify it.

BOX · 201

Raspberry Truffles

Raspberries and chocolate are a classic dessert combination and delicious in every iteration imaginable. Here raspberry is introduced into chocolate in the forms of puree, liqueur, and freeze-dried powder, creating an intensely flavored bite-sized treat.

● MAKES ABOUT 50 TRUFFLES ●

FOR THE GANACHE

6 ounces 38% milk chocolate, finely chopped

6 ounces 61% bittersweet chocolate, finely chopped

³/₄ cup plus 2 tablespoons (5 ounces) raspberry puree (see Resources, page 335)

¹/₄ cup (2 ounces) crème fraîche

4 tablespoons (¹/₂ stick/2 ounces) unsalted butter, softened

2 tablespoons Chambord

¹/₂ cup (2 ounces) 69% bittersweet atomized chocolate (see Resources, page 335)

¹/₂ cup (2.25 ounces) freeze-dried raspberry powder (see Resources, page 335)

1¹/₂ pounds still-molten tempered dark milk chocolate (see page 175)

⟩ To make the ganache: Line a 9-by-13-by-2-inch baking sheet with parchment paper. Set a large bowl on a dish towel and add the chopped chocolates (see Tip, page 201).

⟩ Put the raspberry puree and crème fraîche into a small saucepan and bring just to a boil over medium heat. Pour the mixture over the chocolate and let sit for 1 minute.

⟩ Using a small rubber spatula, stir the puree mixture and chocolate together in one direction, concentrating on the center of the mixture, until smooth and glistening, about 2 minutes. Add the butter and stir until it is completely melted, about 1 minute. Stir in the Chambord.

⟩ Pour the ganache into the prepared baking pan. Cover the ganache with a second piece of parchment paper. Place the pan in the coolest part of the kitchen and let set, 4 to 6 hours.

⟩ Line a baking sheet with parchment paper. Using a melon baller or teaspoon measure, scoop small balls of the ganache onto the lined pan. Let stand at room temperature for 1 to 2 hours. The truffles will develop a thin crust that will make dipping them substantially easier.

⟩ Combine the atomized chocolate and raspberry powder in a baking pan. Dip the truffles in the tempered chocolate, following the directions for the single-fork method on page 190, then roll in the atomized chocolate mixture.

STORING

⟩ The truffles can be stored in an airtight container in the refrigerator for up to 2 weeks.

BOX · 203

PACKAGING CHOCOLATES

———————————

UNWRAPPING A BOX OF CHOCOLATES IS ALMOST AS SATISFYING AS EATING THE CONTENTS. Chocolates, like jewels, elicit a feeling of anticipation when one is presented with a box; there is a true thrill in the process of untying a bow and slowly discovering what lies inside. When Valerie Confections was in its infancy, I allocated an enormous budget to the finest French-milled cotton grosgrain and silk ribbons I could find. As a business expense, my indulgence was grossly irresponsible, but I couldn't resist the thought of those fabulous textures and colors wrapped around our corduroy-embossed boxes. Ultimately, I followed a more practical route and sourced packaging options that satiated my desire for a keepsake ribbon within a sound and frugal budget. But if you share my inclination toward extravagant packaging, the dent in your bank account will be far less dramatic. Forms of packaging to suit a wide variety of budgets and styles are now available online. See Packaging, page 336, for a list of my favorite vendors.

‣ CANDY CUPS help protect chocolates from damage and allow you to handle them in a more sanitary way. They are available in a variety of sizes, shapes, and colors.

‣ FIVE-PLY PADS cushion chocolates and prevent movement in a chocolate box. They are available in gold, brown, and custom patterns.

‣ Using JARS and TINS is a clever (and green!) way to package chocolates and confections.

‣ BIODEGRADABLE CLEAR BAGS are a quick, economical way to package confections and cookies.

‣ HANGTAGS are an easy way to personalize and label confections. They have a modern, utilitarian look when attached with kitchen twine and are very inexpensive.

‣ CUSTOM STICKERS or ADHESIVE LABELS are readily available in fashionable designs. They can give a professional look to your homemade gifts.

‣ STAMPS and STAMP PADS have seen a real resurgence in popularity over the last few years. You can have stamps custom-made or buy designs you like to decorate your packaging.

‣ Traditional BAKERY BOXES, CHOCOLATE BOXES, and TIERED GIFT BOXES are just a few examples of the different containers you might choose to hold your confections.

‣ WAX SEALS add an old-fashioned touch and are a great way to discreetly personalize your creations.

‣ And, of course, there's RIBBON, my raison d'être! The types and styles are endless.

Caramels with Gray Sea Salt

Gray sea salt, or sel gris, is a coarse, unrefined salt harvested from along France's Atlantic coast. The high levels of minerals and nutrients give the salt its distinctive gray hue and potent flavor. The size and texture of the salt crystals allow it to stay solid, rather than dissolving, when stirred into hot caramel, resulting in crunchy bits throughout the candy.

● MAKES ABOUT 50 CARAMELS ●

1³/₄ cups (12.25 ounces) sugar

1 cup plus 1 tablespoon (8.5 ounces) heavy cream

1 tablespoon corn syrup

1 tablespoon (¹/₂ ounce) cold unsalted butter

1¹/₂ teaspoons vanilla extract

1¹/₂ teaspoons gray sea salt

▸ Line a 9-by-13-by-2-inch baking sheet with parchment paper, leaving a 2-inch overhang on both short ends.

▸ Pour the sugar into a large copper or heavy stainless steel saucepan and set over medium heat. Pour the cream and corn syrup into a small saucepan and set over medium-low heat.

▸ As the sugar heats, you will see it start to melt around the edges and then turn golden in color, in 2 to 3 minutes. Using a wooden spoon or heatproof silicone spatula, nudge the sugar slightly on one side. You will see liquid caramel slowly move out from underneath the granular sugar. Very slowly start to move the sugar into the liquid caramel. Do not rush this process—if the caramel starts to look grainy, you are incorporating the sugar too quickly. If the caramel starts to smoke or get very dark, remove the pan from the heat until the smoking subsides or lower the heat.

▸ Meanwhile, watch the cream: You want it to come to a boil when the sugar reaches the liquid caramel stage, so adjust the timing accordingly by raising or lowering the heat under the cream (if the cream comes to a boil too early, just remove it from the heat).

▸ When the sugar has completely melted and is dark amber in color, remove from the heat and pour in the cream—it will bubble substantially. When the caramel has settled down, stir the ingredients together until smooth.

▸ Return the pan to medium heat, attach a digital candy thermometer to the side of the pan, and cook, stirring very occasionally, until the caramel reaches 260°F. Immediately remove from the heat. Stir in the butter, vanilla, and salt, then pour into the lined baking sheet and let cool completely, about 2 hours.

▸ Run a sharp knife along the unlined edges of the pan, then lift the ends of the paper to remove the caramel and put it on a cutting board. Using an oiled pizza cutter or a sharp heavy knife, slice the caramel lengthwise into ¹/₂- to ³/₄-inch-wide strips, then cut crosswise into 1¹/₂-inch pieces. Wrap each caramel in wax paper or a cellophane candy wrapper.

STORING

▸ The caramels can be stored in a cool, dry place for up to 1 month.

BOX · 207

Meringues

Can a confection be described as multipurpose? On their own with a cup of tea, meringues make a fat-free midafternoon treat. They can also be crushed and used as the garnish for a frosted cake, or as the topping for Eton Mess (page 218). They can replace marshmallows on hot chocolate or top a simple, fruit-flavored ice cream. Once you embrace the meringue, I'm sure you'll share my enthusiasm for the little puffs that cost just pennies to make.

● MAKES ABOUT 50 MERINGUES ●

4 large egg whites, at room temperature

1/2 teaspoon cream of tartar

1 cup (7 ounces) sugar

⟩ Heat the oven to 225°F. Line two 13-by-18-by-1-inch baking sheets with parchment paper or silicone baking mats.

⟩ In the bowl of a stand mixer fitted with the whisk attachment (or in a large bowl, using a handheld mixer), whip the egg whites on medium speed until frothy and bubbly. Add the cream of tartar and continue whipping. Once the size of the bubbles starts to diminish, begin streaming in the sugar. When all the sugar is incorporated, increase the speed to high and beat for a few seconds; turn off the mixer when you see tracks from the whisk in the meringue. Remove the whisk (or one of the beaters) and turn it upside down: if the meringue is stiff and remains upright, the meringue is ready for the next step; if not, whip the meringue until it forms stiff peaks.

⟩ Fit a medium piping bag with a plain 1/4-inch tip and fill it with the meringue. Pipe 11/2-inch meringues onto the prepared pans, leaving 2 inches of space between them. Bake for 1 hour and 15 minutes, or until the exterior of the meringues is crisp and the bottom edges show the slightest golden color. Turn off the oven and prop the oven door ajar with an oven mitt or a thick kitchen towel. Leave the meringues in the oven for 11/2 hours.

⟩ Transfer the meringues to a cool, dry area to cool.

STORING

⟩ The meringues can be stored in an airtight container for up to 1 month.

BOX · 208

Chocolate Marshmallows

This is an adaptation of a recipe I found on the popular recipe website Food52.com. I have worked with many marshmallow recipes and found this one to have the best flavor and most consistent results. As an added bonus, the recipe doubles and triples successfully.

1 cup (8 ounces) cold water

2¹/₂ tablespoons powdered gelatin

1¹/₂ cups (10.5 ounces) sugar

1 cup (11 ounces) light corn syrup

¹/₄ teaspoon kosher salt

1 tablespoon vanilla extract

2.5 ounces 72% bittersweet chocolate, finely chopped

¹/₂ cup (2 ounces) 69% bittersweet atomized chocolate (see Resources, page 335)

¹/₂ cup (2.25 ounces) confectioners' sugar

‣ Spray a 9–by-13-by-2-inch baking sheet with nonstick baking spray or lightly brush with a neutral oil such as canola or grapeseed.

‣ Pour ¹/₂ cup of the water into the bowl of a stand mixer fitted with the whisk attachment. Add the gelatin, stir to combine, and allow to soften, about 3 minutes.

‣ Meanwhile, combine the remaining ¹/₂ cup water, the sugar, corn syrup, and salt in a small saucepan and heat over low heat, stirring, until the sugar is dissolved, about 3 minutes. Attach a candy thermometer to the side of the pan, increase the heat to medium, and bring to a boil, without stirring. Keep a wet pastry brush handy, and brush down the sides of the pot if little crystals appear. When the temperature reaches 240°F, remove the pan from the heat.

‣ Turn the mixer onto low speed and slowly pour the hot sugar mixture into the gelatin. Gradually increase the speed to high and beat until the mixture is opaque and thick, about 12 minutes.

‣ Add the vanilla and chopped chocolate and beat on medium speed until thoroughly combined. Immediately transfer the marshmallow to the prepared baking sheet and spread it evenly with an oiled offset spatula. Cover the marshmallow with a piece of parchment and set aside until firm, about 2 hours.

‣ Mix the atomized chocolate and confectioners' sugar in a medium bowl. Lift the marshmallow slab out of the pan. Dip a pair of kitchen shears in the chocolate and sugar mixture to coat and cut the marshmallow into 1¹/₂- or 2-inch squares, dipping the shears again as necessary. Toss the marshmallows in the chocolate and sugar mixture to coat lightly but evenly.

STORING

‣ The marshmallows can be stored in an airtight container for up to 3 weeks.

BOX • 211

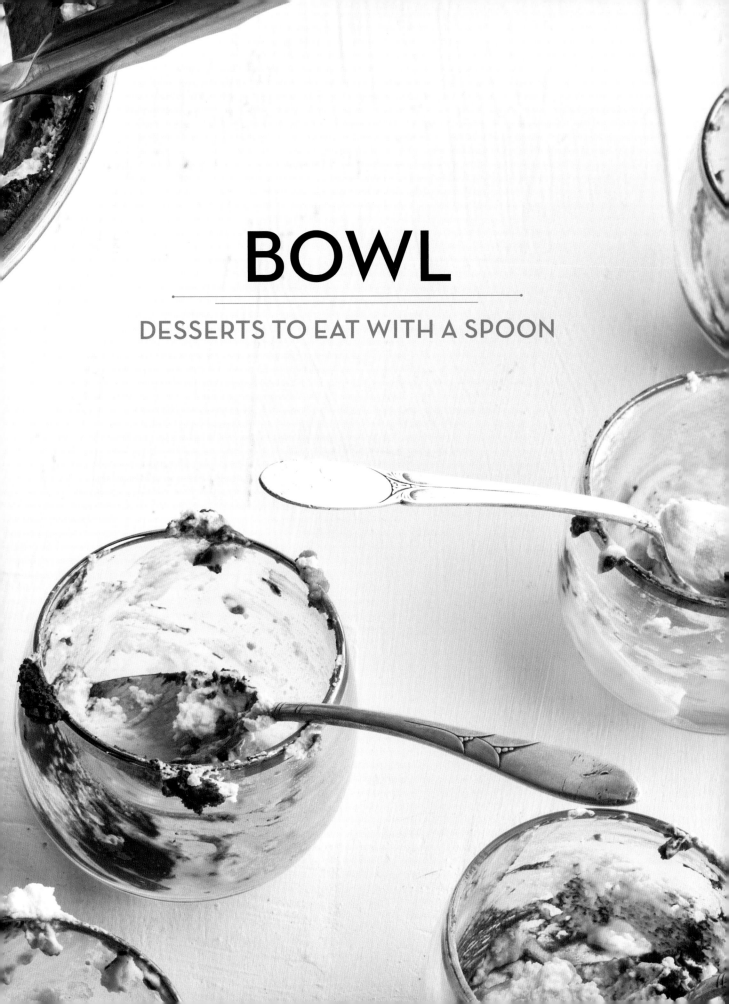

BOWL

DESSERTS TO EAT WITH A SPOON

WHEN asked to bring dessert to a dinner party or a small gathering, I frequently use one of the desserts in this chapter. The first time I presented a hostess with an Eton Mess (page 218), I was a little nervous because as a professional in the dessert field, I felt like I was cheating or being lazy somehow by offering a dessert that required, literally, five minutes of my time. Did it look too easy to make? My insecurities were quickly assuaged, as not only was the entire dessert devoured, but it also extended the dinner party, in a good way. Watching everyone luxuriate with spoonful after spoonful of fruity meringue-dotted cream was reassuring and entertaining. We all love the comforting satisfaction of eating dessert with a spoon, and no one is analyzing "active cooking time" when they are licking up the last bits of dessert.

Soft desserts are the simplest in the canon but frequently elicit the most enthusiastic response from those who indulge, yet I didn't explore the world of making ice creams, gelées, or mousses until I was well into my adult years. When you see a molded plated dessert such as panna cotta, you might assume that it is difficult to prepare or that special training is required to execute it perfectly. And what about homemade ice cream or sorbet? Investing in a piece of kitchen equipment that serves one purpose might seem wasteful, in terms of both the expense and the precious storage space. I was confident making a myriad of desserts, some that had taken many months to perfect, but was still intimidated by gelée.

Eventually, after a little research and some experimentation, I realized that making a fancy panna cotta is easier than making chocolate chip cookies. Over the last few years, my trusty ice cream machine has saved me countless dollars in store-bought pints. And while a gelée may sound downright complex, the recipe has only four ingredients and a handful of cooking steps, and will take just minutes of your time. Whenever I see that golden, quivering dessert (see page 221) shimmering with every spoonful, I still marvel at the elegance and luxurious flavor.

In this chapter, you will find a variety of desserts with irresistible names, such as fool and Eton Mess. Once you master those, move on to panna cotta, pots de crème, mousse, pudding, and a party-sized tiramisu. Make sure you have your ice cream maker handy for two deliciously light sorbets, as well as two ice cream recipes that will give you a year's worth of flavors (see A Variety of Flavors from Your Pantry, page 238).

Although the actual cooking time is very short for these recipes, you do need to plan ahead. The most challenging part of making sorbet or ice cream is remembering to put the bowl in the freezer in advance, so that it's cold enough to use when you need it. And, of course, all of these desserts require a few hours to either set or freeze before serving.

Black-and-Blue Fool

Fool is an English dessert that originated in the fifteenth or sixteenth century. It consists of two components, whipped cream and pureed fruit, and it is one of simplest desserts you will ever make. Top each serving with fresh blueberries and blackberries.

● SERVES 8 ●

2 cups (16 ounces) well-chilled heavy cream

1¼ cups (10 ounces) Black-and-Blue Jam (page 282) or other fruit jam

› In the bowl of a stand mixer fitted with the whisk attachment (or in a large bowl, using a handheld mixer), beat the cream on medium-high speed until medium-soft peaks form, about 3 minutes. Remove the bowl from the mixer stand and fold the jam into the cream until almost incorporated—it looks pretty if you leave ribbons of jam throughout the fool. Cover with plastic wrap and refrigerate for at least 1 hour.

› Spoon into small bowls and serve.

STORING

› The fool is best enjoyed the day it is made.

Eton Mess

A fun British dessert from the nineteenth century, this addictive combination of cream, berries, and meringue is named after the elite Eton College. This is the "pudding" of choice at Eton's annual cricket game against Winchester College, but I say a dessert this divine should be served far more often. Eton Mess is traditionally made with strawberries, but it is equally delicious with sliced stone fruits and other berries, such as the raspberries used here.

● SERVES 8 ●

1 cup (4 ounces) raspberries, rinsed and dried

1 cup (5 ounces) small strawberries, rinsed, hulled, and sliced in half

¼ cup (1.75 ounces) sugar

2 cups (16 ounces) well-chilled heavy cream

12 to 15 meringues, homemade (page 208) or store-bought

3 tablespoons Chambord (optional)

▸ Put the raspberries, strawberries, and sugar in a medium bowl and stir together. Cover and let macerate in the refrigerator for 1 to 4 hours. (If you do refrigerate them for longer, the berries will just break down more.)

▸ In the bowl of a stand mixer fitted with the whisk attachment (or in a large bowl, using a handheld mixer), beat the cream on medium-high speed until medium-soft peaks form, about 3 minutes. Remove the bowl from the mixer stand and gently fold in the macerated fruit, with its juices, until it is just incorporated. Transfer to a serving bowl, top with the meringues, and drizzle the Chambord, if using, over the meringues. (Refrigerate if not serving immediately.)

▸ Spoon into small bowls and serve.

STORING

▸ This dessert is best enjoyed the day it is made.

Champagne Gelée

Gelée sounds so much more sophisticated and elegant than the word "gelatin." We all grew up with the packaged variety in those electric colors with flavors like orange and lime. Dispel that notion of gelatin; this version is far more delicious and impressive. Use your favorite Champagne or sparkling wine.

● SERVES 6 ●

1 tablespoon plus ³/₄ teaspoon powdered gelatin

³/₄ cup plus 3 tablespoons (7.5 ounces) cold water

1 cup (7 ounces) sugar

1 bottle (750 ml) Champagne, chilled

TIP: ADDING STRAWBERRIES, SLICED IF large, and raspberries is a delicious way to vary this recipe. Add the berries to the glasses before refrigerating the gelée. If you add berries, it is best to serve the gelées the day they are made, as the berries can darken and break down, and the effect will not be as pretty.

› Sprinkle the gelatin over the 3 tablespoons water in a small bowl, and let sit for 10 minutes, until the gelatin softens.

› Combine the remaining ³/₄ cup water and the sugar in a medium saucepan over medium heat, and bring to a simmer, stirring to dissolve the sugar. Remove from the heat.

› Add the gelatin to the sugar syrup, stirring until it has dissolved. Pour into a large pitcher. Pour the Champagne into the pitcher and stir with a long spoon.

› Pour the gelée into glasses or small glass bowls and refrigerate for 3 to 4 hours, until set.

STORING

› The gelée can be refrigerated, covered with plastic wrap, for up to 3 days.

Fraises des Bois Mousse

Fraises des bois (literally, "strawberries of the woods") are one of the greatest natural delicacies you can find. Their aroma is almost unreal, perhaps best described as strawberry perfume. The berries are tiny little things, often irregular in shape, and their flavor is memorable. They are quite expensive, but so worth the extravagance.

● SERVES 8 ●

3¹⁄₂ cups (12 ounces) stemmed fraises des bois (see Resources, page 335), plus (optional) extra for garnish

¹⁄₂ cup plus 2 tablespoons (4.375 ounces) sugar

2 teaspoons powdered gelatin

2 cups plus 3 tablespoons (17.5 ounces) cold water

2¹⁄₂ cups (20 ounces) heavy cream

▸ Toss the berries with ¹⁄₂ cup of the sugar in a medium bowl. Cover and let macerate for at least 1 hour in the refrigerator.

▸ Transfer the macerated fruit, with its juices, to a food processor or blender and process to a smooth puree. Set aside.

▸ Sprinkle the gelatin over 3 tablespoons of the water in a small bowl. Let sit for 10 minutes, until the gelatin softens.

▸ Combine 1 cup of the cream, the remaining 2 tablespoons sugar, and the gelatin in a small saucepan and stir over medium-low heat until the gelatin dissolves; do not let the cream boil. Remove from the heat.

▸ Fill a large shallow bowl with ice and the remaining 2 cups water. Put the saucepan directly into the ice bath, and let stand until the gelatin mixture is cool to the touch, about 5 minutes.

▸ In the bowl of a stand mixer fitted with the whisk attachment (or in a large bowl, using a handheld mixer), beat the remaining 1¹⁄₂ cups cream on medium-high speed until soft peaks form. With the mixer running, stream in the gelatin mixture and beat until the cream forms soft to medium peaks. Transfer the whipped cream to a medium bowl and fold in the strawberry puree thoroughly. Cover with plastic wrap and chill for at least 1 hour.

▸ Scoop the mousse into bowls and garnish with additional fraises des bois, if desired.

STORING

▸ The mousse can be refrigerated for up to 2 days.

TIP: IF YOU ARE UNABLE TO FIND FRAISES des bois, omit the sugar from the recipe and use 1¹⁄₂ cups (12 ounces) Strawberry-Vanilla Bean Jam (page 276) or strawberry puree (see Resources, page 335) as a replacement for the berries.

Jasmine Panna Cotta

Panna cotta (literally, "cooked cream") is an Italian dessert that should be a part of everyone's repertoire. You can replace the jasmine tea in this recipe with any other tea or dried herb for the same magnificent results. Serve the panna cotta plain or with fresh fruit on top. The panna cotta needs to set for at least 5 hours, so plan ahead.

● SERVES 8 ●

4 cups (32 ounces) heavy cream

1/3 cup (1 ounce) jasmine pearl tea (see Resources, page 335)

2 teaspoons powdered gelatin

3 tablespoons cold water

3/4 cup plus 1 tablespoon (5.75 ounces) sugar

› Put the cream and tea into a medium saucepan and bring to a boil over medium heat. Turn off the heat, cover the pan with aluminum foil, and poke a few holes into the top to allow steam to release. Let steep for 1 hour.

› Sprinkle the gelatin over the cold water in a small bowl. Let sit for 10 minutes, until the gelatin softens.

› Strain the infused cream through a fine-mesh sieve into a bowl, pressing on the tea leaves with the back of a large spoon to release all the liquid. Pour the cream back into the saucepan, add the sugar and gelatin, and heat, stirring, over medium-low heat until the gelatin is melted; do not let the mixture come to a boil.

› Pour the cream into a pitcher and divide among eight 4-ounce ramekins (or small bowls), filling each ramekin to about 1/2 inch from the top. Chill for at least 5 hours, until set.

› When you are ready to serve, to unmold the panna cotta, dip each ramekin into a bowl of hot water and slowly count to 5, then invert onto a dessert plate and gently agitate the ramekin until the panna cotta releases onto the plate. Serve immediately.

STORING

› The panna cotta can be wrapped individually in plastic wrap and stored in the refrigerator for up to 3 days.

Chocolate Pots de Crème

True to its name, this little custard is nothing more than a pot of chocolate and cream. I love scooping bites of the dessert up with a cookie instead of a spoon. See pages 138–39 for whipped cream variations for topping it.

● SERVES 6 ●

6.5 ounces 72% bittersweet chocolate, finely chopped

1¼ cups (10 ounces) heavy cream

¾ cup (6 ounces) whole milk

5 large egg yolks (see Tip)

⅔ cup (4.5 ounces) sugar

2 teaspoons vanilla bean paste (see Resources, page 335)

‣ Position a rack in the middle of the oven and heat the oven to 325°F.

‣ Put the chocolate into a medium bowl. Combine the cream and milk in a small saucepan and bring to a boil over medium heat. Pour the hot cream over the chocolate. Let sit for 30 seconds or so to allow the chocolate to melt, then stir together until smooth.

‣ In a small bowl, whisk together the egg yolks, sugar, and vanilla paste. Slowly stream the egg mixture into the chocolate mixture, whisking constantly. Strain the custard through a fine-mesh sieve into a bowl or pitcher, then pour into six 4-ounce ramekins or ceramic cups or bowls.

‣ Arrange the ramekins in a baking dish or pan and carefully add enough hot water to come about two-thirds of the way up the sides of the ramekins. Carefully place the baking dish in the oven and bake for 30 minutes. Remove the baking dish from the oven and let the pots de crème sit in the hot water for 5 minutes. If they still appear very jiggly in the middle, let them sit for another 5 minutes in the hot water. You want the custards to be very firm around the edges and to barely move toward the center when gently shaken.

‣ Remove the ramekins from the hot water and let cool in a cool area of the kitchen before serving, or chill to serve cold.

STORING

‣ The pots de crème can be wrapped individually in plastic wrap and stored in the refrigerator for up to 3 days.

TIP: USE THE LEFTOVER EGG WHITES TO make Meringues (page 208).

Matcha Pots de Crème

The unmistakable bright green color from the matcha creates a can't-miss dessert. I like making these custards in small white or ivory teacups to highlight the color. Top with strawberries and whipped cream (see pages 138–39), if desired.

● SERVES 6 ●

1¼ cups (10 ounces) heavy cream

3 tablespoons sifted matcha tea (see Resources, page 335)

¾ cup (3.75 ounces) 31% white chocolate chips or fèves (see Resources, page 335) or chopped 31% white chocolate

¾ cup (6 ounces) whole milk

5 large egg yolks (see Tip)

⅓ cup (2.25 ounces) sugar

1½ teaspoons vanilla bean paste (see Resources, page 335)

▸ Position a rack in the center of the oven and heat the oven to 325°F.

▸ Stir together ¼ cup of the heavy cream and the matcha in a small bowl to make a paste. Set aside. Put the white chocolate in a medium bowl.

▸ Combine the remaining 1 cup cream and the milk in a small saucepan and bring to a boil over medium heat. Pour the hot cream over the white chocolate. Let sit for 30 seconds or so, to allow the chocolate to melt, then stir together until smooth. Whisk in the matcha paste until just combined.

▸ In a small bowl, whisk together the egg yolks, sugar, and vanilla paste. Slowly stream the egg mixture into the chocolate mixture, whisking constantly. Strain the custard through a fine-mesh sieve into a bowl or pitcher, then pour into six 4-ounce ramekins or ceramic cups or bowls.

▸ Arrange the ramekins in a baking dish or pan and carefully add enough hot water to come about two-thirds of the way up the sides of the ramekins. Carefully place the baking dish in the oven and bake for 30 minutes. Remove the baking dish from the oven and let the pots de crème sit in the hot water for 10 minutes. If they still appear very jiggly in the middle, let them sit for another 5 minutes in the hot water. You want the custards to be very firm around the edges and barely move toward the center when gently shaken.

▸ Remove the ramekins from the hot water and let cool in a cool area of the kitchen before serving, or chill to serve cold.

STORING

▸ The pots de crème can be wrapped individually in plastic wrap and stored in the refrigerator for up to 3 days.

TIP: USE THE LEFTOVER EGG WHITES TO make Meringues (page 208).

Tiramisu Trifle

Tiramisu is a layered Italian dessert made of sweetened mascarpone, espresso, and ladyfingers. This version is a bit grander—it's constructed with chiffon cake and incorporates more layers than a traditional tiramisu, making it a perfect centerpiece dessert. Use a 9-inch trifle bowl or a deep glass bowl for maximum effect. If you don't want to make the chiffon cake, the recipe works equally well with store-bought ladyfingers.

● SERVES 10 TO 14 ●

2 cups (16 ounces) mascarpone

3/4 cup (3 ounces) confectioners' sugar, sifted

2 teaspoons vanilla bean paste (see Resources, page 335)

2 tablespoons brandy

2 1/4 cups (18 ounces) heavy cream

3 tablespoons (1.5 ounces) granulated sugar

1 teaspoon instant coffee granules or espresso powder

1 1/2 to 2 cups (12 to 16 ounces) chilled espresso or strong coffee (to taste)

Chiffon Cake (page 31) or 26 store-bought ladyfingers (see Resources, page 335)

2 tablespoons cocoa nibs (see Resources, page 335)

2.5 ounces 72% bittersweet chocolate, chopped

2 tablespoons atomized 69% bittersweet chocolate (see Resources, page 335)

▸ In the bowl of a stand mixer fitted with the paddle attachment (or in a large bowl, using a handheld mixer), beat the mascarpone, confectioners' sugar, vanilla paste, and brandy until the mascarpone softens and the ingredients are just combined, about 1 minute. If using a stand mixer, transfer the mascarpone to a medium bowl and wash and dry the mixer bowl.

▸ Using the whisk attachment (or clean beaters and another large bowl), whip 1 cup of the heavy cream until soft peaks form. Gently fold the whipped cream into the mascarpone mixture; set aside.

▸ Put the remaining 1 1/4 cups heavy cream, the granulated sugar, and the instant coffee into the mixer bowl (or large bowl)—no need to wash the bowl or whisk/beaters—and whip until the coffee crystals have dissolved and soft peaks form. Leave the whipped coffee cream in the bowl.

▸ Pour the chilled espresso into a shallow bowl.

▸ *If using the chiffon cake,* with a long serrated knife, carefully trim the sides of the cake to remove the golden exterior. Then slice the cake horizontally in half. Put one half of the cake in the bottom of a 9-inch trifle bowl or deep glass bowl, cut side up. Using a pastry brush, generously paint the surface of the cake with half of the chilled espresso until the espresso is absorbed by the cake. (I find 1 1/2 cups of espresso is the perfect amount for this recipe, but if you prefer a very strong espresso flavor, use up to 1/2 cup more.)

▸ *Or, if using ladyfingers,* immerse a ladyfinger in the espresso and then quickly move it to the bottom of the trifle bowl. Continue with 12 more ladyfingers, laying them close together so the bottom of the bowl is covered.

▸ Scoop the mascarpone on top of the cake/ladyfinger layer and spread it evenly, using an offset spatula. Sprinkle the cocoa nibs and chopped chocolate evenly over the mascarpone. Lay the second layer of cake on top of the chocolate and press down with both hands to slightly compress the layers. Or repeat the instructions above to add a second layer of ladyfingers. Using a pastry brush, generously paint the surface of the cake/ladyfingers with the remaining chilled espresso until the espresso is absorbed by the cake.

▸ Using an offset spatula, spread the coffee whipped cream evenly over the top of the tiramisu. Sift the atomized chocolate over the coffee whipped cream, covering the entire surface.

▸ Cover and refrigerate for at least 4 hours before serving.

STORING

▸ The trifle can be refrigerated for up to 2 days.

Salted Caramel Pudding Parfaits

At some point in the last decade, the marriage of caramel and salt became a perennial one on dessert menus. What took us so long? Here is a luscious representation. Serve it in parfait glasses or a clear serving dish so the layers are visible.

● SERVES 6 ●

1½ cups (12 ounces) heavy cream

3 tablespoons cornstarch

1 teaspoon vanilla bean paste (see Resources, page 335)

1 cup plus 1 tablespoon (7.5 ounces) sugar

3 cups (24 ounces) whole milk, at room temperature

½ cup (5 ounces) Caramel Sauce (recipe follows)

1½ teaspoons fleur de sel

› Whisk together ½ cup of the heavy cream, the cornstarch, and vanilla paste in a small bowl. Set aside.

› Put 1 cup of the sugar into a medium copper or heavy stainless steel saucepan and set over medium heat. As the sugar heats, you will see it start to melt around the edges and then turn golden in color, in 2 to 3 minutes. Using a wooden spoon or heatproof silicone spatula, nudge the sugar slightly on one side. You will see liquid caramel slowly move out from underneath the granular sugar. Very slowly start to move the sugar into the liquid caramel. Do not rush this process—if the caramel starts to look grainy, you are incorporating the sugar too quickly. If the caramel starts to smoke or get very dark, remove the pan from the heat until the smoking subsides or lower the heat.

› When the sugar has completely melted and is dark amber in color, turn off the heat and pour in the milk—it will bubble up. When the bubbles settle down, turn the heat on to low and whisk the milk and caramel together, then cook, whisking, to dissolve any hardened bits of caramel.

› Whisk the cornstarch mixture into the caramel and continue cooking, stirring, until the pudding thickens and coats the back of the spoon, 2 to 3 minutes. Remove from the heat.

› Pour the pudding through a fine-mesh sieve into a medium bowl. Cover the surface of the pudding with plastic wrap so the pudding doesn't form a skin and refrigerate until cold, about 2 hours. (The pudding can be refrigerated, covered, for up to 2 days.)

TO ASSEMBLE THE PARFAITS

› In the bowl of a stand mixer fitted with the whisk attachment (or in a large bowl, using a handheld mixer), whip the remaining 1 cup cream with the remaining 1 tablespoon sugar until firm peaks form.

› Spoon 1 to 2 teaspoons of caramel sauce into the bottom of each parfait glass. Scoop about ½ cup of pudding into the glass, drizzle with another 1 to 2 teaspoons caramel sauce, and top with a large dollop of whipped cream. Drizzle a little more caramel sauce over the whipped cream, finish with a sprinkling of fleur de sel, and serve immediately.

Continued ›

Caramel Sauce

MAKES ABOUT 1 CUP

1¹/₃ cups (9.25 ounces) sugar

³/₄ cup (6 ounces) heavy cream

¹/₄ cup (2.75 ounces) light corn syrup

4 tablespoons (¹/₂ stick/2 ounces) unsalted butter, cubed and chilled

¹/₂ teaspoon kosher salt

▸ Put the sugar into a medium copper or heavy stainless steel saucepan and set over medium heat. Pour the cream and corn syrup into a small saucepan and set over medium-low heat.

▸ As the sugar heats, you will see it start to melt around the edges and then turn golden in color, in 2 to 3 minutes. Using a wooden spoon or heatproof silicone spatula, nudge the sugar slightly on one side. You will see liquid caramel slowly move out from underneath the granular sugar. Very slowly start to move the sugar into the liquid caramel. Do not rush this process—if the caramel starts to look grainy, you are incorporating the sugar too quickly. If the caramel starts to smoke or get very dark, re-move the pan from the heat until the smoking subsides or lower the heat.

▸ Meanwhile, watch the cream: You want it to come to a boil when the sugar reaches the liquid caramel stage, so adjust the timing accordingly by raising or lowering the heat under the cream (if the cream comes to a boil too early, just remove it from the heat).

▸ When the sugar has completely melted and is dark amber in color, remove from the heat and pour in the cream—it will bubble substantially. When the caramel has settled down, stir the ingredients together until smooth. Add the butter and salt and stir until smooth, about 30 seconds.

▸ Pour the hot caramel into a heatproof jar or container and let cool completely.

▸ The caramel sauce can be stored, covered, in the refrigerator for up to 4 weeks. Bring to room temperature or reheat gently before serving.

TIP: TRY THIS SAUCE DRIZZLED OVER A slice of Vanilla Bean Cake (page 75) or with your favorite ice cream.

Angelino Plum Ice Cream

The crème fraîche and buttermilk in this recipe provide an exceptional backdrop for the flavor of fall plums. Serve with Tangy Whipped Cream (page 139).

● MAKES JUST OVER 1 QUART ●

³/₄ cup (6 ounces) crème fraîche

³/₄ cup (6 ounces) heavy cream

³/₄ cup (5.25 ounces) sugar

4 medium egg yolks

1¹/₂ cups (12 ounces) buttermilk

2 cups (16¹/₂ ounces) Angelino Plum Jam
    (page 293)

› Combine the crème fraîche, heavy cream, and ¹/₂ cup of the sugar in a medium saucepan over medium heat and bring to a boil, stirring to dissolve the sugar.

› Meanwhile, whisk together the egg yolks and the remaining ¹/₄ cup sugar in a small bowl.

› When the cream boils, reduce the heat and then slowly stream approximately ¹/₂ cup of the hot cream into the egg yolks, whisking constantly. Pour the egg yolks into the saucepan, stirring constantly, and cook, stirring, until the mixture thickens enough to coat the back of the spoon, about 3 minutes. Pour the mixture into a 1-quart container and let cool, then chill completely, about 3 hours.

› Stir the buttermilk into the chilled ice cream base. Pour into an ice cream maker and freeze according to the manufacturer's directions.

› When the ice cream is almost ready, with the machine running, pour in the jam. When the ice cream is a uniform color and thick, it is ready.

› Serve immediately, or transfer to a covered plastic or paper container (see Resources, page 335) and freeze.

STORING

› The ice cream can be frozen for up to 2 months.

Blenheim Apricot Ice Cream

There are so many ways to serve this ice cream. For example, spoon freshly whipped cream (see pages 138–39) and more apricot jam over a generous serving to create a summertime sundae, or blend 2 cups of the ice cream with 1½ cups whole milk for an inspired milk shake.

●━━━ **MAKES 1 QUART** ━━━●

2 cups (16 ounces) heavy cream

1 cup (8 ounces) whole milk

½ cup (3.5 ounces) sugar

4 large egg yolks

1½ cups (12.5 ounces) Blenheim Apricot Jam (page 285)

▸ Combine the heavy cream, milk, and ¼ cup of the sugar in a medium saucepan over medium heat and bring to a boil, stirring to dissolve the sugar.

▸ Meanwhile, whisk together the egg yolks and the remaining ¼ cup sugar in a small bowl.

▸ When the cream boils, reduce the heat and then slowly stream approximately ½ cup of the hot cream into the egg yolks, whisking constantly. Pour the egg yolks into the saucepan, stirring constantly, and cook, stirring, until the mixture thickens enough to coat the back of the spoon, about 4 minutes. Pour the mixture into a 1-quart container and let cool, then chill completely, about 3 hours.

▸ Pour the ice cream base into an ice cream maker and freeze according to the manufacturer's directions.

▸ When the ice cream is almost ready, with the machine running, pour in the jam. When the ice cream is a uniform color and thick, it is ready.

▸ Serve immediately, or transfer to a covered plastic or paper container (see Resources, page 335) and freeze.

STORING

▸ The ice cream can be frozen for up to 2 months.

A VARIETY OF FLAVORS FROM YOUR PANTRY

ALTHOUGH THE TERM IS A CLICHÉ, I can't deny that the two ice cream recipes in this chapter use "mix-ins." The apricot recipe has a sweet base and the plum recipe has a tart base; see below for ways to customize either one. The options are infinite.

To make a sweet ice cream, start with the recipe on page 237. Omit the apricot jam and replace with the same amount of one of the following ingredients:

› STRAWBERRY–VANILLA BEAN JAM (page 276)

› BLACK-AND-BLUE JAM (page 282)

› APRICOT AND RAINIER CHERRY JAM (page 286)

› PEACH MELBA JAM (page 288)

› WHITE FIG, FUJI APPLE, AND VANILLA BEAN JAM (page 294)

› BLACK MISSION FIG, PEAR, AND PORT JAM (page 297)

› BLOOD ORANGE MARMALADE (page 302)

To make a tart ice cream, start with the recipe on page 235. Omit the plum jam and replace with the same amount of one of the following ingredients:

› STRAWBERRY RHUBARB JAM (page 278)

› BLUSHING BERRY JAM (page 281)

› WHITE NECTARINE AND LEMON VERBENA JAM (page 287)

› MANGO JAM (page 292)

› KUMQUAT MARMALADE (page 298)

Cocktail-Grapefruit and Champagne Sorbet

Cocktail grapefruits are the sweetest, juiciest grapefruits I have ever tasted. They are a hybrid citrus that is a combination of the mandarin orange and the pomelo. This sorbet is wonderfully refreshing on a hot day and, unlike most homemade sorbets, the texture is so yielding that you can enjoy it straight from the freezer.

● MAKES 1 QUART ●

2 cups (16 ounces) Cocktail-grapefruit juice (from about 6 grapefruits)

1 cup (7 ounces) sugar

³/₄ cup (6 ounces) Champagne

¹/₄ cup (2 ounces) cold water

2 tablespoons fresh lemon juice

1 tablespoon Campari

TIP: IF COCKTAIL GRAPEFRUITS ARE NOT available, use a mixture of equal parts pink grapefruit juice and mandarin or orange juice.

› Combine 1 cup of the grapefruit juice and the sugar in a small saucepan and heat over medium heat, stirring constantly, until the sugar is completely dissolved. Pour the mixture into a bowl or other container, add the remaining ingredients, and stir to combine. Refrigerate for 1 to 2 hours, until cold.

› Pour the chilled sorbet base into an ice cream maker and freeze according to the manufacturer's instructions.

› Serve immediately, or transfer to a covered plastic or paper container (see Resources, page 335) and freeze.

STORING

› The sorbet can be frozen for up to 3 weeks.

Cucumber, Lime, and Mint Sorbet

These three flavors complement one another equally well in a salad, in a Vietnamese sandwich, and in this sorbet. It might sound crazy, but it tastes great.

1¼ cups (8.75 ounces) sugar

1¼ cups (10 ounces) water

1 cup (1 ounce) mint leaves

4 to 6 Persian cucumbers (18 ounces) (see Tip)

⅓ cup (2.66 ounces) fresh lime juice (from 3 to 4 limes)

TIP: PERSIAN CUCUMBERS HAVE AN EDIBLE skin, small seeds, and a more mellow flavor than standard cucumbers. If they are unavailable, use 18 ounces standard cucumbers (about 3), peeled, halved lengthwise, seeded, and sliced.

› Combine the sugar and water in a medium saucepan and bring to a boil over medium heat, stirring to dissolve the sugar. Remove from the heat, add the mint, and muddle (mash) with a wooden spoon or silicone spatula to release the mint flavor into the sugar syrup. Cover the pan with aluminum foil, poke a few holes in the top to release steam, and let the syrup steep for 20 minutes.

› Peel the cucumbers and slice into disks approximately ½ inch thick. Put the cucumbers into a food processor or blender and puree for 2 minutes, or until very smooth.

› Pour the lime juice into a medium bowl or other container. Strain the mint syrup, add the pureed cucumber and syrup to the lime juice, and stir until thoroughly combined. Chill the sorbet mixture for 1 to 2 hours or until cold.

› Pour the chilled sorbet base into an ice cream maker and freeze according to the manufacturer's instructions.

› Serve immediately, or transfer to a covered plastic or paper container (see Resources, page 335) and freeze. Remove the sorbet from the freezer about 10 minutes before serving.

STORING

› The sorbet can be frozen for up to 3 weeks.

JAR

COOKIES AND BARS

suspect many baking careers begin with cookies. They are simpler to make than most items in the dessert repertoire and require little, if any, special equipment. I had my first baking experience with my mother when I was eight years old. She decided we should make Christmas cookies and give them to people as gifts. It struck me as strange that we were making gifts instead of buying something from the store. When I asked her why, she said, simply, "Because it's nice." I loved cookie baking immensely and by the age of nine, I had truly mastered the chocolate chip cookie and made a batch every Wednesday afternoon. Then on Thursdays, I'd take a Ziploc bag filled with my handmade treats to school and share with my friends. It's amazing how small lessons from childhood can inform our lives. By the time I was eighteen, I was creating holiday gift bags for friends filled with an assortment of cookies and confections; I suppose in a way it was the unofficial launch of Valerie Confections. Cookies are a major part of my story, both personally and professionally; I still find a day incomplete if it passes without a cookie.

From inspiration to execution, cookies provide near-instant gratification. There are three basic types of cookies in this chapter: scooped, rolled, and bar. I believe a simple cookie is the best kind. A rolled cookie covered in piped royal icing with intricate décor may have strong visual impact, but I promise you an oatmeal raisin cookie tastes infinitely better.

But simple in creation doesn't translate to basic or boring in execution. Cookies are excellent templates for innovative ingredients; for example, see page 263 for a number of ideas on how to flavor classic shortbread. The smallest inclusion of tea, spice, or citrus zest in a cookie batter results in memorable flavors and colors.

Once you find comfort in cookie making, do consider giving them as gifts. In a world where so much of our lives is conducted online—shopping, reading, even our personal communication—it's extremely comforting to receive a handmade gift. There is no comparison between a lovely box of homemade cookies and a mundane gift card. And homemade cookies are far less expensive. A batch of Classic Shortbread (page 263), for example, will cost about $3.50 to make. Add the box and a ribbon, for a grand total of $6. Of course, the added bonus of gifting cookies is keeping a few for yourself.

Durango Cookies

Sometimes you hit on a recipe that just resonates with people, and this is one of them. The combination of smoked salt, roasted almonds, and milk chocolate in these cookies is impossible to resist. I have watched customers buy one Durango, only to return five minutes later and ask for a whole box. Make a double batch—it won't go to waste.

● MAKES 30 LARGE COOKIES ●

2 cups plus 3 tablespoons (11 ounces) all-purpose flour

1 teaspoon kosher salt

1 teaspoon baking soda

2 sticks plus 2 tablespoons (9 ounces) unsalted butter, softened

1³/₄ cups (10.5 ounces) light brown sugar

³/₄ cup (5.25 ounces) granulated sugar

2 large eggs

1 teaspoon vanilla extract

3 cups (1 pound) large milk chocolate chips

1 cup (4.4 ounces) roasted almonds, roughly chopped

¹/₂ cup (2 ounces) cocoa nibs (see Resources, page 335)

Durango smoked salt for sprinkling (see Resources, page 335)

▸ Sift together the flour, salt, and baking soda into a medium bowl. Set aside.

▸ In the bowl of a stand mixer fitted with the paddle attachment (or in a large bowl, using a handheld mixer), cream the butter and both sugars on medium speed until light and fluffy, about 4 minutes.

▸ Using a fork or small whisk, beat the eggs and vanilla together in a small bowl. With the mixer on medium speed, alternately add the dry ingredients and eggs and continue beating until the batter is smooth. Scrape the bottom and sides of the bowl and beat for an additional minute. Add the chocolate chips 1 cup at a time, mixing for 30 seconds after each addition. Add the almonds and cocoa nibs and beat until combined, 30 to 45 seconds. Transfer the batter to a large bowl (if it's not already in a mixing bowl), cover with plastic wrap or parchment paper, and chill for 1 hour.

▸ Position the racks in the upper and lower thirds of the oven and heat the oven to 350°F. Line two large heavy baking sheets with parchment paper or silicone liners.

▸ Using a 2¹/₂-inch ice cream scoop (or a ¹/₃-cup measure), scoop the dough onto the lined baking sheets, spacing the cookies 3 inches apart (the cookies will spread considerably while baking). Sprinkle each ball with Durango salt. Bake for 15 minutes, or until slightly golden on the edges. Let the cookies cool on the baking sheets on cooling racks for 10 minutes.

▸ Using an offset spatula, transfer the cookies to a cooling rack to cool completely.

STORING

▸ The cookies can be stored in an airtight container for up to 4 days or transferred to Ziploc freezer bags and frozen for up to 2 months.

Gingersnap Cookies

I make gingersnaps year-round, not just during the holidays. I love
the chewiness of these cookies, and because of their yielding
texture, they are especially good for ice cream sandwiches.

● MAKES 24 COOKIES ●

2 cups (14 ounces) granulated sugar

1 cup (6 ounces) light brown sugar

3¹/₂ cups (17.5 ounces) all-purpose flour

1 tablespoon baking soda

1¹/₂ teaspoons kosher salt

2 teaspoons ground ginger

2 teaspoons ground cinnamon

2 tablespoons finely chopped candied ginger
  (see Resources, page 335)

3 sticks (12 ounces) unsalted butter, softened

2 large eggs

¹/₂ cup (5.5 ounces) unsulphured molasses

› Position the racks in the upper and lower thirds of the oven and heat the oven to 350°F. Line two large heavy baking sheets with parchment paper or silicone liners.

› In a small bowl, mix together ¹/₂ cup each of the granulated and brown sugars. Set aside.

› Sift together the flour, baking soda, salt, ground ginger, and cinnamon into a medium bowl. Mix in the candied ginger.

› In the bowl of a stand mixer fitted with the paddle attachment (or in a large bowl, using a handheld mixer), combine the butter, the remaining 1¹/₂ cups granulated sugar, and the remaining ¹/₂ cup brown sugar, and beat on medium speed until light and fluffy, about 4 minutes. Add the eggs one at a time, beating well after each addition, then add the molasses, beating until no streaks remain. Add the flour mixture 1 cup at a time, beating just until the batter is smooth.

› Using a 2¹/₂-inch ice cream scoop (or a ¹/₃-cup measure), scoop the dough onto the lined baking sheets, spacing the cookies 3 inches apart. Sprinkle the cookies with the sugar mixture. Bake for 15 minutes, or until the surface is cracked and flat. Let the cookies cool on the baking sheets on cooling racks for 10 minutes.

› Using an offset spatula, transfer the cookies to a cooling rack to cool completely.

STORING

› The cookies can be stored in an airtight container for up to 4 days or transferred to Ziploc freezer bags and frozen for up to 2 months.

VARIATION

CHOCOLATE GINGERSNAPS: For an indulgent variation, add 1 cup (5¹/₂ ounces) 61% bittersweet chocolate chips (see Resources, page 335) after the dry ingredients are incorporated.

Matcha White Chocolate Macadamia Cookies

Matcha, powdered green tea, was originally used in Japanese tea ceremonies. There are many grades of matcha. The finest is made with young leaves and is extravagantly priced. Use a baking-grade or ingredient-grade matcha for this recipe; "cooking" matcha comes from older leaves, and the stronger flavor complements the other ingredients in the recipe.

● MAKES 24 COOKIES ●

1³/₄ cups plus 2 tablespoons (9 ounces) all-purpose flour

1 teaspoon kosher salt

1 teaspoon baking soda

1 tablespoon plus 1 teaspoon matcha tea (see Resources, page 335)

2 sticks plus 2 tablespoons (9 ounces) unsalted butter, softened

1 cup (6 ounces) light brown sugar

²/₃ cup (4.65 ounces) granulated sugar

2 large eggs

1 teaspoon vanilla bean paste (see Resources, page 335)

2 cups (11 ounces) 31% white chocolate chips (see Resources, page 335)

1 cup (4.25 ounces) roasted macadamia nuts

▸ Sift together the flour, salt, baking soda, and matcha into a medium bowl. Set aside.

▸ In the bowl of a stand mixer fitted with the paddle attachment (or in a large bowl, using a handheld mixer), cream the butter and both sugars on medium speed until light and fluffy, about 4 minutes.

▸ Using a fork or small whisk, beat the eggs and vanilla paste together in a small bowl. With the mixer on medium speed, alternately add the dry ingredients and the eggs in batches and continue beating until the batter is smooth. Add the white chocolate chips 1 cup at a time, mixing for 30 seconds after each addition. Add the macadamia nuts and mix until combined. Transfer the dough to a large bowl (if it's not already in a mixing bowl), cover with plastic wrap or parchment paper, and chill for 1 hour.

▸ Position the racks in the upper and lower thirds of the oven and heat the oven to 350°F. Line two large heavy baking sheets with parchment paper or silicone liners.

▸ Using a 2¹/₂-inch ice cream scoop (or a ¹/₃-cup measure), scoop the dough onto the lined baking sheets, spacing the cookies 3 inches apart (the cookies will spread considerably while baking). Bake for 15 minutes, or until slightly golden on the edges. Let the cookies cool on the baking sheets on cooling racks for 10 minutes.

▸ Using an offset spatula, transfer the cookies to a cooling rack to cool completely.

STORING

▸ The cookies can be stored in an airtight container for up to 4 days or transferred to Ziploc freezer bags and frozen for up to 2 months.

TURN A COOKIE INTO A SANDWICH

DO SANDWICH COOKIES OFFER DOUBLE THE ENJOYMENT? As a child, I viewed sandwich cookies as a special treat—they were bigger and better than single cookies, because you could disassemble them and have two cookies to nibble. As an adult, I like the interesting flavor combinations sandwich cookies offer and the textural complexity of a soft filling hugged by two crunchy cookies. Try a few of these delicious combinations. You'll need a half recipe of the ganache or buttercream of your choosing for one full recipe of cookies. Cool the cookies completely, then use 1 to 2 tablespoons of room-temperature filling to sandwich them together. Store at room temperature in an airtight container for up to 4 days.

‣ Durango Cookies (page 247) with Single-Malt-Scotch Truffles ganache (page 198)

‣ Matcha White Chocolate Macadamia Cookies (opposite) with Lemon Ganache (page 96) or Lemon Verbena Ganache (page 101)

‣ Sugar Cookies (page 257) with Cassis Ganache (page 113)

‣ Oatmeal Raisin Cookies (page 253) with Ginger Ganache (page 105)

‣ Coconut–Finger Lime Cookies (page 259) with Passion Fruit Buttercream Filling (page 55)

‣ Gingersnap Cookies (page 248) with Lemon Ganache (page 96)

Oatmeal Raisin Cookies

Oatmeal cookies have two distinct styles: One is chunky, almost like a soft granola bar, with tons of nuts and fruits. The other is like this one, buttery and chewy, with crisp edges. If you prefer the first style, add 1 cup of nuts and an additional ½ cup raisins to the recipe.

● MAKES 24 COOKIES ●

1½ cups (7.5 ounces) all-purpose flour

1 teaspoon baking soda

1 teaspoon kosher salt

1 teaspoon ground cinnamon

2 sticks plus 2 tablespoons (9 ounces) unsalted butter, softened

1½ cups (9 ounces) light brown sugar

½ cup plus 2 tablespoons (4.375 ounces) granulated sugar

2 large eggs

1 teaspoon vanilla bean paste (see Resources, page 335)

2 cups (6.5 ounces) quick-cooking oats

1 cup (6 ounces) raisins

> Position the racks in the upper and lower thirds of the oven and heat the oven to 350°F. Line two large heavy baking sheets with parchment paper or silicone liners.

> Sift together the flour, baking soda, salt, and cinnamon into a medium bowl. Set aside.

> In the bowl of a stand mixer fitted with the paddle attachment (or in a large bowl, using a handheld mixer), cream the butter and both sugars on medium speed until light and fluffy, about 4 minutes. Add the eggs one at a time, mixing well after each addition. Add the vanilla paste and mix for 30 seconds. Add the flour mixture, mixing until fully combined. Add the oats 1 cup at a time, mixing for about 30 seconds after each addition. Fold in the raisins.

> Using a 2½-inch ice cream scoop (or a ⅓-cup measure), scoop the dough onto the lined baking sheets, spacing the cookies 3 inches apart (the cookies will spread considerably while baking). Bake for 15 minutes, or until slightly golden on the edges. Let the cookies cool on the baking sheets on cooling racks for 10 minutes.

> Using an offset spatula, transfer the cookies to a cooling rack to cool completely.

STORING

> The cookies can be stored in an airtight container for up to 4 days or transferred to Ziploc freezer bags and frozen for up to 2 months.

TIP: REPLACE THE RAISINS WITH A different dried fruit, such as chopped dried apricots, pears, or peaches.

Snowballs
(Mexican Wedding Cookies)

When I think of Christmas cookies, this is the first cookie that comes to mind. I started gifting these in my late teens and I still receive requests from old friends eager for a delivery of snowballs near December 25. This recipe also works well with pecans, walnuts, or hazelnuts, if you prefer those flavors.

● MAKES 36 COOKIES ●

2 sticks (8 ounces) unsalted butter, softened

2¼ cups (10.13 ounces) confectioners' sugar

2 teaspoons vanilla bean paste (see Resources, page 335)

2 cups (10 ounces) all-purpose flour

1 cup (4.4 ounces) roasted almonds, finely chopped

› In the bowl of a stand mixer fitted with the paddle attachment (or in a large bowl, using a handheld mixer), cream the butter on medium speed until light and fluffy, about 3 minutes. Add ¾ cup of the confectioners' sugar and the vanilla paste and mix until combined. Add the flour ½ cup at a time, mixing until thoroughly combined. Fold in the almonds.

› Turn the dough out onto a cool surface and divide it into 3 portions. Form each one into a disk. Wrap individually in plastic wrap or wax paper and chill for 1 hour.

› Position the racks in the upper and lower thirds of the oven and heat the oven to 350°F. Line two large heavy baking sheets with parchment paper or silicone liners.

› To form the cookies, break off a piece of chilled dough approximately the size of a measuring tablespoon, roll the dough between your palms into a ball, and place on the lined baking sheets, leaving 1 inch between the cookies. Bake for 17 to 20 minutes, until the bottom of the cookies is slightly golden—lift one of the cookies with an offset spatula and check to be sure. Let the cookies cool on the baking sheets on cooling racks for 5 minutes.

› Put the remaining 1½ cups confectioners' sugar in a small bowl. Drop one warm cookie at a time into the confectioners' sugar and roll until it's completely covered in sugar, then shake off any excess and put on a cooling rack. Let cool completely.

STORING

› The cookies can be stored in an airtight container for up to 5 days.

Sugar Cookies

When our son, August, was three years old, we started hosting an annual Christmas cookie party for him and his friends. I make an enormous batch of sugar cookie dough, set it in the middle of our kitchen worktable along with bowls of sprinkles and other cookie décor, and let the kids have at it. I suppose these parties are more arts and crafts than baking, but the cookies taste substantially better than Play-Doh!

● MAKES 50 COOKIES ●

2 cups (10 ounces) all-purpose flour

1/2 teaspoon baking powder

1/4 teaspoon kosher salt

12 tablespoons (1 1/2 sticks/6 ounces) unsalted butter, softened

1 1/4 cups (8.75 ounces) sugar, plus sugar for sprinkling

1 large egg

1 teaspoon vanilla bean paste (see Resources, page 335)

> Sift together the flour, baking powder, and salt into a medium bowl. Set aside.

> In the bowl of a stand mixer fitted with the paddle attachment (or in a large bowl, using a handheld mixer), cream the butter and sugar on medium speed until light and fluffy, about 4 minutes. Add the egg and vanilla paste and mix until fully combined. Add the dry ingredients 1 cup at a time, mixing thoroughly after each addition.

> Turn the dough out onto a cool surface and divide it into 3 portions. Form each one into a disk. Wrap individually in plastic wrap or wax paper and chill for 1 hour.

> Position the racks in the upper and lower thirds of the oven and heat the oven to 350°F. Line two large heavy baking sheets with parchment paper or silicone liners.

> To form the cookies, break off a 2-tablespoon-sized piece of chilled dough, roll the dough between your palms into a ball, and place on the lined baking sheets, spacing the cookies about 2 inches apart. With a small offset spatula, flatten each cookie to about 1/2 inch thick. Sprinkle the cookies with sugar.

> Bake for 15 minutes, or until the edges of the cookies are golden brown. Let the cookies cool on the baking sheets on cooling racks for 10 minutes.

> Using an offset spatula, transfer the cookies to a cooling rack to cool completely.

STORING

> The cookies can be stored in an airtight container for up to 5 days or transferred to Ziploc freezer bags and frozen for up to 2 months.

TIP: KEEP COOKIE DECORATING WITH kids simple. Sprinkles, nuts, dried fruits, and chocolate chips are all fun and easy toppers for sugar cookies; omit the sugar for sprinkling. To frost the cookies, leave them plain and use Chocolate Buttercream (page 81) or White Chocolate Buttercream Frosting (page 55).

Chocolate Cookies

Some people might call this a brownie in a cookie, because it tastes as chocolaty as a fudgy brownie. Follow the directions closely— the cookies are exceptionally delicate when warm and will break if you try to move them too soon after baking.

● MAKES 50 COOKIES ●

1 cup (5 ounces) all-purpose flour

$1/3$ cup (1.3 ounces) unsweetened cocoa powder

$1/4$ teaspoon baking powder

$1^{1}/_{2}$ teaspoons kosher salt

2 sticks (8 ounces) unsalted butter, softened

$1^{1}/_{2}$ cups (10.5 ounces) sugar

1 large egg

1 tablespoon whole milk

1 teaspoon vanilla extract

$1^{1}/_{2}$ cups (8.25 ounces) 61% bittersweet chocolate chips (see Resources, page 335), finely chopped, or finely chopped 61% bittersweet chocolate

> Sift together the flour, cocoa powder, baking powder, and salt into a medium bowl. Set aside.

> In the bowl of a stand mixer fitted with the paddle attachment (or in a large bowl, using a handheld mixer), cream the butter and sugar on medium speed until light and fluffy, about 4 minutes. Add the egg, mixing well. Add the dry ingredients and continue beating until the batter is smooth. Add the milk and vanilla, then add the chocolate chips, beating until combined.

> Turn the dough out onto a cool surface, form it into a disk, and wrap in plastic wrap. Refrigerate until firm, approximately 2 hours.

> Position the racks in the upper and lower thirds of the oven and heat the oven to 350°F. Line two large heavy baking sheets with parchment paper or silicone liners.

> Using a 1-ounce scoop, scoop the dough onto the lined baking sheets, spacing the cookies 2 inches apart; or use a measuring spoon to scoop heaping tablespoons of dough onto the sheets. Let the dough come to room temperature.

> Bake the cookies for 11 minutes, or until they lose their shine. Let cool on the baking sheets on cooling racks for 10 minutes.

> Using an offset spatula, transfer the cookies to a cooling rack to cool completely.

STORING

> The cookies can be stored in an airtight container for up to 4 days (these cookies are quite fragile and do not freeze well).

Coconut–Finger Lime Cookies

The pairing of coconut and lime, tasting vaguely tropical, is a fantastic flavor combination. Finger limes are originally from Australia and have more acidity and less bitterness than a traditional lime—flavor notes that make this cookie doubly exciting. If you are unable to get finger limes, substitute four Yuzu or Key limes.

● **MAKES 50 COOKIES** ●

1¹/₂ cups (5.62 ounces) sweetened shredded coconut

8 finger limes (see Resources, page 335)

3 sticks (12 ounces) unsalted butter, softened

1 cup (7 ounces) sugar

1¹/₂ teaspoons kosher salt

1 teaspoon vanilla bean paste (see Resources, page 335)

2²/₃ cups (13.3 ounces) all-purpose flour

› Heat the oven to 300°F.

› Spread the coconut evenly on a baking sheet and toast until golden, about 8 minutes. Set aside to cool.

› Zest the finger limes and put the zest in a small bowl. Cut the limes in half with a sharp knife and squeeze the pulp into the bowl. (If using Yuzu or Key limes, juice them and add the juice to the zest.)

› In the bowl of a stand mixer fitted with the paddle attachment (or in a large bowl, using a handheld mixer), cream the butter and sugar on medium speed until light and fluffy, about 4 minutes. Add the salt and vanilla paste and mix for 30 seconds. Add the flour in three additions, mixing well after each addition. Add the toasted coconut and mix thoroughly. Add the lime zest and pulp and beat for 1 minute. Scrape down the sides and bottom of the bowl and mix for 1 minute.

› Turn the dough out onto a cool surface and divide it into quarters. Roll each piece into a log measuring about 1¹/₂ inches thick and 6 to 7 inches long. Wrap the logs in plastic wrap or parchment paper and refrigerate for 2 hours.

› Position the racks in the upper and lower thirds of the oven and heat the oven to 325°F. Line two large heavy baking sheets with parchment paper or silicone liners.

› Slice the logs into rounds about ¹/₂ inch thick and place on the lined baking sheets, spacing them 2 inches apart. Bake the cookies for 10 minutes, then rotate the pans and bake for 8 minutes, or until golden on the edges. Let the cookies cool on the baking sheets on cooling racks for 10 minutes.

› Using an offset spatula, transfer the cookies to a cooling rack to cool completely.

STORING

› The cookies can be stored in an airtight container for up to a week or transferred to Ziploc freezer bags and frozen for up to 2 months.

FREEZING COOKIE DOUGH

***

AS A MOTHER OF TWO YOUNG CHILDREN, I find my time is frequently interrupted. Just when I think I'll have a full hour in the kitchen, my plans are dashed and I am forced to improvise. Those constant disruptions have taught me to find ways to make the most out of those random ten or fifteen minutes. Freezing cookie doughs is one of my favorite shortcuts. Follow these guidelines for preserving cookie doughs to use when you know you'll be suffering from a time deficit later.

> **SCOOPED COOKIES:** Scoop the cookies onto the lined baking sheets as directed, but instead of baking them, freeze, uncovered, for 1 hour, or until firm, then transfer to a Ziploc freezer bag and freeze for up to 2 months. When you are ready to bake the cookies, place the frozen cookies on lined baking sheets and let sit at room temperature for 30 to 40 minutes before baking; the dough should be cold but not rock hard.

> **CHILLED LOGS:** After wrapping the dough logs in plastic wrap, freeze them for up to

2 months. Transfer the logs from the freezer to the refrigerator about 3 hours before you plan to bake.

> **BAR COOKIES:** After spreading the dough in the baking sheet, lay a sheet of parchment paper over the dough and then wrap the entire pan in plastic wrap. Freeze for up to 2 months. When you are ready to bake the bars, remove the pan of dough from the freezer and let sit at room temperature for 30 to 40 minutes before baking; the dough should be cold but not rock hard.

Classic Shortbread

I always marvel at how the combination of just four basic ingredients can be so completely satisfying. Although this basic shortbread recipe is probably my favorite, it is also fun to use the shortbread as a template for fruits, herbs, and other flavors. See the variations suggested below, or try your hand at creating your own.

● MAKES 48 COOKIES ●

2 sticks (8 ounces) unsalted butter, softened
½ cup (2.25 ounces) confectioners' sugar
1 teaspoon kosher salt
2 cups (10 ounces) all-purpose flour

› In the bowl of a stand mixer fitted with the paddle attachment (or in a large bowl, using a handheld mixer), cream the butter on medium speed until light and fluffy, about 3 minutes. Add the confectioners' sugar and beat until thoroughly incorporated.

› Stir the salt into the flour and add to the butter mixture ½ cup at a time, mixing thoroughly after each addition.

› Turn the dough out onto a cool surface and divide it into quarters. Roll each piece into a log measuring about 1 inch thick and 6 inches long. Wrap the logs in plastic wrap or parchment paper and refrigerate until firm, about 1 hour.

› Position the racks in the upper and lower thirds of the oven and heat the oven to 325°F.

› Slice the logs into rounds approximately ½ inch thick and place them on an ungreased large heavy baking sheet, spacing them about 1½ inches apart. Bake for 10 to 12 minutes, until the edges are slightly golden. Let the cookies cool on the baking sheets on cooling racks for 10 minutes.

› Using an offset spatula, transfer the cookies to a cooling rack to cool completely.

STORING

› The cookies can be stored in an airtight container for up to 5 days or transferred to Ziploc freezer bags and frozen for up to 2 months.

VARIATIONS

Add 3 tablespoons of any of the following ingredients to the flour and proceed as directed: grated lemon, orange, tangerine, or lime zest; fresh thyme leaves; finely chopped fresh rosemary; slivered mint leaves, or dried mint; finely chopped dried organic rose petals; crushed tea leaves, such as Earl Grey or Lapsang souchong; lemon verbena.

Here are some suggestions for flavor combinations: 2 tablespoons grated lime zest and 1 tablespoon dried mint; 2 tablespoons finely chopped organic rose petals and 1 tablespoon dried mint; 2 tablespoons crushed Earl Grey tea leaves and 1 tablespoon grated lemon zest.

Almond Shortbread

This cookie is like a well-made cardigan: it always presents handsomely and requires very little fuss. Almond flour gives the cookie a tender bite and a subtle nutty flavor. Replace the almond flour with hazelnut, pecan, or pistachio flour if you prefer. I make these cookies year-round and always have a log or two in the freezer.

● **MAKES 50 COOKIES** ●

1 cup (5 ounces) all-purpose flour

³/₄ cup (2.63 ounces) raw almond flour (see Resources, page 335), toasted (see page 20)

8 tablespoons (1 stick/4 ounces) unsalted butter, softened

¹/₄ cup (1.5 ounces) light brown sugar

¹/₄ cup (1.75 ounces) granulated sugar

¹/₂ teaspoon kosher salt

1 teaspoon vanilla extract

❯ Whisk together both flours in a small bowl. Set aside.

❯ In the bowl of a stand mixer fitted with the paddle attachment (or in a large bowl, using a handheld mixer), cream the butter and both sugars on medium speed until light and fluffy, about 4 minutes. Add the flours ¹/₂ cup at a time, mixing thoroughly after each addition. Add the salt and vanilla and mix for 30 seconds.

❯ Turn the dough out onto a cool surface and divide it into quarters. Roll each piece into a log measuring about 1 inch thick and 6 inches long. Wrap the logs in plastic wrap and refrigerate until firm, about 1 hour.

❯ Position the racks in the upper and lower thirds of the oven and heat the oven to 350°F.

❯ Slice the logs into rounds approximately ¹/₃ inch thick and place them on an ungreased large heavy baking sheet, spacing them about 2 inches apart. Bake for 10 to 12 minutes, until the edges appear golden. Let the cookies cool on the baking sheets on cooling racks for 10 minutes.

❯ Using an offset spatula, transfer the cookies to a cooling rack to cool completely.

STORING

❯ The cookies can be stored in an airtight container for up to a week or transferred to Ziploc freezer bags and frozen for up to 2 months.

VARIATION

CHOCOLATE-COVERED ALMOND SHORTBREAD WITH FLEUR DE SEL: Temper 1 pound 61% bittersweet chocolate (see page 174). Dip the almond short-bread cookies in the chocolate and top them with a sprinkling of fleur de sel.

Brownies

This recipe delivers all the best parts of a brownie: crispy edges, a chewy center, and a slight crunch to the crust. In order to maximize the best brownie attributes, the batter is spread thin for a better crust, and brown sugar is blended with white to increase the chewiness factor.

12 tablespoons (1¹/₂ sticks/6 ounces) unsalted butter

3 ounces 99% unsweetened chocolate, chopped

1 cup (7 ounces) granulated sugar

¹/₂ cup (3 ounces) light brown sugar

3 large eggs

³/₄ cup (3.75 ounces) all-purpose flour

1 teaspoon vanilla bean paste (see Resources, page 335)

1 teaspoon kosher salt

› Heat the oven to 350°F. Butter the bottom and sides of a 9-by-9-by-2-inch square baking pan and line the bottom with parchment paper or aluminum foil.

› Melt the butter and chocolate in a double boiler or a medium heatproof bowl set over a pot of boiling water, stirring occasionally with a small whisk until smooth. Remove from the heat and let cool for 2 to 3 minutes. If you used a double boiler, transfer the chocolate to a medium bowl.

› Stir both sugars into the chocolate mixture until fully combined. Using a rubber spatula or a wooden spoon, mix in the eggs one at a time. Add the flour, vanilla paste, and salt, and stir until thoroughly combined.

› Spread the batter into the prepared baking pan. Bake for 25 to 30 minutes, until a crust forms and the center appears dry. Check the brownies with a toothpick—small crumbs should adhere (do not bake until a toothpick inserted in the center comes out totally clean). Let the brownies cool in the pan for at least 10 minutes on a cooling rack before cutting with a sharp knife.

STORING

› Once cooled, the brownies can be stored in an airtight container for up to 5 days; or leave the brownies, uncut, in the pan, wrap in a double layer of plastic wrap, and freeze for up to 2 months.

Caramelized Crispies

This cross between Rice Krispies Treats and caramel corn tastes both familiar and new at the same time. Dip small pieces of the crispies in tempered 38% milk chocolate (see page 175; use 9 ounces chocolate) to make an even more decadent treat.

● MAKES 48 CRISPIES ●

10 cups (10 ounces) crisped rice cereal, such as Rice Krispies

2 cups (13 ounces) light brown sugar

1/2 cup (5.5 ounces) light corn syrup

2 sticks (8 ounces) unsalted butter, cut into chunks

1 1/2 teaspoons gray sea salt (see Resources, page 335)

2 1/2 cups (4.6 ounces) mini-marshmallows

1 tablespoon vanilla extract

1 teaspoon baking soda

> Heat the oven to 250°F.

> Spread the crisped rice on an unlined baking sheet and heat in the oven for about 10 minutes. While the crisped rice is warming, butter a very large bowl and set aside.

> Line a 13-by-18-by-1-inch baking sheet with parchment paper and set aside. Whisk together the brown sugar, corn syrup, butter, and 1 teaspoon of the sea salt in a medium saucepan, set over medium heat, and attach a candy thermometer to the side of the pan. Bring the mixture to a simmer, whisking frequently. When the caramel is at about 240°F, pour the crisped rice into the buttered bowl. Mix in the mini marshmallows until evenly distributed. Set aside.

> When the caramel reaches 250°F, quickly remove the thermometer, remove from the heat, and whisk in the vanilla and baking soda. Pour the caramel over the cereal and mix everything together with a large wooden spoon; work quickly so the caramel stays soft enough to cover all the cereal and marshmallows. Spread the mixture into the prepared baking sheet. Using your hands, press the mixture into the baking sheet to create a level surface. Sprinkle with the remaining 1/2 teaspoon sea salt. Let the crispies cool for 5 minutes.

> Using a very sharp heavy knife, cut the crispies into 2-inch squares, then let cool completely.

STORING

> The crispies can be stored in an airtight container for up to 6 days.

TIP: CHOP THE CRISPIES INTO BITS FOR A delicious topping on ice cream or pudding.

Salted-Peanut Blondies

I like peanuts best when they are well salted and paired with something sweet. Bazzini peanuts from New York City have an exceptional crunch, a good roasted flavor, and a pleasing level of saltiness, which makes them the perfect addition to buttery blondies studded with milk chocolate chips. This recipe makes small blondies; you can cut them bigger if you like.

• MAKES 48 BLONDIES •

2 cups (10 ounces) all-purpose flour

1 teaspoon baking powder

1 teaspoon kosher salt

12 tablespoons (1½ sticks/6 ounces) unsalted butter, softened

2 cups (12 ounces) light brown sugar

2 teaspoons vanilla bean paste (see Resources, page 335)

2 large eggs

¾ cup (4.13 ounces) 38% milk chocolate chips (see Resources, page 335)

¾ cup (3.5 ounces) high-quality salted peanuts (such as Bazzini; see Resources, page 335), chopped

1 teaspoon fleur de sel

› Heat the oven to 350°F. Coat the bottom and sides of a 9-by-13-by-2-inch baking sheet with nonstick baking spray.

› Sift together the flour, baking powder, and salt into a medium bowl. Set aside.

› In the bowl of a stand mixer fitted with the paddle attachment (or in a large bowl, using a handheld mixer), cream the butter and brown sugar on medium speed until light and fluffy, about 4 minutes. Add the vanilla paste and beat for 30 seconds. Add the eggs one at a time, mixing thoroughly after each addition. Add the dry ingredients ½ cup at a time, beating well after each addition. Scrape down the bottom and sides of the bowl. Add the chocolate chips and beat until evenly distributed, about 1 minute.

› Spread the batter into the prepared baking sheet. Sprinkle the chopped peanuts and fleur de sel over the top. Bake for 45 to 55 minutes, until the edges appear crisp and the top is slightly golden. A toothpick inserted in the center should come out with a few moist crumbs clinging to it. Let the blondies cool completely in the pan on a cooling rack before cutting with a sharp knife.

STORING

› Once cooled, the blondies can be stored in an airtight container for up to 4 days; or leave the blondies, uncut, in the pan, wrap in a double layer of plastic wrap, and freeze for up to 2 months.

LARDER

JAMS AND MARMALADES

A few years ago, homemade preserves seemed to burst into our collective consciousness in an exciting new way. A hobby that had been regarded as antiquated suddenly felt unabashedly hip. The combination of an economic collapse and readily available top-caliber fruits created the perfect storm for a jamming renaissance. When I go to the farmers' market, almost every fruit I look at becomes a jar of something fabulous in my mind, and it seems people all across the country are having the same experience.

And yet many people are still intimidated by the thought of making preserves. I must confess I shared that fear when I started: standing over a huge pot of boiling fruit and sugar was fraught with anxiety. On one particularly stressful day, I was called to the phone in the middle of an intense jam session. I hesitantly turned off the flame and walked away. When I returned to the pot, I expected to see some kind of crystallized mess, but that wasn't the case at all—in fact, the fruit and sugar appeared to have progressed a bit in the cooking stage. Curious. I could turn off the heat and walk away, and nothing bad would happen! It was a day of jam liberation.

So, here's a comforting thing to remember as you start to play with preserves: it is very difficult to ruin what you are making. Think of your jams and marmalades as you would savory sauces or, better yet, soups. You are essentially doing the same thing: combining ingredients in a pot and attempting to extract the best flavor possible—though with preserves, when you are cooking, you are removing the water from the fruit and replacing it with sugar.

After gaining a bit of jam confidence, I threw caution to the wind. What would happen if I used extra sugar—not even simple syrup—near the end of the cooking process? What if I left fruit and sugar macerating for, say, five days in the refrigerator before cooking it? My results were still good. Once the rules are gone, jam making becomes fun, even addictive.

I urge you to play with this chapter, adjusting the recipes to your taste as you find your jam personality, or jam voice. Know that you can skip the canning process entirely and just refrigerate these preserves if that better suits your needs. They'll keep for up to 2 weeks refrigerated.

I now crave my time in front of the massive pot, intoxicated with thoughts of new flavor combinations. My collection of flavor possibilities has grown exponentially, from classic Strawberry–Vanilla Bean Jam (page 276) to hybrid flavors such as Blushing Berry Jam (page 281). I hope you will come to experience the same affection for jam making that I feel.

STERILIZING AND CANNING INSTRUCTIONS

———◦———

HOME PRESERVING IS COMPLETELY SAFE AND EASY TO EXECUTE, as long as you follow some basic guidelines. For more details on chemical balance, safety, and alternative canning methods, check the website of the USDA National Center for Home Food Preservation, nchfp.uga.edu/index.html. Here is the basic process for home canning; do read through the instructions before you begin, to ensure a safe canning session.

1. Heat the oven to 250°F.

2. Wash the canning jars with soap and warm water, or run them through a cycle in a dishwasher.

3. Set the jars right side up on a baking sheet and put them in the hot oven for 15 minutes to sterilize them.

4. Meanwhile, prepare a boiling-water canner, or fill a large deep pot halfway with water and bring to a low boil.

5. Bring a small saucepan of water to a low boil, then remove it from the heat and drop in the jar lids (and bands). Heating the lids before canning will soften the wax seal and result in a tighter seal.

6. Remove the jars from the oven and set them on a stable work surface. When the jam is cooked, fill the jars one at a time using a funnel or sterilized heat-resistant pitcher, leaving 1/2 inch headspace.

7. Using a clean damp cloth, wipe the rims of the jars clean.

8. Carefully remove the lids from the small saucepan and seal the jars. If using lids and bands, put the lid on top of the jar and screw the band on until it is secure.

9. Using a jar lifter, carefully put the jars into the boiling-water canner (or large pot), making sure the water covers the jars by at least 1 inch.

10. Place the lid on the canner (or pot) and bring the water to a full boil. Boil the jam for 10 minutes, then turn off the heat.

11. Lay two large dish towels on a flat surface. Using the jar lifter, carefully remove the jars from the canner (or pot) and put on the towels. Leave the jars undisturbed for at least 12 hours. Check the seals; if they're secure, store the jars in your larder. If any seal is loose, refrigerate the jar immediately and consume the contents within the appropriate timetable.

Jams can be stored in a cool area away from direct sunlight for up to 1 year; marmalades will keep for up to 1 1/2 years. Once they've been opened, store all preserves in the refrigerator. Jams keep well for up to 3 weeks in the refrigerator, marmalades for up to 2 months.

Strawberry-Vanilla Bean Jam

This is one of the first jams I ever made, and it is a perennial best seller at Valerie Confections. The vanilla bean rounds out the sweetness of the strawberry and takes the jam to an almost candy-like level. Pair it with your favorite peanut butter for the best PB&J ever.

6 pints (about 4 pounds) strawberries, rinsed, hulled, and quartered

3 cups (21 ounces) sugar, or more to taste

1 to 2 vanilla beans, split

› Mix the strawberries with the sugar in a medium bowl.

› Using a small paring knife, split 1 vanilla bean lengthwise and scrape the seeds out. Add the seeds and bean to the strawberries, cover, and set aside for 30 minutes, or macerate for as long as overnight in the refrigerator.

› Sterilize six 12-ounce canning jars and lids (see page 275).

› Put two small ceramic plates in the freezer.

› Pour the strawberry mixture into a large pot and set over high heat. Cook, stirring with a large wooden spoon or a heatproof silicone spatula, scraping the edges and bottom of the pot to prevent scorching, until the berries soften and begin to break down, approximately 15 minutes. If the jam bubbles up too much, lower the heat to medium. Once the bubbling subsides, after 5 to 10 minutes, the jam will begin to thicken.

› Taste the jam for sweetness. If you want, add a little more sugar ¼ cup at a time, taste, and cook for an additional 2 to 3 minutes. If you want a stronger vanilla flavor, add the second vanilla bean.

› Check the set of the jam by putting a small dollop of hot jam on one of the chilled plates. Run a finger through it: if your finger leaves a track, the jam is ready; if not, continue cooking for a few minutes and repeat the test. Remove from the heat.

› Remove the vanilla bean(s). Pour the jam into the sterilized jars and seal with the warm lids. Let cool to room temperature and refrigerate for up to 2 weeks, or follow the canning instructions for long-term storage on page 275.

Strawberry Rhubarb Jam

I have an aversion to working with standard flavor combinations: I can't help but change recipes or add my own twist. So, when I started making jams, I resisted the traditional combination of strawberry and rhubarb like the plague. I experimented with a number of rhubarb jam recipes that didn't include strawberries, but guess what? Nothing was as delicious as strawberry and rhubarb together.

MAKES SIX 12-OUNCE JARS

1½ pounds rhubarb (about 15 stalks), rinsed, trimmed, and cut into 1-inch pieces

2¾ cups (18 ounces) sugar, or more to taste

Grated zest and juice of 1 lemon, preferably a Meyer lemon

3 pints (about 2¼ pounds) strawberries, rinsed, hulled, and sliced into quarters

› Mix the rhubarb with 1¼ cups of the sugar, the lemon zest, and juice in a medium bowl. Mix the strawberries with the remaining 1½ cups sugar in another medium bowl. Cover and set aside for 30 minutes, or macerate for as long as overnight in the refrigerator.

› Sterilize six 12-ounce canning jars and lids (see page 275).

› Put two small ceramic plates in the freezer.

› Pour the rhubarb into a large pot and set over high heat. Cook, stirring with a large wooden spoon or a heatproof silicone spatula, scraping the edges and bottom of the pot to prevent scorching, until the rhubarb softens, approximately 10 minutes. Add the strawberries and continue cooking, stirring, until the strawberries soften and break down, about 15 minutes. If the jam bubbles up too much, lower the heat to medium and continue stirring. Once the bubbling subsides, after about 10 minutes, the jam will begin to thicken.

› Taste the jam for sweetness. If you want, add a little more sugar ¼ cup at a time, taste, and cook for an additional 2 to 3 minutes.

› Check the set of the jam by putting a small dollop of hot jam on one of the chilled plates. Run a finger through it: if your finger leaves a track, the jam is ready; if not, continue cooking for a few minutes and repeat the test. Remove from the heat.

› Pour the jam into the sterilized jars and seal with the warm lids. Let cool to room temperature and refrigerate for up to 2 weeks, or follow the canning instructions for long-term storage on page 275.

READING FRUIT

FRUIT CAN VARY TREMENDOUSLY IN FLAVOR, texture, and, most important, water and sugar content. Today, for example, you can find a variety of peaches, such as June Gold, Donut, Elberta, and white, at the same farmers' market. Each type is slightly different, so it is important to adjust a preserving recipe to best suit the fruit. A very large peach with light coloring is likely to have a higher water content and a lower sugar content than a small peach. Size and color are two of the clues fruits give as to the best way to cook them, but the most important clue is taste. The larger peach will probably have less flavor than the smaller one. It might seem logical to add more sugar to larger peaches when cooking, but the opposite is the best route with jam making. The larger peach will actually require less sugar by weight to create a delicious jam because the water in the fruit will boil off during cooking. The smaller, sweeter peach, with its lower water content, requires more sugar by weight to attain the desired level of sweetness.

When you purchase fruit at the market, read it for clues and then experiment a bit when you make preserves. As a starting point, you might make the Peach Melba Jam (page 288) with small dark, sweet fruit, then make a jam with the same weight of large peaches with a lighter color. I bet you will find you need less sugar with the larger peaches to make a jam that tastes similar to the one you made with the small peaches.

Blushing Berry Jam

The "blush" in this jam is a nod to the generous amount of alcohol it contains. Chambord, a liqueur made of red and black raspberries, vanilla, citrus peel, honey, and Cognac, has a pleasing sweetness. Raspberries and rhubarb have tart flavors; here the Chambord softens the acidity, balancing the jam. To make great favors for bridal showers, tie ribbons and hangtags around jars to personalize them (see Packaging, page 336).

● MAKES SIX 12-OUNCE JARS ●

4 pints (about 2 pounds) raspberries, rinsed

4 cups (28 ounces) sugar, or more to taste

50 to 60 organic rose petals (see Resources, page 335), rinsed

2¼ pounds rhubarb (about 20 stalks), rinsed, trimmed, and cut into ½-inch pieces

½ cup (4 ounces) Chambord

▶ Mix the raspberries with 2 cups of the sugar and the rose petals in a medium bowl. Mix the rhubarb with the remaining 2 cups sugar in another bowl and stir well; you want to see the sugar dissolve and the rhubarb release a bit of juice. Cover and set aside for 1 hour, or macerate for as long as overnight in the refrigerator.

▶ Sterilize six 12-ounce canning jars and lids (see page 275).

▶ Put two small ceramic plates in the freezer.

▶ Pour the rhubarb into a large pot and set over high heat. Cook, stirring with a large wooden spoon or a heatproof silicone spatula, scraping the edges and bottom of the pot to prevent scorching, until the rhubarb softens, approximately 10 minutes. Add the raspberries and rose petals and continue cooking until the berries soften and break down, approximately 10 minutes. If the jam bubbles up too much, lower the heat to medium and continue stirring. Once the bubbling subsides, after about 10 minutes, the jam will begin to thicken. Add the Chambord to the jam and stir; you will see the jam loosen a bit.

▶ Taste the jam for sweetness. If you want, add a little more sugar ¼ cup at a time, taste, and cook for an additional 2 to 3 minutes.

▶ Check the set of the jam by putting a small dollop of hot jam on one of the chilled plates. Run a finger through it: if your finger leaves a track, the jam is ready; if not, continue cooking for a few minutes and repeat the test. Remove from the heat.

▶ Pour the jam into the sterilized jars and seal with the warm lids. Let cool to room temperature and refrigerate for up to 2 weeks, or follow the canning instructions for long-term storage on page 275.

Black-and-Blue Jam

Blueberries and blackberries complement each other beautifully, with the perfect balance of sweet and tart flavors. The jam has many uses—try it in the Black-and-Blue Fool (page 217) or as the flavoring of an ice cream (see page 238), or spread it on toast or biscuits. The catchy name is an added bonus.

● MAKES SIX 12-OUNCE JARS ●

3 pints (about 1½ pounds) blueberries, rinsed and stemmed

3 pints (about 1½ pounds) blackberries, rinsed

2½ cups (17.5 ounces) sugar, or more to taste

› Mix the blueberries and blackberries with the sugar in a medium bowl. Cover and set aside for 30 minutes, or macerate for as long as overnight in the refrigerator.

› Sterilize six 12-ounce canning jars and lids (see page 275).

› Put two small ceramic plates in the freezer.

› Pour the berry mixture into a large pot and set over high heat. Cook, stirring with a large wooden spoon or a heatproof silicone spatula, scraping the edges and bottom of the pot to prevent scorching, until the berries soften and break down, approximately 20 minutes. If the jam bubbles up too much, lower the heat to medium and continue stirring. Once the bubbling subsides, after about 10 minutes, the jam will begin to thicken.

› Taste the jam for sweetness. If you want, add a little more sugar ¼ cup at a time, taste, and cook for an additional 2 to 3 minutes. If you want a chunky, old-fashioned jam, continue stirring with the spoon or spatula. If you like a jam with a smoother texture, switch to a large whisk and stir more rapidly.

› Check the set of the jam by putting a small dollop of hot jam on one of the chilled plates. Run a finger through it: if your finger leaves a track, the jam is ready; if not, continue cooking for a few minutes and repeat the test. Remove from the heat.

› Pour the jam into the sterilized jars and seal with the warm lids. Let cool to room temperature and refrigerate for up to 2 weeks, or follow the canning instructions for long-term storage on page 275.

Blenheim Apricot Jam

Blenheim apricots have a very short season—often it's just two or three weeks in July. They are smaller than other apricots, and the skin is covered with small brown specks. The flavor of this exceptional apricot is incomparable in preserves. Whenever I develop a recipe, I always look for an arc in the flavor that provides a beginning, a middle, and an end to the sensory experience. Blenheim apricots do this naturally, imparting a tart-sweet creaminess that is pure enjoyment. Serve Blenheim jam with La Tur, a lusciously creamy goat-, cow-, and sheep's-milk cheese, and a crusty baguette for a memorable savory pairing.

◆ MAKES SIX 12-OUNCE JARS ◆

About 5 pounds Blenheim apricots (60 to 70), rinsed, pitted, and thinly sliced

3¹/₂ cups (24.5 ounces) sugar, or more to taste

▶ Mix the sliced apricots with the sugar in a large bowl. Cover and set aside for 1 hour, or macerate for as long as overnight in the refrigerator.

▶ Sterilize six 12-ounce canning jars and lids (see page 275).

▶ Put two small ceramic plates in the freezer.

▶ Pour the apricots into a large pot and set over high heat. Cook, stirring with a large wooden spoon or a heatproof silicone spatula, scraping the edges and bottom of the pot to prevent scorching, until the apricots soften and begin to break down, approximately 20 minutes. If the jam bubbles up too much, lower the heat to medium and continue stirring. Once the bubbling subsides, after about 10 minutes, the jam will begin to thicken.

▶ Taste the jam for sweetness. If you want, add a little more sugar ¹/₄ cup at a time, taste, and cook for an additional 2 to 3 minutes. Then stir the jam vigorously with a whisk until very smooth, approximately 5 minutes.

▶ Check the set of the jam by putting a small dollop of hot jam on one of the chilled plates. Run a finger through it: if your finger leaves a track, the jam is ready; if not, continue cooking for a few minutes and repeat the test. Remove from the heat.

▶ Pour the jam into the sterilized jars and seal with the warm lids. Let cool to room temperature and refrigerate for up to 2 weeks, or follow the canning instructions for long-term storage on page 275.

Apricot and Rainier Cherry Jam

Rainier cherries are one of the sweetest and most delectable summer fruits. Unfortunately, they are also one of the most delicate fruits of the season. They brown and scar easily, so treat Rainiers with the utmost care. After pitting and slicing the cherries for this recipe, get them into the sugar as fast as possible to reduce the discoloration.

● MAKES SIX 12-OUNCE JARS ●

About 3 pounds apricots (35 to 40), rinsed, pitted, and thinly sliced

4 pints (about 2 pounds) Rainier cherries, rinsed, cut in half, and pitted

3 1/2 cups (24.5 ounces) sugar, or more to taste

1/2 cup (4 ounces) water

› Mix the apricots and cherries with the sugar in a large bowl. Cover and set aside for 1 hour, or macerate for as long as overnight in the refrigerator.

› Sterilize six 12-ounce canning jars and lids (see page 275).

› Put two small ceramic plates in the freezer.

› Pour the fruit into a large pot, add the water, and set over high heat. Cook, stirring frequently with a large wooden spoon or a heatproof silicone spatula, scraping the edges and bottom of the pot to prevent scorching, until the fruit comes to a boil. If the jam bubbles up too much, lower the heat to medium and continue stirring. Once the bubbling subsides, after about 10 minutes, the jam will begin to thicken.

› Taste the jam for sweetness. If you want, add a little more sugar 1/4 cup at a time, taste, and cook for an additional 2 to 3 minutes.

› Check the set of the jam by putting a dollop of hot jam on one of the chilled plates. Run a finger through it: if your finger leaves a track, the jam is ready; if not, continue cooking for a few minutes and repeat the test. Remove from the heat.

› Pour the jam into the sterilized jars and seal with the warm lids. Let cool to room temperature and refrigerate for up to 2 weeks, or follow the canning instructions for long-term storage on page 275.

White Nectarine and Lemon Verbena Jam

Nectarines are a close relative of peaches, but while peaches have
a thick, fuzzy skin that must be removed, nectarines have a smooth,
thin skin that cooks down easily in a pot of jam. White nectarines
are very juicy, with an incredibly bright flavor, combining perfectly
with a citrusy herb such as lemon verbena.

● MAKES SIX 12-OUNCE JARS ●

About 5 pounds white nectarines (25 to 30),
rinsed, pitted, and sliced into 1-inch wedges
2½ cups (17.5 ounces) sugar, or more to taste
25 dried or fresh lemon verbena leaves (see
Resources, page 335)
Grated zest and juice of 1 lemon

▸ Mix the nectarines with the sugar in a medium bowl. Add the lemon verbena, lemon zest, and juice and mix well. Cover and set aside for 1 hour,
or macerate for as long as overnight in the refrigerator.

▸ Sterilize six 12-ounce canning jars and lids (see page 275).

▸ Put two small ceramic plates in the freezer.

▸ Pour the nectarines into a large pot and set over high heat. Cook, stirring frequently with a large wooden spoon or a heatproof silicone spatula,
scraping the edges and bottom of the pot to prevent scorching, until the
nectarines soften and break down, 10 to 15 minutes. If the jam bubbles
up too much, reduce the heat to medium and continue stirring. Once the
bubbling subsides, after about 10 minutes, the jam will begin to thicken.

▸ Taste the jam for sweetness. If you want, add a little more sugar ¼ cup
at a time, taste, and cook for an additional 2 to 3 minutes. Remove the
jam from the heat. Carefully remove the larger pieces of lemon verbena
with a spoon and discard; it is fine to leave smaller pieces (less than
¼ inch) in the jam.

▸ Check the set of the jam by putting a small dollop of hot jam on one
of the chilled plates. Run a finger through it: if your finger leaves a track,
the jam is ready; if not, continue cooking for a few minutes and repeat
the test.

▸ Pour the jam into the sterilized jars and seal with the warm lids. Let cool
to room temperature and refrigerate for up to 2 weeks, or follow the canning instructions for long-term storage on page 275.

Peach Melba Jam

Peach Melba is a classic dessert of vanilla ice cream, raspberry sauce, and peaches, originally created by the great Auguste Escoffier. This recipe puts all those wonderful flavors in a jar.

● MAKES SIX 12-OUNCE JARS ●

About 4 pounds yellow peaches (10 to 12), rinsed

$3^1/_2$ cups (24.5 ounces) sugar, or more to taste

1 vanilla bean, split, seeds scraped out, seeds and bean reserved

2 pints (about 1 pound) raspberries, rinsed

▸ Fill a large pot with water and bring to a boil. Cut a small X in the bottom of each peach. Fill a large bowl with ice water and set it close to the stove.

▸ Plunge 2 peaches at a time into the boiling water and leave them in the water for 1 minute; you will see the skin start to pull away at the X marks. Using tongs or a slotted spoon, transfer the peaches to the ice water. When all the peaches have been blanched, drain and remove the skins; they should slip off easily.

▸ Halve and pit the peaches and cut into 1-inch-thick wedges. Mix with $1^1/_2$ cups of the sugar in a medium bowl. Add the vanilla bean and seeds and cover the bowl. Combine the raspberries with the remaining 2 cups sugar in another bowl and cover the bowl. Set the fruit aside for 30 minutes, or macerate for as long as overnight in the refrigerator.

▸ Sterilize six 12-ounce canning jars and lids (see page 275).

▸ Put four small ceramic plates in the freezer.

▸ Pour the peaches and sugar into a large pot and set over high heat. Cook, stirring with a large wooden spoon or a heatproof silicone spatula, scraping the edges and bottom of the pot to prevent scorching, until the fruit comes to a boil. If the jam bubbles up too much, lower the heat to medium and continue stirring. Once the bubbling subsides, after about 10 minutes, the jam will begin to thicken.

▸ Taste the jam for sweetness. If you want, add a little more sugar $^1/_4$ cup at a time, taste, and cook for an additional 2 to 3 minutes.

▸ Check the set of the jam by putting a small dollop of hot jam on one of the chilled plates. Run a finger through it: if your finger leaves a track, the jam is ready; if not, continue cooking for a few minutes and repeat the test. Remove from the heat and set aside.

▸ Pour the raspberries and sugar into another pot and set over high heat. Cook, stirring with a large wooden spoon or a heatproof spatula, scraping the edges and bottom of the pot to prevent scorching, until the mixture starts to thicken and the major bubbling has given way to smaller bubbles, 10 to 12 minutes.

▸ Taste the jam for sweetness. If you want, add a little more sugar $^1/_4$ cup at a time, taste, and cook for an additional 2 to 3 minutes. The raspberry jam should taste tarter and brighter than the peach jam.

› Check the set of the raspberry jam. When it is ready, remove from the heat.

› Pour the peach jam into the sterilized jars, filling each one about halfway. Wearing a heatproof glove or an oven mitt, pick up each jar and carefully tap it on the work surface to remove any air bubbles in the jam. Caution—the contents and jars are very hot!

› Then fill the jars with raspberry jam and seal with the warm lids. (It is not necessary to tap the jars with the second layer of jam.) Let cool to room temperature and refrigerate for up to 2 weeks, or follow the canning instructions for long-term storage on page 275.

FRUIT SAUCES

———————————•———————————

THESE FRUIT SAUCES are essentially fluid versions of the jams. Use the sauces in marinades, dressings, cocktails, and natural sodas.

White Nectarine Sauce

Make White Nectarine and Lemon Verbena Jam (page 287), but reduce the sugar by 1/2 cup (3.5 ounces). When the jam is ready, stir 1 1/2 cups (13 ounces) hot Simple Syrup (see below) into the pot. Using an immersion blender, blend until completely smooth. The canning and storing instructions are the same as for the jam.

Strawberry–Vanilla Bean Sauce

Make Strawberry–Vanilla Bean Jam (page 276), but reduce the sugar by 1 cup (7 ounces). When the jam is ready, stir 2 cups hot Simple Syrup (see below) into the pot. Using an immersion blender, blend the mixture until completely smooth. The canning and storing instructions are the same as for the jam.

Black-and-Blue Sauce

Make Black-and-Blue Jam (page 282), but reduce the sugar by 1 cup (7 ounces). When the jam is ready, stir 2 cups hot Simple Syrup (see below) into the pot. Using an immersion blender, blend until completely smooth. The canning and storing instructions are the same as for the jam.

Simple Syrup

MAKES 3 CUPS

2 cups (14 ounces) sugar
2 cups (16 ounces) water

Combine the sugar and water in a medium saucepan and cook over medium heat, stirring occasionally, until the sugar dissolves and the syrup is clear. Use immediately, or cool to room temperature and store, covered, in the refrigerator for up to 2 weeks.

Mango Jam

Wong Family Farms sets up shop at the Santa Monica Farmers' Market every August and creates a flurry of excitement with their Keitt mangoes. If you happen to be in the Southland in the late summer, pick up a few. I have also made this jam with mangoes from different growers or even with mangoes from the grocery store, all with delicious results. Try the jam on ice cream or in a smoothie, or pair it with goat cheese.

● MAKES SIX 12-OUNCE JARS ●

5½ pounds ripe mangoes (about 8 large)
3 cups (21 ounces) sugar, or more to taste
Grated zest and juice of 1 lime

▸ Rinse the mangoes and peel them. Cut the flesh off the large seeds and then cut it into small cubes.

▸ Mix the mango flesh with the sugar in a large bowl. Cover and set aside for 1 hour, or macerate for as long as overnight in the refrigerator.

▸ Sterilize six 12-ounce canning jars and lids (see page 275).

▸ Put two small ceramic plates in the freezer.

▸ Pour the mangoes into a large pot and bring to a boil over high heat, stirring frequently with a large wooden spoon or a heatproof silicone spatula, scraping the edges and bottom of the pot to prevent scorching. The jam will bubble but not as high as other jams because of the low water content of the fruit; lower the heat slightly if necessary. Continue stirring as the jam boils to break down the fruit, approximately 15 minutes. Add the lime zest and juice and stir the jam aggressively with a large whisk until it is very smooth.

▸ Taste the jam for sweetness. If you want, add a little more sugar ¼ cup at a time, taste, and cook for an additional 2 to 3 minutes.

▸ Check the set of the jam by putting a small dollop of hot jam on one of the chilled plates. Run a finger through it: if your finger leaves a track, the jam is ready; if not, continue cooking for a few minutes and repeat the test. Remove from the heat.

▸ Pour the jam into the sterilized jars and seal with the warm lids. Let cool to room temperature and refrigerate for up to 2 weeks, or follow the canning instructions for long-term storage on page 275.

Angelino Plum Jam

Angelinos are a late-season plum with beautiful dark purple flesh and skin. If you can't find them, you can make this jam with Damson or Italian prune plums. Plum jam pairs beautifully with duck and goose. Put up a double batch in September—you'll devour it with your holiday meals a few months later.

About 5 pounds Angelino plums (60 to 70), rinsed, pitted, and thinly sliced

3 cups (21 ounces) granulated sugar, or more to taste

1 cup (6 ounces) light brown sugar

› Mix the sliced plums and sugars in a large bowl. Cover and set aside for 1 hour, or macerate for as long as overnight in the refrigerator.

› Sterilize six 12-ounce canning jars and lids (see page 275).

› Put two small ceramic plates in the freezer.

› Pour the plums into a large pot and set over high heat. Cook, stirring with a large wooden spoon or a heatproof silicone spatula, scraping the edges and bottom of the pot to prevent scorching, until the plums soften and begin to break down, approximately 20 minutes. If the jam bubbles up too much, lower the heat to medium. Once the bubbling subsides, after about 10 minutes, the jam will begin to thicken.

› Taste the jam for sweetness. If you want, add a little more granulated sugar ¼ cup at a time, taste, and cook for an additional 2 to 3 minutes. Then stir the jam vigorously with a whisk until very smooth, approximately 5 minutes.

› Check the set of the jam by putting a small dollop of hot jam on one of the chilled plates. Run a finger through it: if your finger leaves a track, the jam is ready; if not, continue cooking for a few minutes and repeat the test. Remove from the heat.

› Pour the jam into the sterilized jars and seal with the warm lids. Let cool to room temperature and refrigerate for up to 2 weeks, or follow the canning instructions for long-term storage on page 275.

White Fig, Fuji Apple, and Vanilla Bean Jam

White figs are actually light green or yellow, with gorgeous bright pink flesh. In contrast to berries and stone fruits, figs are more flesh than water, so you need to add water to cook them into a jam. The water acts as a conduit for heat; without liquid, the figs get very pasty and can burn quickly. The water evaporates during the cooking process, leaving behind smooth preserves. White figs have a unique nutty flavor, making them exceptionally good with cheeses and meats. Try this jam with a rich, creamy cheese (such as bleu d'Auvergne), a drizzle of truffle honey, and a thin slice of prosciutto; it's one of my favorite combinations.

• MAKES SIX 12-OUNCE JARS •

About 1 pound Fuji apples (2 large)

2 tablespoons fresh lemon juice

About 5 pounds white figs, such as Calimyrna, rinsed, stemmed, and quartered

4 cups (1 pound 12 ounces) sugar, or more to taste

1 vanilla bean, split, seeds scraped out, seeds and bean reserved

2 cups (16 ounces) water

3 tablespoons Cognac

▸ Peel, core, and finely dice the apples. Put in a large bowl and toss with the lemon juice. Add the figs to the apples, then mix with the sugar. Add the vanilla seeds and bean. Cover and set aside for 1 hour, or macerate for as long as overnight in the refrigerator.

▸ Sterilize six 12-ounce canning jars and lids (see page 275).

▸ Put two small ceramic plates in the freezer.

▸ Pour the macerated fruit into a large pot and set over high heat. Cook, stirring with a large wooden spoon or a heatproof silicone spatula, scraping the edges and bottom of the pot to prevent scorching, until the fruit softens and the flesh of the figs starts to appear pasty. Add 1 cup of the water and continue stirring until the fruit starts to boil. Add the second cup of water and continue cooking, stirring frequently, for approximately 20 minutes. If the jam bubbles up too much, lower the heat to medium and continue stirring. Once the bubbling subsides, after about 5 minutes, the jam will begin to thicken.

▸ Add the Cognac and continue cooking for 2 to 3 minutes.

▸ Taste the jam for sweetness. If you want, add a little more sugar ¼ cup at a time, taste, and cook for an additional 2 to 3 minutes.

▸ Check the set of the jam by putting a small dollop of hot jam on one of the chilled plates. Run a finger through it: if your finger leaves a track, the jam is ready; if not, continue cooking for a few minutes and repeat the test. Remove from the heat.

▸ Remove the vanilla bean. Pour the jam into the sterilized jars and seal with the warm lids. Let cool to room temperature and refrigerate for up to 2 weeks, or follow the canning instructions for long-term storage on page 275.

VALERIE
at the market

Black Mission Fig
Pear & Port

NET WEIGHT 8 oz (226 grams)

Black Mission Fig, Pear, and Port Jam

Dark, rich, and a little boozy, this is a great jam for holiday gifting. It's
not a jam you're going to crave on a hot summer day, but is something
to indulge in on a cold winter night with a platter of charcuterie.

● MAKES SIX 12-OUNCE JARS ●

About 3½ pounds Black Mission figs, rinsed,
 stemmed, and sliced

About 2 pounds pears (3 to 4 large), peeled,
 cored, and finely diced

4 cups (1 pound 12 ounces) sugar

1 cup (8 ounces) water

1 cup (8 ounces) port

Grated zest and juice of 1 lemon

› Mix the figs and pears with the sugar in a large bowl. Cover and set aside for 1 hour, or macerate for as long as overnight in the refrigerator.

› Sterilize six 12-ounce canning jars and lids (see page 275).

› Put two small ceramic plates in the freezer.

› Pour the macerated fruit into a large pot and set over high heat. Cook, stirring with a large wooden spoon or a heatproof silicone spatula, scraping the edges and bottom of the pot to prevent scorching, until the fruit softens and the flesh of the figs starts to appear pasty. Add the water and continue stirring until the jam comes to a high boil. If the jam bubbles up too much, lower the heat to medium. Once the bubbling subsides, after about 10 minutes, the jam will begin to thicken.

› Add the port, lemon zest, and juice and continue cooking for 5 minutes.

› Taste the jam for sweetness. If you want, add a little more sugar ¼ cup at a time, taste, and cook for an additional 2 to 3 minutes.

› Check the set of the jam by putting a small dollop of hot jam on one of the chilled plates. Run a finger through it: if your finger leaves a track, the jam is ready; if not, continue cooking for a few minutes and repeat the test. Remove from the heat.

› Pour the jam into the sterilized jars and seal with the warm lids. Let cool to room temperature and refrigerate for up to 2 weeks, or follow the canning instructions for long-term storage on page 275.

TIP: IF YOU PREFER THE FLAVOR OF RED wine over port, substitute your favorite Pinot Noir, Gamay, or Sangiovese.

Kumquat Marmalade

Preparing kumquats requires lots of patience. The time it takes to trim these adorable and flavorful fruits is extreme, so put on a good audiobook before sitting down with your paring knife for a long session of meditative slicing and seeding. The end product will be worth every minute.

About 3 pounds kumquats, stemmed and rinsed

5 to 7 cups (35 to 49 ounces) sugar

▸ Using a very sharp paring knife, slice each kumquat lengthwise in half. Remove the seeds and set them aside in a small bowl. Put the kumquat halves cut side down and thinly slice (approximately 10 slices per half). Transfer to a medium bowl.

▸ Mix the kumquats with 5 cups of sugar. Cover the bowl and macerate overnight in the refrigerator. Cover the bowl of seeds as well and refrigerate overnight.

▸ The next day, fill a tea ball with approximately 2 tablespoons of the kumquat seeds; make sure the ball is tightly closed. Or, if you don't have a tea ball, cut a square of cheesecloth, wrap the seeds in it, and tie securely.

▸ Sterilize six 12-ounce canning jars and lids (see page 275).

▸ Put two small ceramic plates in the freezer.

▸ Pour the macerated kumquats into a large pot and set over high heat. Drop in the tea ball or cheesecloth sachet. Cook, stirring frequently with a large wooden spoon or a heatproof silicone spatula, scraping the edges and bottom of the pot to prevent scorching, for approximately 30 minutes. The marmalade will bubble very high midway through the cooking; if it starts to bubble too high, reduce the heat slightly.

▸ Taste the marmalade for sweetness. It should have a bit of tang in the finish, but if your mouth puckers, add up to 2 cups more sugar 1/2 cup at a time, taste, and cook for an additional 3 to 4 minutes or so. The marmalade will have a slightly gelatinous quality and shine on the surface when it is ready. Remove the seed sachet from the pot.

▸ Check the set of the marmalade by putting a small dollop of hot marmalade on one of the chilled plates. Run a finger through it: if your finger leaves a track, the marmalade is ready; if not, continue cooking for a few minutes and repeat the test. Remove from the heat.

▸ Pour the marmalade into the sterilized jars and seal with the warm lids. Let cool to room temperature and refrigerate for up to 2 weeks, or follow the canning instructions for long-term storage on page 275.

TIPS: MANDARINQUATS, ORANGEQUATS, and limequats are hybrid relatives of the kumquat that would make interesting versions of this marmalade. The marmalade recipes here require longer cooking (and stirring) times than the jams; if you need a break, you can lower the heat as the marmalade cooks and then stir less frequently.

Marsh Grapefruit and Earl Grey Marmalade

Marsh grapefruits are very juicy and tremendously flavorful, with less bitterness than other grapefruits. Their growing season peaks in the winter, but they are generally available during late fall and early spring as well. Enjoy this marmalade the old-fashioned way—on a large slice of toast with butter accompanied by a hot cup of tea on a cold winter afternoon.

● MAKES SIX 12-OUNCE JARS ●

About 10 pounds grapefruits (12 to 18), rinsed

7 cups (3 pounds 1 ounce) sugar, or more to taste

2 tablespoons Earl Grey tea

1 vanilla bean, split, seeds scraped out, seeds and bean reserved

1 tablespoon fresh lemon juice

▸ Using a vegetable peeler, remove the zest from the grapefruit in long strips approximately 1 inch wide and put in a small bowl. Using a sharp paring knife, slice off the top and bottom of each grapefruit, exposing the flesh. Then stand the grapefruit upright and carefully remove all the white pith in wide strips, working from the bottom and following the shape of the fruit.

▸ Put a cutting board inside a baking sheet slightly larger than the board, to catch the grapefruit juice. One at a time, slice down the membranes on either side of each grapefruit segment to release the segment. Remove the seeds and reserve in a small bowl; transfer the segments to a large bowl. Discard the membranes. Pour the juice in the baking pan into the bowl of grapefruit segments.

▸ Fill a medium pot with water and bring to a boil. Drop approximately 1 cup of the grapefruit zest into the boiling water and let it soften, 3 to 4 minutes. Using tongs or a slotted spoon, remove the blanched zest and put it in a bowl. Repeat with the remaining zest.

▸ Stack 4 strips of grapefruit zest on a cutting board and slice into very thin strips, approximately 1 inch by 1/8 inch. Add the zest to the grapefruit segments. Repeat with the remaining zest.

▸ Mix the sugar and tea into the grapefruit, then add the vanilla bean and seeds. Cover the bowl and macerate overnight in the refrigerator. Cover the bowl of seeds as well and refrigerate overnight.

▸ The next day, fill a tea ball with approximately 2 tablespoons of the grapefruit seeds; make sure the ball is tightly closed. Or, if you don't have a tea ball, cut a square of cheesecloth, wrap the seeds in it, and tie securely.

▸ Sterilize six 12-ounce canning jars and lids (see page 275).

▸ Put two small ceramic plates in the freezer.

▸ Pour the macerated grapefruit into a large pot and set over high heat. Drop in the tea ball or cheesecloth sachet. Cook, stirring frequently with a large wooden spoon or a heatproof silicone spatula, scraping the edges and bottom of the pot to prevent scorching, for approximately 40 minutes. The marmalade will bubble very high midway through the cooking; if it starts to bubble too high, reduce the heat slightly.

> When the marmalade starts to thicken, add the lemon juice and continue cooking for 2 to 3 minutes.

> Taste the marmalade for sweetness. If you want, add a little more sugar $1/2$ cup at a time, taste, and cook for an additional 2 to 3 minutes. The marmalade will have a slightly gelatinous quality and shine on the surface when it is ready. Remove the seed sachet from the pot.

> Check the set of the marmalade by putting a small dollop of hot marmalade on one of the chilled plates. Run a finger through it: if your finger leaves a track, the marmalade is ready; if not, continue cooking for a few minutes and repeat the test. Remove from the heat.

> Remove the vanilla bean. Pour the marmalade into the sterilized jars and seal with the warm lids. Let cool to room temperature and refrigerate for up to 2 weeks, or follow the canning instructions for long-term storage on page 275.

Blood Orange Marmalade

Blood oranges are gorgeous orbs with pink-orange skin and crimson flesh. In contrast to most winter fruits, they are also refreshing and literally exploding with sweet juice. A couple spoonfuls of this marmalade over Vanilla Bean Cake (page 75) or drizzled on Chocolate Pots de Crème (page 226) make an elegant and seasonal dessert.

● MAKES SIX 12-OUNCE JARS ●

10 to 12 pounds blood oranges
(30 oranges), rinsed
6 cups (2 pounds 10 ounces) sugar, or more to taste

▸ Using a vegetable peeler, remove the zest from the blood oranges in long strips approximately ½ inch wide and put in a medium bowl. Using a sharp paring knife, slice off the top and bottom of each orange, exposing the flesh. Then stand the orange upright and carefully remove all the white pith in wide strips, working from top to bottom and following the shape of the fruit.

▸ Put a cutting board inside a baking sheet slightly larger than the board, to catch the blood orange juice. One at a time, slice down the membranes on either side of each orange segment to release the segment. Remove the seeds and reserve the larger seeds in a small bowl; transfer the segments to a large bowl. Discard the membranes. Pour the juice in the baking pan into the bowl of orange segments.

▸ Fill a medium pot with water and bring to a boil. Drop approximately 1 cup of the blood orange zest into the boiling water and let it soften, 2 to 3 minutes. Using tongs or a slotted spoon, remove the blanched zest and put it in a small bowl. Repeat with the remaining zest.

▸ Stack 4 strips of blood orange zest on a cutting board and slice into very thin strips, approximately ½ inch by ⅛ inch. Add the zest to the orange segments. Repeat with the remaining zest.

▸ Mix the fruit with the sugar. Cover the bowl and macerate overnight in the refrigerator. Cover the bowl of seeds as well and refrigerate overnight.

▸ The next day, fill a tea ball with approximately 2 tablespoons of the blood orange seeds; make sure the ball is tightly closed. Or, if you don't have a tea ball, cut a square of cheesecloth, wrap the seeds in it, and tie securely.

▸ Sterilize six 12-ounce canning jars and lids (see page 275).

▸ Put two small ceramic plates in the freezer.

▸ Pour the macerated oranges into a large pot and set over high heat. Drop in the tea ball or cheesecloth sachet. Cook, stirring frequently with a large wooden spoon or a heatproof silicone spatula, scraping the edges and bottom of the pot to prevent scorching, for approximately 30 minutes. The marmalade will bubble very high midway through the cooking; if it starts to bubble too high, reduce the heat slightly.

▸ Taste the marmalade for sweetness. If you want, add a little more sugar ½ cup at a time, taste, and cook for an additional 2 to 3 minutes. The marmalade will have a slightly gelatinous quality and shine on the surface when it is ready. Remove the seed sachet from the pot.

▸ Check the set of the marmalade by putting a small dollop of hot marmalade on one of the chilled plates. Run a finger through it: if your finger left a track, the marmalade is ready; if not, cook for a few minutes and repeat the test. Remove from the heat.

▸ Pour the marmalade into the sterilized jars and seal with the warm lids. Let cool to room temperature and refrigerate for up to 2 weeks, or follow the canning instructions for long-term storage on page 275.

GIFTS FROM THE LARDER

JAMS ARE A PERENNIAL FAVORITE GIFT, and you can make your jam jars look even more special if you put some time and thought into the packaging. The packaging should complement the flavor and style of the jam you're giving. For example, if your jam is chunky and rustic, use a traditional jar by Ball with a lid and band top capped with a "kerchief" (see below) and a hangtag. If your jam is more elegant, try a modern jar by Weck, labeled with a small sticker displaying a discreet logo (see below) or message. Preserves are also popular as wedding favors. Use the elements to create a look you like (see Packaging, page 336).

There are many types of **jars** available for preserving today. Try a few styles.

Hangtags are a traditional and practical way to label your preserves. They are available in a variety of sizes that allow for messages and personalization.

Custom-designed **stickers** are easy to create and give your packaging a professional look. Have a little fun and name your "preserve company"— maybe even design a logo for it.

A range of **stamps** and **stamp pads** has become available in the last few years. You can have stamps custom-made or use an existing design to decorate your packaging.

Ribbon or **twine** tied around a jam jar with a bow adds a festive touch to preserves; also use to attach hangtags and kerchiefs.

The square or circular bit of **fabric,** or kerchief, that often covers the lids of preserves is an endearing reference to a country kitchen. You can purchase these ready-made or cut your own. Coordinating the fabric with the color of the jam results in a pleasing composition. Place the fabric over the lid and secure it with a rubber band, ribbon, or twine.

HAND

BREAKFAST AND SNACKS
TO EAT ON THE GO

THIS chapter is dedicated to all the people who are short on time but have the desire to bake. The thought of baking something for the fund-raiser or, I don't know, say, breakfast, might seem a little extreme to people. Sure, it's faster to grab a dozen muffins from Whole Foods than to bake them, but the satisfaction of the aroma of muffins as they come out of the oven is incomparable. We all have to eat on the run—I certainly consume more breakfasts in my car than anywhere else. Is it ideal? Of course not, but I console myself with the knowledge that what I'm eating is delicious, sometimes healthy, and almost always homemade.

When we think of home cooking, the meal that comes to mind is dinner. Many of us go to great lengths to peel locally grown carrots for salads and braise ethically raised meats for stews. So why is breakfast so often neglected within the construct of making more of the foods we eat? Even for the most die-hard locavores, breakfast frequently comes from a box or a Mylar wrapper. We might bake a pie or a cake for a special occasion, but making scones for breakfast seems unusual or even unrealistic. So how do we integrate homemade into our morning ritual? The recipes in this chapter will show you how.

Most of these are easier than most of the other recipes in this book—they are designed for people with a hectic modern lifestyle. And all of the recipes can be doubled or tripled, so I urge you to make a big batch when you finally claim an extra hour or two of baking time. Then the next time you need muffins for breakfast on the run or quick bread for a bake sale, you'll have something in your freezer to save you. All the baked goods freeze and defrost beautifully, and the granolas store well in sealed jars or bags, giving you delicious homemade desserts and breakfast for several days or weeks.

I can't imagine my life without Muesli (page 311); it's a great quick meal and I seem to stash little bags of it all over the place. Every other week I make a batch and it takes 15 to 20 minutes of active time. On a luxurious day I might fill a bowl with yogurt and fruit and a generous heap of nutty, fruity cereal for a sit-down breakfast with my family, but more often than not I am running out the door, breakfast in hand.

Chocolate Granola

Granola has taken on a new identity of late; I see it frequently on salads or cheese platters. This one is for dessert. It includes all the defining ingredients of granola, but then it goes in a different direction. With the chocolate, it is best served on ice cream or pudding or another sweet.

● MAKES ABOUT 12 CUPS ●

4 cups (13 ounces) rolled oats

1¹/₂ cups (5.25 ounces) sliced raw almonds

1 cup (3.5 ounces) raw hazelnuts, halved

¹/₄ cup (1 ounce) cocoa nibs (see Resources, page 335)

¹/₃ cup (1.3 ounces) unsweetened cocoa powder

³/₄ cup (4.5 ounces) light brown sugar

¹/₄ cup (2.75 ounces) honey

¹/₃ cup (2.36 ounces) canola oil

2 teaspoons vanilla bean paste (see Resources, page 335)

8.25 ounces 61% bittersweet chocolate, finely chopped

1¹/₂ teaspoons fleur de sel

▸ Heat the oven to 250°F. Line two 13-by-18-by-1-inch baking sheets with parchment paper or silicone liners.

▸ Mix together the oats, almonds, hazelnuts, and cocoa nibs in a large bowl.

▸ Mix the cocoa powder, sugar, honey, oil, and vanilla paste in a small bowl, stirring well. Pour over the dry ingredients and stir with a rubber spatula until the dry ingredients are evenly moistened.

▸ Spread the granola evenly on one of the prepared baking sheets. Bake for about 1 hour, stirring every 15 minutes, until the nuts are slightly golden.

▸ Quickly pour the hot granola onto the second baking sheet and spread it evenly. Sprinkle the chopped chocolate evenly over the granola and wait for 1 to 2 minutes; the chocolate will melt. Spread the chocolate evenly with an offset spatula, then sprinkle the fleur de sel over the chocolate and move the pan to a cool area. Allow the granola to cool for 15 to 20 minutes. If the chocolate has not set, put the pan in the refrigerator until it is firm to touch, 5 to 10 minutes, then bring back to room temperature. Break up the granola.

STORING

▸ The granola can be stored in an airtight container for up to 3 weeks.

Granola

This granola is not the kind you find at the health food store—it's more fitting for a bakery. The brown sugar results in a texture similar to that of old-fashioned brittle. Make sure to cool the granola for at least 2 hours; storing it before it is completely cool will alter the texture. Eat it by itself as a snack or break into small pieces and enjoy as a cereal with yogurt or milk.

● MAKES ABOUT 10 CUPS ●

3 cups (9.75 ounces) rolled oats

1 cup (3.5 ounces) sliced raw almonds

1 cup (4.5 ounces) cashews, roughly chopped

1 cup (5.25 ounces) raw pumpkin seeds

3/4 cup (2.5 ounces) sweetened shredded coconut

1/2 cup (3 ounces) light brown sugar

1/2 cup (5.5 ounces) honey

1/2 cup (3.55 ounces) canola oil

1 teaspoon kosher salt

2 teaspoons vanilla extract

1 cup (5 ounces) dried apricots, roughly chopped

› Heat the oven to 250°F. Line two 13-by-18-by-1-inch baking sheets with parchment paper or silicone liners.

› Mix together the oats, almonds, cashews, pumpkin seeds, and coconut in a large bowl.

› Combine the brown sugar, honey, canola oil, salt, and vanilla in a small bowl. Pour over the dry ingredients and mix thoroughly with your hands. Make sure all the dry ingredients are evenly moistened, and scrape the sides and bottom of the bowl to incorporate all of the ingredients.

› Spread the granola evenly onto one of the prepared baking sheets. Bake for 1 hour. Stir the granola with a wooden spoon, spread it out evenly with an offset spatula, and bake for an additional 30 minutes, or until golden brown. Quickly stir in the chopped apricots.

› Transfer the granola to the second baking sheet, spreading it evenly with an offset spatula. Set aside in a cool area for at least 2 hours, until completely cool. Break up the cooled granola.

STORING

› The granola can be stored in an airtight container for up to 2 weeks.

Muesli

Muesli was created around 1900 by Maximilian Bircher-Benner, a Swiss doctor who believed in a diet rich in grains and fresh fruits. Unlike traditional muesli recipes, which call for raw oats, this recipe allows for toasted oats, imparting a satisfying texture and nutty flavor to the cereal.

● MAKES ABOUT 12 CUPS ●

2 cups (6.5 ounces) rolled oats (not quick-cooking)

2 cups (11 ounces) stone-cut oats, such as Anson Mills (see Resources, page 335)

1 cup (8 ounces) unsweetened applesauce

¹/₂ cup (4 ounces) unsweetened apple juice

1 cup (5.5 ounces) dried cherries

1 cup (4.5 ounces) dried pears, roughly chopped

1¹/₂ cups (5.25 ounces) roasted sliced almonds

TIP: THIS IS ALSO WONDERFUL SERVED hot, topped with a small pat of butter: Combine 1 cup muesli and ¹/₂ cup water in a small saucepan, bring to a boil, and simmer for 2 to 3 minutes.

› Heat the oven to 250°F. Line a 13-by-18-by-1-inch baking sheet with parchment paper or a silicone liner.

› Combine the rolled and stone-cut oats, applesauce, and apple juice in a large bowl and stir until the oats are evenly moistened. Spread on the prepared baking sheet and bake for about 1 hour, stirring every 20 minutes, until the oats are completely dry and golden brown. Remove from the oven and let cool completely.

› Mix the oats with the cherries, pears, and almonds in a large bowl.

STORING

› The muesli can be stored in an airtight container for up to 4 weeks.

Butternut Squash Bread

When the air turns crisp, I crave the nutty sweetness of butternut squash
in soups, stews, and, especially, this bread. A generous slice slathered
with butter signifies the fall season to me like nothing else.

• MAKES 1 LOAF; 8 TO 10 SLICES •

1 small butternut squash (6 to 7 inches long)

1/3 cup (2.36 ounces) canola oil, plus more if
    needed

1 1/2 cups (7.5 ounces) all-purpose flour

1/2 teaspoon baking powder

1/2 teaspoon baking soda

1/2 teaspoon kosher salt

2 teaspoons Spice Mix (page 44)
    or ground cinnamon

5 tablespoons (2.5 ounces) unsalted butter,
    softened

1/2 cup (3.5 ounces) granulated sugar

2/3 cup (4 ounces) light brown sugar

2 large eggs

1/2 teaspoon vanilla extract

› Heat the oven to 350°F. Line a baking sheet with parchment paper. Coat the bottom and sides of a 9 1/2-by-5 1/2-inch loaf pan with nonstick baking spray and line the bottom with parchment paper.

› Halve the butternut squash lengthwise, peel it, and scoop out the seeds. Reserve one half for another use (or cook all the squash and reserve half the cooked squash for another use). Cut the squash into 1-inch cubes. Spread the cubes on the prepared baking sheet and roast for about 50 minutes, until the flesh is soft. Let cool completely.

› Puree the squash with the oil in a food processor until smooth, about 4 minutes; if the squash is too dry to puree, add an additional tablespoon of oil. Measure out 1 1/4 cups of the pureed squash.

› Whisk together the flour, baking powder, baking soda, salt, and spice mix in a medium bowl.

› In the bowl of a stand mixer fitted with the paddle attachment (or in a large bowl, using a handheld mixer), cream the butter and both sugars on medium speed until light and fluffy, about 3 minutes.

› Mix the eggs and vanilla together in a small bowl with a fork or small whisk. With the mixer on medium speed, alternately add the dry and wet ingredients to the creamed butter in batches, beating until the batter is smooth. Fold in the 1 1/4 cups pureed squash.

› Pour the batter into the prepared loaf pan and smooth the top with an offset spatula. Bake for 50 to 60 minutes, until the top is golden brown and a wooden skewer inserted in the center comes out clean. Cool the bread completely on a cooling rack before unmolding. Wrap leftovers in plastic wrap or wax paper.

STORING

› Wrapped in plastic wrap, the bread keeps well at room temperature for up to 4 days and can be frozen for up to 2 months.

TIP: IF YOU USE A 9-BY-5-INCH LOAF PAN, reserve 2/3 cup of the batter and reduce the baking time by 5 to 10 minutes. You can use the extra batter to make griddle cakes: Just heat a large skillet, lightly butter it, and proceed as if making pancakes.

Zucchini Bread

Zucchini is beautifully abundant during the spring and summer months. It's one of those miracle ingredients that can be used in every meal of the day, but there are few things in life as satisfying as eating a thick slice of zucchini bread. When choosing the zucchini, go for smaller squash; they will impart better color and flavor to your bread.

MAKES 1 LOAF; 8 TO 10 SLICES

1½ cups (7.5 ounces) all-purpose flour

1 teaspoon baking soda

1 teaspoon kosher salt

½ teaspoon baking powder

1¼ teaspoons ground cinnamon

5 tablespoons (2.5 ounces) unsalted butter, softened

¾ cup (5.25 ounces) granulated sugar

⅔ cup (4 ounces) light brown sugar

⅓ cup (2.36 ounces) canola oil

2 large eggs

1¾ teaspoons vanilla extract

1¼ teaspoons grated lemon zest

1½ cups (8 ounces) shredded zucchini

> TIP: IF YOU USE A 9-BY-5-INCH LOAF PAN, reserve ⅔ cup of the batter and reduce the baking time by 5 to 10 minutes. You can pour the extra batter into a muffin tin and bake for 25 to 30 minutes.

› Heat the oven to 350°F. Coat the bottom and sides of a 9½-by-5½-inch loaf pan with nonstick baking spray and line the bottom with parchment paper.

› Whisk together the flour, baking soda, salt, baking powder, and cinnamon in a medium bowl.

› In the bowl of a stand mixer fitted with the paddle attachment (or in a large bowl, using a handheld mixer), cream the butter and both sugars on medium speed until light and fluffy, about 3 minutes.

› Mix the oil, eggs, vanilla, and lemon zest together in a small bowl with a fork or small whisk. With the mixer on medium speed, alternately add the dry and wet ingredients to the creamed butter in batches, then continue beating until the batter is smooth. Fold in the shredded zucchini.

› Pour the batter into the prepared loaf pan and smooth the top with an offset spatula. Bake for 60 to 70 minutes, until the top is golden brown and a wooden skewer inserted in the center comes out clean. Cool the bread completely on a cooling rack before unmolding. Wrap leftovers in plastic wrap or wax paper.

STORING

› Wrapped in plastic wrap, the bread keeps well at room temperature for up to 5 days and can be frozen for up to 2 months.

Multigrain Muffins

This recipe might read like an ambitious laundry list, but the combination of whole grains, dairy, and fruits makes a healthy, hearty muffin that is a nutritious meal in itself. Whole wheat flour is flavorful but can be heavy on its own; the lighter almond flour balances the texture, and the addition of millet provides a surprising crunch in every bite.

● MAKES 12 MUFFINS ●

1¼ cups (5.87 ounces) whole wheat pastry flour (see Resources, page 335)

1 cup (3.5 ounces) raw almond flour (see Resources, page 335)

2 teaspoons baking soda

1 teaspoon baking powder

1 teaspoon kosher salt

1¼ cups (4.06 ounces) quick-cooking oats

½ cup (3.35 ounces) millet (see Resources, page 335)

2 large eggs

¾ cup (6 ounces) plain yogurt

⅓ cup (2.36 ounces) canola oil

⅓ cup (3.63 ounces) honey

⅓ cup (2 ounces) light brown sugar

1½ teaspoons vanilla bean paste (see Resources, page 335)

¼ cup (2 ounces) buttermilk

2 large ripe bananas

⅔ cup (3.5 ounces) dried plums or apricots, chopped into ¼-inch pieces

▸ Position a rack in the center of the oven and heat the oven to 350°F. Line a muffin tin with muffin liners.

▸ Whisk together the whole wheat flour, almond flour, baking soda, baking powder, and salt in a large bowl. Stir in the oats and millet.

▸ Gently whisk the eggs, yogurt, oil, honey, brown sugar, vanilla paste, and buttermilk in a medium bowl until just combined. Using a large spoon or rubber spatula, fold the wet ingredients into the dry ingredients.

▸ Mash the bananas in a small bowl, then fold into the batter, along with the chopped fruit, scraping down the sides and bottom of the bowl.

▸ Using an ice cream scoop or a large spoon, scoop about ½ cup batter into each muffin cup. Pick up the muffin tin and knock it firmly against the work surface a couple of times to level the batter and release any air pockets.

▸ Bake the muffins for 25 minutes; do not open the oven door to check before 25 minutes, or the muffins will sink. Then insert a toothpick in the center of a muffin to check, and remove the muffins from the oven when it comes out clean. Cool in the pan on a cooling rack for 15 to 20 minutes.

STORING

▸ The muffins can be stored for up to 2 days in an airtight container or frozen for up to 3 months in Ziploc freezer bags.

Raspberry–Vanilla Bean Crumble Muffins

Is this a muffin or cake? The line between breakfast pastry and dessert is sometimes hazy at best, and here we have an excellent example of that conundrum.

● MAKES 12 MUFFINS ●

FOR THE CRUMBLE

3/4 cup (3.75 ounces) all-purpose flour

1 cup (6 ounces) light brown sugar

1 teaspoon ground cinnamon

1/2 teaspoon kosher salt

5 tablespoons (2.5 ounces) unsalted butter, cubed and chilled

FOR THE MUFFINS

2 cups (10 ounces) all-purpose flour

2 teaspoons baking powder

1/2 teaspoon kosher salt

5 tablespoons (2.5 ounces) unsalted butter, softened

1 cup (7 ounces) granulated sugar

1 large egg

1/2 cup (4 ounces) heavy cream

2 teaspoons vanilla bean paste (see Resources, page 335)

2 cups (8 ounces) raspberries, rinsed and dried

‣ Position a rack in the center of the oven and heat the oven to 350°F. Line a muffin tin with muffin liners.

TO MAKE THE CRUMBLE

‣ Combine the flour, brown sugar, cinnamon, and salt in food processor, and pulse to blend. With the processor running, add the butter, pulsing until the mixture looks like sand, about 2 minutes. Set aside.

TO MAKE THE MUFFINS

‣ Sift together the flour, baking powder, and salt into a medium bowl.

‣ In the bowl of a stand mixer fitted with the paddle attachment (or in a large bowl, using a handheld mixer), cream the butter and sugar on medium speed until light and fluffy, about 3 minutes.

‣ Mix the egg, heavy cream, and vanilla paste together in a small bowl with a fork or small whisk. Add to the creamed butter and mix until fully combined, about 2 minutes; the batter will appear a little lumpy. Add the dry ingredients in two batches, mixing well after each addition. Scrape down the sides and bottom of the bowl and the paddle attachment. Use a rubber spatula to fold in the raspberries to avoid crushing them.

‣ Using an ice cream scoop or a large spoon, scoop about 1/3 cup batter into each muffin cup. Pick up the muffin tin and knock it firmly against the work surface a couple of times to level the batter and release any air pockets. Cover the top of each muffin with 1 tablespoon of the crumble.

‣ Bake for 13 minutes, then rotate the muffin tin and bake for an additional 14 minutes, or until a toothpick inserted in the center of a muffin comes out clean. Cool the muffins in the pan on a cooling rack for 15 to 20 minutes before removing them.

STORING

‣ The muffins can be stored for up to 2 days in an airtight container or frozen for up to 2 months in Ziploc freezer bags.

Blueberry–Meyer Lemon Muffins

This muffin has the texture of a coffee cake; it is dense and moist, not fluffy, like a lot of muffins. Its heft allows it to hold large amounts of fruit, so every bite is bursting with sweet fresh blueberries. During the fall and winter months, use the same recipe with seasonal fruits. For example, omit the lemon and blueberries and add 2 cups peeled and diced apples. Top with brown sugar instead of white.

• MAKES 12 MUFFINS •

2 cups (10 ounces) all-purpose flour

2 teaspoons baking powder

1/2 teaspoon kosher salt

6 tablespoons (3/4 stick/3 ounces) unsalted butter, softened

1 cup (7 ounces) sugar, plus 1 tablespoon for sprinkling

1 large egg

1/2 cup (4 ounces) crème fraîche

2 tablespoons grated Meyer lemon zest

2 tablespoons Meyer lemon juice

2 cups (8 ounces) blueberries, rinsed and dried

› Position a rack in the center of the oven and heat the oven to 350°F. Coat the cups of a muffin tin with nonstick baking spray or brush generously with melted butter.

› Sift together the flour, baking powder, and salt into a medium bowl.

› In the bowl of a stand mixer fitted with the paddle attachment (or in a large bowl, using a handheld mixer), cream the butter and sugar on medium speed until light and fluffy, about 3 minutes.

› Mix the egg, crème fraîche, lemon zest, and juice together in a small bowl with a fork or small whisk. Add to the creamed butter and mix until fully combined, about 2 minutes; the batter will appear a little lumpy. Add the dry ingredients in two batches, mixing well after each addition. Scrape down the sides and bottom of the bowl and the paddle attachment. Use a rubber spatula to fold in the blueberries to avoid crushing them.

› Using an ice cream scoop or a large spoon, scoop about 1/3 cup batter into each muffin cup. Pick up the muffin tin and knock it firmly against the work surface a couple of times to level the batter and release any air pockets. Sprinkle the top of each muffin with 1/4 teaspoon sugar.

› Bake for 13 minutes, then rotate the muffin tin and bake for an additional 13 minutes, or until a toothpick inserted in the center of a muffin comes out clean. Cool the muffins in the pan on a cooling rack for 15 to 20 minutes before removing them.

STORING

› The muffins can be stored for up to 2 days in an airtight container or frozen for up to 2 months in Ziploc freezer bags.

Corn and Cherry Scones

Every time I go home to San Francisco, I stop into Arizmendi Bakery in the Sunset District for their delicious breads and scones. My favorite is the corn and dried cherry scone; here is my take on that recipe.

2 cups (10 ounces) all-purpose flour

1¹/₂ cups (8.25 ounces) yellow cornmeal

2 teaspoons baking powder

¹/₂ teaspoon baking soda

1 teaspoon kosher salt

²/₃ cup plus 2 tablespoons (5.5 ounces) sugar, plus more for sprinkling

2 sticks (8 ounces) unsalted butter, cubed and chilled

2 cups (10 ounces) Bing cherries, rinsed, pitted, and halved

1¹/₄ cups (10 ounces) buttermilk

> Position a rack in the center of the oven and heat the oven to 400°F. Line a 13-by-18-by-1-inch baking sheet with parchment paper or a silicone liner.

> Whisk together the flour, cornmeal, baking powder, baking soda, salt, and ²/₃ cup of the sugar in a large bowl. Using a pastry cutter, cut in the butter until the butter is in pea-sized pieces, about 4 minutes.

> Toss the cherries with the remaining 2 tablespoons sugar in a small bowl, then fold into the dough with a wooden spoon or rubber spatula. Pour the buttermilk over the center of the dough and gently mix the dough together with your hands; be careful not to overwork the dough—this should take only 1 to 2 minutes. The dough will appear very crumbly and dry. Let it sit for 5 minutes: the cornmeal will absorb some buttermilk and cherry juice, making the dough more cohesive.

> Transfer the dough to a lightly floured cool work surface. Use a rolling pin to roll out the dough very gently until it is ³/₄ inch thick; do not over-work the dough. Cut the dough into six 4-inch squares and then cut the squares diagonally into long triangles.

> Using an offset spatula, transfer the triangles to the prepared baking sheet, spacing them 2 inches apart. If the scones break apart, just press the dough back together. Sprinkle the scones generously with sugar. Bake for 17 minutes, or until the scones are crackly on top and dark yellow. Transfer the scones to a cooling rack and cool completely.

STORING

> The scones can be stored for up to 2 days in an airtight container or frozen for up to 2 months in Ziploc freezer bags.

TIP: THIS RECIPE ALSO WORKS VERY WELL with fresh apricots in place of the cherries. Use 2 cups chopped apricots (cut into pieces the size of halved cherries).

Crème Fraîche Scones

The generous portion of crème fraîche in this recipe gives the scones a pleasing tart flavor and a yielding texture. Serve at room temperature or toasted, with a small mountain of marmalade (see pages 298–302).

2 cups (10 ounces) all-purpose flour

1/3 cup (2.33 ounces) sugar, plus extra for sprinkling

2 teaspoons baking powder

1/2 teaspoon kosher salt

5 tablespoons (2.5 ounces) unsalted butter, cut into cubes and chilled

1 cup (8 ounces) crème fraîche

2 large eggs

1 tablespoon grated lemon zest

1 tablespoon fresh lemon juice

> Position a rack in the center of the oven and heat the oven to 375°F. Line a 13-by-18-by-1-inch baking sheet with parchment paper or a silicone liner.

> Sift together the flour, sugar, baking powder, and salt into a medium bowl. Cut in the butter with a pastry cutter until the butter is in pea-sized pieces, about 4 minutes.

> Whisk together the crème fraîche, 1 egg, the lemon zest, and juice in a small bowl, then fold into the flour mixture until just combined; do not overmix—you want to see bits of butter in the dough.

> Transfer the dough to a lightly floured cool work surface. Use a rolling pin to roll out the dough very gently until it is 3/4 inch thick; be careful not to overwork the dough. Using a 3-inch round cookie cutter, cut out scones and place them 2 inches apart on the prepared baking sheet. Gather the dough scraps together, reroll, and cut out more scones.

> Whisk the remaining egg in a small bowl. Using a pastry brush, lightly brush the tops of the scones with the egg. Sprinkle with sugar.

> Bake for 15 minutes, or until the scones are lightly golden. Transfer the scones to a cooling rack and cool completely.

STORING

> The scones can be stored in an airtight container for up to 2 days.

TIP: IF YOU WANT TO FREEZE THE SCONES, reduce the baking time by 2 minutes, pulling them from the oven before they turn golden. Cool completely, then store in Ziploc freezer bags for up to 2 months. Reheat the frozen scones in a 300°F oven for 10 minutes.

Hazelnut, Blue Cheese, and Date Scones

This scone, both sweet and savory, is appropriate for breakfast, lunch, or dinner. In the morning, try it with softly scrambled eggs; at lunch, toast the scones and serve with soup or salad; and in the evening, pair a scone with serrano ham and a glass of wine.

● MAKES 12 SCONES ●

2 cups (10 ounces) all-purpose flour

1/4 cup (1.5 ounces) light brown sugar, plus more for sprinkling

2 teaspoons baking powder

8 tablespoons (1 stick/4 ounces) unsalted butter, cubed and chilled

1/2 cup (2.5 ounces) crumbled blue cheese, preferably bleu d'Auvergne

2 large eggs

1/2 cup (4 ounces) heavy cream

1/2 cup (3 ounces) chopped raw hazelnuts

2/3 cup (4.5 ounces) chopped pitted dates, tossed with 1 tablespoon flour

▸ Position a rack in the center of the oven and heat the oven to 350°F. Line a baking sheet with parchment paper or a silicone liner.

▸ Sift together the flour, brown sugar, and baking powder and transfer to the bowl of a stand mixer fitted with the paddle attachment (or a large bowl, if using a handheld mixer). Add the butter and mix on low speed for about 30 seconds. With the mixer running, crumble in the blue cheese and mix for about 30 seconds. Add 1 egg and the heavy cream and mix just until everything looks crumbly, about 30 seconds; do not overmix.

▸ Transfer the dough to a lightly floured cool work surface. Use a rolling pin to roll out the dough gently until it is about 1 inch thick; it will be sticky and moist. Sprinkle half the chopped hazelnuts and dates over the dough. Fold the dough in half as best you can and sprinkle the top with the remaining nuts and dates.

▸ Dust the dough with a little flour and use a rolling pin to roll it out to 3/4 inch thick. Using a sharp knife, cut the dough into twelve 2 1/2- to 3-inch squares.

▸ Using an offset spatula, place the scones at least 1 inch apart on the prepared baking sheet.

▸ Whisk the remaining egg in a small bowl. Using a pastry brush, lightly brush the tops of the scones with egg. Sprinkle generously with brown sugar. Bake for 20 minutes, or until the scones are golden brown around the edges.

▸ Transfer the scones to a cooling rack and cool completely.

STORING

▸ The scones can be stored for up to 2 days in an airtight container or frozen for up to 2 months in Ziploc freezer bags.

Hazelnut Orange Cakes with Orange Glaze

Sourcing the best ingredients can make for an exceptional cake. I use hazelnuts from Trufflebert Farms in Oregon (see Resources, page 335)—the flavor and texture of their nuts is truly exceptional. I grind the nuts for this recipe, which infuses every bite of cake with their meaty deliciousness.

● MAKES 18 INDIVIDUAL CAKES ●

FOR THE CAKES

1 cup (3.5 ounces) raw hazelnut flour (see Resources, page 335)

³/4 cup plus 2 tablespoons (4.38 ounces) all-purpose flour

1 teaspoon kosher salt

9 tablespoons butter (4.5 ounces), softened

1 cup (7 ounces) sugar

²/3 cup (5.45 ounces) packed hazelnut paste (see Resources, page 335)

3 large eggs

1 large egg yolk

¹/2 teaspoon vanilla bean paste (see Resources, page 335)

¹/4 teaspoon orange oil (see Resources, page 335)

1 tablespoon minced dried orange (see Resources, page 335, and Tip)

FOR THE ORANGE GLAZE

1¹/2 cups (6.75 ounces) confectioners' sugar

3 tablespoons orange juice

TO MAKE THE CAKES

▸ Position a rack in the center of the oven and heat the oven to 350°F. Coat the cups of two popover pans with nonstick baking spray or melted butter.

▸ Whisk together the hazelnut flour, flour, and salt in a small bowl.

▸ In the bowl of a stand mixer fitted with the paddle attachment (or in a large bowl, using a handheld mixer), cream the butter and sugar until light and fluffy, about 3 minutes. With the mixer on low, crumble in the hazelnut paste, then increase the speed to medium and beat until the paste breaks into very small bits.

▸ Whisk together the eggs, egg yolk, vanilla paste, and orange oil in a small bowl. Add to the mixer and beat until fully combined, about 2 minutes. Add the dry ingredients and beat until the batter is smooth, with tiny dots of hazelnut paste. Add the dried orange, scrape the bowl, and mix for 1 minute.

▸ Using an ice cream scoop or a large spoon, scoop approximately ¹/4 cup of the batter into each popover cup. Bake for 10 minutes, then rotate the pans and bake for an additional 10 minutes, or until the cakes are light brown and a toothpick inserted in the center of one cake comes out clean. Let the cakes sit for 5 minutes in the pans on a cooling rack, then invert the pans and remove the cakes. Cool completely before glazing.

TO MAKE THE GLAZE

▸ Sift the confectioners' sugar into a medium bowl. Add the orange juice and stir with a small rubber spatula until completely smooth. Let the glaze sit at room temperature for 5 minutes.

TO GLAZE THE CAKES

▸ Place the cakes top side down on a cooling rack set over a baking sheet. If they stand crooked, trim the tops so the surface is flat. Using a small spoon, gently drizzle approximately 2 teaspoons of glaze over each cake; you may need to smooth the top of the glaze gently with the back of the spoon. Put the cakes on a plate or small tray and set aside in a cool, dry area until the glaze loses its sheen and sets, about 1 hour.

STORING

▸ The glazed cakes can be stored for up to 4 days in an airtight container; unglazed, they can be frozen for up to 2 months in Ziploc freezer bags.

TIP: IF YOU ARE UNABLE TO FIND DRIED oranges, use 2 teaspoons grated orange zest.

Meyer Lemon Tea Cakes with Pomegranate Glaze

We feature this cake every spring and summer at our farmers' market booths, and time and again I hear the same question, "What is *that*?!" The jolt of pretty, pastel pink glaze always elicits a response from children and adults alike. Mini-cake pans, with 12 cups each, are available online; see Resources, page 335.

• MAKES 24 INDIVIDUAL CAKES •

FOR THE CAKES

3 1/3 cups (17.3 ounces) all-purpose flour

3/4 teaspoon baking powder

3/4 teaspoon kosher salt

3 3/4 sticks (15 ounces) unsalted butter, softened

2 1/4 cups (15.75 ounces) sugar

1/2 cup (4 ounces) crème fraîche

6 large eggs

1/3 cup grated Meyer lemon zest

1/2 cup (4 ounces) Meyer lemon juice

FOR THE POMEGRANATE GLAZE

2 cups (9 ounces) confectioners' sugar

2 tablespoons fresh lemon juice

1 tablespoon unsweetened pomegranate juice

TIP: IF YOU WANT TO FREEZE SOME OR ALL of these cakes for future use, freeze them unglazed and then glaze them only after they are completely defrosted. This recipe makes a lot of little cakes—feel free to halve it if you like.

TO MAKE THE CAKES

› Heat the oven to 350°F. Coat 24 large muffin cups or 3-inch mini-cake pans with nonstick baking spray or butter.

› Sift together the flour, baking powder, and salt into a medium bowl.

› In the bowl of a stand mixer fitted with the paddle attachment (or in a large bowl, using a handheld mixer), cream the butter and sugar on medium speed until light and fluffy, about 3 minutes.

› Mix the crème fraîche, eggs, lemon zest, and juice together in a small bowl with a fork or small whisk. With the mixer on medium speed, alternately add the dry and wet ingredients in batches and continue beating until the batter is smooth, occasionally scraping down the sides of the bowl, about 3 minutes.

› Using a large ice cream scoop or a large spoon, scoop approximately 1/2 cup batter into each prepared muffin or cake cup. Bake for 18 minutes, or until the tops of the cakes appear matte and the shiny center has disappeared; do not bake until the cakes turn golden. Let the cakes cool in the pans for 5 minutes before removing them. Cool the cakes completely on a cooling rack before glazing, about 1 hour.

TO MAKE THE GLAZE

› Sift the confectioners' sugar into a medium bowl. Add the lemon juice and pomegranate juice and stir with a small spatula until completely smooth. Let the glaze sit at room temperature for 10 minutes before using.

TO GLAZE THE CAKES

› Pour the glaze into a wide shallow bowl. One at a time, pick up each cake, rotate the cake so the top is facing down, and dip it into the glaze. Carefully move the cake in a slow, circular motion so the entire surface is coated with glaze, then shake the cake gently so any excess glaze falls back in the bowl and put on a baking sheet. Put the cakes in a cool, dry area and let stand until the glaze loses its sheen and sets, about 20 minutes.

STORING

› Once the glaze has set, the cakes can be stored in an airtight container for up to 3 days.

Upside-down Apple and Almond Cakes

Enjoy these little cakes at room temperature for a breakfast pastry or slightly warm with a dollop of fresh whipped cream (see pages 138–39) for a plated dessert. You can replace the apple with slices of pear, fig, or banana for delectable variations. If you have mini-cake pans (see headnote, page 328), use them for this recipe.

12 tablespoons (1¹/₂ sticks/6 ounces) unsalted butter, softened

³/₄ cup plus 2 tablespoons (4.38 ounces) all-purpose flour

1 cup (3.5 ounces) blanched almond flour (see Resources, page 335)

1 teaspoon kosher salt

1 cup (7 ounces) granulated sugar

²/₃ cup (5.45 ounces) Almond Paste (page 44), made with blanched almond flour

3 large eggs

1 large egg yolk

¹/₂ teaspoon vanilla bean paste (see Resources, page 335)

1 tablespoon amaretto (optional)

¹/₄ teaspoon almond extract

¹/₄ cup (1.5 ounces) dark brown sugar

2 medium baking apples, such as Pink Lady or Granny Smith, peeled, halved, cored, and cut into ¹/₂-inch-thick slices

▸ Position a rack in the center of the oven and heat the oven to 350°F. Using a pastry brush, thickly coat 12 muffin cups with 3 tablespoons of the butter. Line a 13-by-18-by-1-inch baking sheet with parchment paper; set aside.

▸ Whisk together the flour, almond flour, and salt in a medium bowl.

▸ In the bowl of a stand mixer fitted with the paddle attachment (or in a large bowl, using a handheld mixer), cream the remaining 9 tablespoons butter and the granulated sugar on medium speed until light and fluffy, about 3 minutes. With the mixer on low speed, crumble in the almond paste, then increase the speed to medium and continue mixing until the paste has broken down to very small bits.

▸ Whisk together the eggs, egg yolk, vanilla paste, amaretto, if using, and almond extract in a small bowl, then add to the mixer and beat until fully combined. Add the dry ingredients and beat until the batter is smooth, with tiny dots of almond paste, about 2 minutes. Scrape the sides and bottom of the bowl and mix for 1 minute.

▸ Sprinkle 1 teaspoon of the brown sugar into the bottom of each muffin cup. Place 3 to 4 slices of apple on top of the brown sugar, slightly overlapping them. Using an ice cream scoop or a large spoon, scoop approximately ¹/₃ cup of cake batter into each cup.

▸ Bake for 10 minutes, then rotate the tin and bake for an additional 10 minutes, or until the cakes appear light brown on the edges and a toothpick inserted in the center of one cake comes out clean. Allow the cakes to cool for 2 to 3 minutes in the tin.

▸ Run a small paring knife or offset spatula around the edges of each cake. Place the parchment-lined baking sheet on top of the muffin tin and, holding both pans together, quickly invert them. Strongly knock on the bottom of each cup to help the cakes release, and remove the tin. (If the cakes stick to the muffin tin, put the pan directly over low heat and move the pan around so all of the cakes receive equal amounts of heat. After 1 or 2 minutes, invert the pan again and release the cakes.) Serve warm or at room temperature.

STORING

▸ The cakes can be stored in an airtight container for up to 4 days.

TIP: TO FREEZE THE CAKES, PLACE THEM on a baking sheet and cover with parchment paper, then wrap the entire pan tightly in plastic wrap and freeze for up to 2 months; or wrap individual cakes in plastic wrap.

Tangerine Sour Cream Pound Cake

Birthdays are a big deal at Valerie Confections. We have had some interesting cake requests over the years, but the most popular cake is so old-fashioned that it almost feels new—a sour cream pound cake. The tangerine zest and juice enhance the cake's sour cream tang.

● SERVES 12 ●

FOR THE CAKE

3 cups (15 ounces) all-purpose flour

1/2 teaspoon baking soda

1/2 teaspoon kosher salt

2 sticks (8 ounces) unsalted butter, softened

3 cups (1 pound 5 ounces) sugar

6 large eggs

1 cup (8 ounces) sour cream

2 tablespoons grated tangerine zest (from approximately 8 tangerines)

1 teaspoon vanilla extract

FOR THE GLAZE

1/2 cup (4 ounces) fresh tangerine juice

2 tablespoons fresh lemon juice

1/4 cup (1.75 ounces) granulated sugar

2 cups (9 ounces) confectioners' sugar, sifted

TO MAKE THE CAKE

› Position a rack in the center of the oven and heat the oven to 325°F. Coat the inside of a tube pan with nonstick baking spray or butter.

› Sift together the flour, baking soda, and salt into a medium bowl.

› In the bowl of a stand mixer fitted with the paddle attachment (or in a large bowl, using a handheld mixer), cream the butter on medium speed until light and fluffy, about 3 minutes.

› Add the sugar and beat until light and fluffy, about 5 minutes. Add the eggs one at a time, mixing well after each. Add the dry ingredients, 1 cup at a time, mixing well after each addition. Scrape the sides of the bowl.

› Mix the sour cream, tangerine zest, and vanilla together in a small bowl with a fork or small whisk. Add to the batter and mix until smooth. Fill the prepared tube pan with the batter and smooth the surface with an offset spatula. Bake for 45 minutes, then rotate the cake and bake for an additional 30 minutes, or until the top of the cake is cracked and golden brown and a toothpick inserted in the middle of the cake comes out clean. Cool the cake in the pan on a cooling rack for 45 minutes.

› Invert the cake onto a cooling rack set on top of a baking sheet, to catch any glaze drippings. The cake should still be a little warm to the touch.

TO MAKE THE FIRST GLAZE

› Mix 1/4 cup of the tangerine juice, the lemon juice, and granulated sugar together in a small bowl. Using a pastry brush, paint the entire surface of the cake with this clear glaze, continuing until all the glaze has been used. Let the cake cool completely, about 1 hour.

TO MAKE THE SECOND GLAZE

› Whisk together the confectioners' sugar and the remaining 1/4 cup of tangerine juice in a bowl. Let sit at room temperature for 10 minutes.

› Pour the glaze very slowly over the top of the cake, so it drips down the sides. Leave the cake uncovered until the glaze sets, about 20 minutes.

STORING

› The cake can be stored, in a cake box or under a cake dome, at room temperature for up to 3 days; the unglazed cake can be wrapped well in plastic wrap and frozen for up to 2 months.

Pansies

Mint

Roses

Roses

Ingredients and Equipment

Anson Mills
www.ansonmills.com
Toasted stone-cut oats, cornmeal, and an array of high-quality organic grains

Artisanal Cheese
www.artisanalcheese.com
A wide selection of cheeses available for shipping across the country, including bleu d'Auvergne, goat cheeses, La Tur, mascarpone, Aged Gouda, and many more

Bazzini
www.bazzininuts.com
Delicious roasted salted peanuts and other salted nut products

Bob's Red Mill Natural Foods
www.bobsredmill.com
Whole wheat pastry flour and just about every other grain and flour you could desire

Boyajian
www.boyajianinc.com
Lemon oil, orange oil, peppermint oil, and a variety of natural flavorings

Canning Pantry
www.canningpantry.com
Canning equipment

Chef Rubber
www.chefrubber.com
Chocolate of all percentages, dipping forks, depositors, and other chocolate-making supplies

Cuisinart
www.cuisinart.com
Their Frozen Yogurt, Ice Cream, and Sorbet Maker is the machine I used to make the ice creams and sorbets in this book

i.Gourmet
igourmet.com
Ladyfingers

Just Tomatoes
www.justtomatoes.com
Freeze-dried raspberries and a large assortment of other freeze-dried fruits and vegetables, as well as freeze-dried berry powders

Lagier Ranches
www.lagierranches.com
Whole organic almonds, raw and roasted

Local Harvest
www.localharvest.org
A useful guide to finding locally grown produce (including fraises des bois) around the country

Perfect Puree
www.perfectpuree.com
A large selection of fruit purees and concentrates, including black currant (cassis), passion fruit, and raspberry

Spice Station
www.spicestationsilverlake.com
Black sesame seeds, dried lavender, Durango salt, fleur de sel, gray sea salt, sweet smoked paprika, urfa biber, and other spices and dried herbs

Surfas
www.culinarydistrict.com
Almond flours, almond paste, chocolates in a wide range of percentages, candied (crystallized) ginger, edible gold leaf, vanilla beans, vanilla bean paste, and a large assortment of other specialty baking and confection ingredients, as well as equipment

Sur La Table
www.surlatable.com
Paper ice cream containers

Trufflebert Farms
www.trufflebertfarms.com
Exceptional hazelnuts, raw and roasted

Valerie Confections
www.valerieconfections.com
Many of the specialty items called for in this book, including atomized 69% chocolate, almond flours, almond paste, dried oranges, Durango salt, fleur de sel, gray sea salt, hazelnut flour, hazelnut paste, teas (including matcha and jasmine pearl), spices, vanilla beans, and more

Valrhona
www.valrhona-chocolate.com
Exceptional chocolates for baking and all chocolate work, including cocoa nibs

Wong Farms
Tel: 760-265-9167
E-mail: wongfarms@aol.com
The best mangoes I know

Décor

Commune Design
www.communedesign.com
Flatware, linens, tabletop items, and other handcrafted goods for the home

Heath Ceramics
www.heathceramics.com
Tabletop, flatware, tiles, and an extensive collection of midcentury ceramics

TableArt
www.tableartonline.com
Cake stands, flatware, tabletop items, and a bespoke collection of home décor

Packaging

Ball Canning
www.freshpreserving.com
A comprehensive selection of canning jars and equipment, and a source of information

Bell'occhio
www.bellocchio.com
Exquisite ribbons and other packaging options

Britex Fabrics
www.britexfabrics.com
A large selection of ribbons and fabrics for kerchiefs

Kate's Paperie
www.katespaperie.com
Ribbons, tags, and other packaging supplies

Nashville Wraps
www.nashvillewraps.com
Biodegradable candy and cookie bags and a large selection of other packaging necessities

PaperMart
www.papermart.com
Baking cups, cake boxes, cake boards, parchment circles, and an extensive selection of packaging supplies

Paper Source
www.paper-source.com
Boxes, labels, ribbons, stamps, and tags with custom options for personalization

Specialty Bottle
www.specialtybottle.com
Jars in every size, tins, and more

Weck
www.weckcanning.com
Well-designed jars for canning and food storage

ACKNOWLEDGMENTS

To August and Lee, Mommy loves you madly; you are my sweetest treats. To my parents, thank you for teaching me the route to an unpaved path.

Judy Pray: Patience be thy name! Through deadline after deadline, you carefully and thoughtfully guided me along this journey, and I'm forever grateful for your tolerance and your efforts. Cheers to you and everyone else at Artisan, especially Judith Sutton for her impeccable edits; Michelle Ishay-Cohen, the designer extraordinaire; Sibylle Kazeroid; Nancy Murray; Allison McGeehon; Molly Erman; and, most important, Ann Bramson.

Chris Brock and Paul Fortune, many thanks for the years of tasting . . . nothing goes public without your approval. And, of course, thank you for providing me with the most fabulous writing retreat on the hill; I love you dearly.

Chelsea Scott, Michelle Youssefzadeh Davey, Ernesto Morales, Alberto Ceron, Megan Bailey, and Christopher Wu: thank you all for your assistance in testing, re-testing, and shooting the recipes on these pages. Thank you, thank you.

Colleen Riley, Elizabeth Setton, Roxana Jullapat, and the darling Sarah Hirata, you each contributed to this book in so many ways. Thank you all!

Peggy Giffin, my dedicated and diligent recipe tester—you have found your true calling! I will never question your commitment to Sparkle Motion.

Bob Wyman, the patron saint of Valerie Confections: your assistance in every chapter of our company and this book renders me (almost) speechless. Your constant generosity, friendship, and unflagging support are truly humbling. Thank you.

Jen and Taylor: your photos bring fantasies to life. Thank you, *thank you*, for making this happen.

David Kuhn and team: you are the chicest and most tenacious agency a girl could ever want. Many thanks for your guidance and talent.

Ingrid Abramovitch, Jodi Rappaport, and Lora Zarubin: in different and equally important ways, you all propelled this book into a reality; thank you for opening the doors.

Kevin West: thank you for the camaraderie and support through this entire process. You are such a talent; I am always elated to stir fruit by your side.

Aaron Jupiter Stapley and everyone at Stapley Hildebrand, thank you endlessly for all the last-minute stunning, irreplaceable design work over the years. Your artistry surrounds me every day.

Bruce and Tani Isaacs, Pen Densham and Wendy Savage, Corinna Cotsen and Lee Rosenbaum, and Deborah Rosenthal and RJ Comer: thanks for taking a chance.

Coco Iverson and the staff of Heath Ceramics Los Angeles: endless thanks for accommodating my numerous shoots with such graciousness. You're a lovely group of people.

Thanks to Roman Alonso, Stephen Johanknecht, Lisa Neil, and everyone at Commune Design for your collaborative and generous spirits; you're always a pleasure and an inspiration.

And a special thanks to Greta Meroni, Broderick Eddy, Finnegan Toohey, and Jonathan Chou.

I'd also like to thank the following companies for supplying props for our photo shoot.

Commune: pages 188 (linen), 219 (Victoria Morris bowl), 242–243 (jar and lid), and 313–43 (linen).

Heath Ceramics: pages 5 (ivory bowl), 47 (rectangular plate), 53 (ivory platter), 76 (round platter), 82 (square plate), 90 (rectangular plate), 111 (bowls), 122–23 (all ceramic plates, platters, and bowl), 160 (platter), 165 (bowls), 177 (ramekins), 188 (square plate), 223 (bowl and plate), 227 (sugar bowl and lid), 232 (small Weck jars), 236 (bowl), 238 (Canada drink glasses), 277 (bowl), and 277 (plate).

TableArt: pages 26–27 (cake stands), 70–71 (plate with gold detail and gold fork), 80 (cake stand), 86 (cake stand), and 220 (gold spoon).

Valerie Confections: pages 60 (teak cake stand), 122–23 (teak cake stands), 256 (cookie jar), 277 (teak spreader), and 284 (tiered cake stand).